D1442786

HAPPINESS BY DESIGN

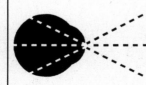

HAPPINESS BY DESIGN

CHANGE WHAT YOU DO,
NOT HOW YOU THINK

PAUL DOLAN, PhD

Foreword by
Daniel Kahneman, PhD

THORNDIKE PRESS
A part of Gale, Cengage Learning

Farmington Hills, Mich • San Francisco • New York • Waterville, Maine
Meriden, Conn • Mason, Ohio • Chicago

GALE
CENGAGE Learning®

LIBRARY OF CONGRESS CATALOGING-IN-PUBLICATION DATA

Dolan, Paul, 1968–
    Happiness by design : change what you do, not how you think / by Paul Dolan, PhD ; foreword by Daniel Kahneman. — Large print edition.
      pages cm. — (Thorndike Press large print health, home & learning.)
    Includes bibliographical references.
    ISBN 978-1-4104-7845-0 (hardcover) — ISBN 1-4104-7845-9 (hardcover)
    1. Happiness—Psychological aspects. I. Title.
    BF575.H27D65 2015
    158—dc23   2015001665

Published in 2015 by arrangement with Hudson Street Press, an imprint of Penguin Publishing Group, a division of Penguin Random House LLC

Printed in Mexico
1 2 3 4 5 6 7 19 18 17 16 15

CONTENTS

FOREWORD 9
A NOTE TO THE READER 13
A LITTLE WARM-UP 19
INTRODUCTION: STUTTERING
   INTO HAPPINESS 21

PART 1. DEVELOPING HAPPINESS
1. What Is Happiness? 35
   Happiness as Evaluation 36
   Happiness as Feelings 39
   The Pleasure-Purpose Principle . . 43
   The PPP for Life 63
2. What Do We Know About
   Happiness? 69
   Experience Sampling 71
   German Days 72
   American Episodes 82
   Other Evidence on Happiness . . 90
   The Measure Matters 101

3. What Causes Happiness? 106
    From Widgets to Happiness . . . 107
    Above and Below the Surface . . 117
    Behavioral Spillovers 125
    The Shifting Sands of Attention . . 133
    Attending to Happiness 147
4. Why Aren't We Happier? 148
    Mistaken Desires 149
    Mistaken Projections 168
    Mistaken Beliefs 185
    Reallocating Attention 197

PART 2. DELIVERING HAPPINESS
5. Deciding Happiness 201
    Pay Attention to Your Own
      Feedback 201
    Pay Attention to the Feedback
      of Others 222
    Don't Try Too Hard 231
    Happier by Deciding 236
6. Designing Happiness 239
    Priming 243
    Defaults 248
    Commitments 251
    Social Norms 260
    Designing Habits 268
    Happier by Designing 272

7. Doing Happiness 275
   Pay Attention to What You Are
     Doing 275
   Pay Attention to Who You Are
     Doing It With 290
   Don't Get Distracted 293
   Happier by Doing 313
8. Decide, Design, and Do 315
   Dither Less 316
   Distribute More 326
   Efficient Production 349

   CONCLUSION 351
   ACKNOWLEDGMENTS . . . 361
   NOTES 365

FOREWORD

There are two central issues in the study of happiness (I tend to prefer the label of subjective well-being). The first is a classic distinction, which goes back at least to Aristotle, between two views of the good life: a life of pleasure, contentment, and other positive feelings, or one that is well-lived and meaningful. A clear choice of one over the other has its problems. A preference for joy over meaning gets you labeled a hedonist, which is not a compliment. On the other hand, you are properly called a scold if you proclaim that pleasure is frivolous and that only virtue and meaning matter. How should you define happiness if you wish to be neither a hedonist nor a scold? The other great question about happiness is how to measure it. Should we study how people feel as they go about their life, whether they mostly experience happiness or misery? Or should we ask people to stop and think about their life, and report whether or not they are satisfied with it?

The two questions appear to be related. It seems natural to use measurements of life satisfaction to study whether people find meaning in their life, and to identify happy feelings by measuring ongoing experience. That was also my view for many years, but Paul Dolan has a different idea. To begin with, he is much more interested in people's experiences of life than in their evaluations of their life. The novel idea is to consider "meaningful" and "meaningless" as experiences, not judgments. Activities, in his view, differ in a subjective experience of purposefulness — volunteer work is associated with a sense of purpose that channel-surfing lacks. For Dolan, purpose and pleasure are both basic constituents of happiness. This is a bold and original move.

The question "What does happiness consist of?" is not answered by listing facts about happiness. It is about the proper use of the word: when people speak of "happiness," what do they have in mind? No answer can be completely satisfactory, because people do not always have the same idea in mind when they use the word. Among the imperfect definitions of happiness, the pleasure-purpose concept that

Dolan offers is, I believe, a strong contender. It is a good description of what I wish for my grandchildren: a life that is rich in activities that are both pleasurable and meaningful.

Paul Dolan is an inveterate optimist who has overcome many obstacles on his way to becoming an internationally recognized expert on well-being. The optimism shows on every page of this book. In particular, Paul is optimistic about you, his reader. He believes that you can make your life both pleasurable and meaningful with deliberate choices, about the environment you create for yourself and about the aspects of life that deserve your attention. He offers a great deal of sound advice on how to make these choices and how to follow through with them. The rest, he says, is up to you.

Daniel Kahneman

A NOTE TO THE READER

I'd like to thank you for buying my book. It makes me happy, and I hope it will make you happy, too. I'm fascinated by happiness and human behavior, professionally and personally, and I get plenty of opportunities to fuel my fascination. Before writing an entire book on happiness, I was asked to devise the questions that are now being used in large surveys of happiness in the UK and also to advise the UK government on how to design better behavior change interventions. I am now increasingly being asked to advise charities, multinational companies, and other governments about how they can improve happiness and influence behavior.

My professional fascination with happiness came about largely by chance. I had spent a decade conducting academic research into how we should measure and value the benefits of health care spending. This work was recognized with a Philip Leverhulme Prize in 2002 for my contribution to health economics, which meant that I could take some time out from teaching at the University of Sheffield and attend a few conferences. One such conference, on the economics of happiness and held in Milan in March 2003, turned out to be the most significant event of my academic life. On the way to the conference dinner, I sat next to a man who introduced himself as Daniel (Danny) Kahneman. I knew exactly who he was. As many of you know, too, Danny is a psychologist who won the Nobel Prize in Economic Sciences in 2002. He has subsequently written *Thinking, Fast and Slow*, which is a brilliant book about human behavior and decision making.

Danny was immediately engaging and interested to hear about what I was working on. After a few minutes, he said, "Why not come to Princeton [where he worked] and we can work together?" I thought about that for about a nanosecond and said, "Yes, please." Beyond being one of the nicest people I have ever met, Danny is my intellectual hero. In fact, that whole conference was pretty life changing as I also met Richard Layard, one of the most famous happiness researchers in the world and author of *Happiness: Lessons from a New Science.*

Richard was instrumental in my move to the London School of Economics in 2010.

Since meeting Danny and Richard, I have been conducting research into happiness and its causes. Sometimes this has involved analyzing existing data sets; other times it requires me to gather my own data. This has quite naturally led to research into understanding human behavior, using experiments conducted in the lab and in the real world. A large part of how you feel is determined by what you do, what you do is largely motivated by the expected impact on your happiness, and happiness is the feedback you receive about the impact of what you do. You can see how it's all very cyclical.

As one of the small number of researchers working on *both* happiness and behavior, one of the main aims of this book is to demonstrate the links between these two research fields, and in so doing to bring the latest insights from happiness research and behavioral science to bear directly on the questions of what you are trying to achieve (more happiness) and how you can bring it about (by behaving differently). I was trained as an economist but I am now a professor of behavioral science, which probably gives me more in common with psychologists these days. My research, and now this book, seeks to combine the best bits from these two disciplines: the formal and explicit consideration of costs and benefits from economics alongside the recognition from psychology that our behavior is heavily influenced by context and situation.

I also bring a distinctive personal perspective to the book. My dad had many low- or semiskilled manual jobs over the years, and my mum worked in clerical roles to supplement the family income. I grew up in social housing and attended run-of-the-mill state schools. Money was tight, but not too tight to mention. We did not go on holiday very often, but my parents made sure we were always well fed and wore pretty decent clothes, too. Many of my current friends have not attended university, while others have had privileged backgrounds. I therefore continue to have experiences that are different from many of those who write about human happiness and behavior. A good understanding of the academic research matters, but so, too, does a little knowledge of the complexities and quirks of the real lives of people from a range of different backgrounds.

As I'm sure you are only too well aware, managing other people's expectations of you is an important skill, and so I won't make any promises to change your life; but I do hope to provide some insights into how you can change what you do. Behavioral science teaches us that what you are told matters a bit but *who* it is that tells you matters a lot. You listen more to some people than to others. Ideally, good messengers have three attributes: they can be trusted; they are experts; and they are like you. As a consequence of my academic work and my personal background, I would like to think I have all three attributes. All the more reason to pay attention to what follows.

A LITTLE WARM-UP

Before we move ahead, I'd like you to look at the following list of twenty items that could potentially make you happier.

From this list, what are the four items that would make you happiest? Place an X in the "make me happiest" column alongside the four items. For each of the four items you chose, please rate how difficult it would be to achieve on a scale from 0 to 10, where 0 represents "not at all difficult" and 10 means "very difficult indeed."

You might want to keep your selections in the back of your head as you read on.

		Make me happiest	Difficulty in achieving (0–10)
1	More money		
2	New experiences		
3	Children		
4	More time with the kids		
5	The kids leaving home		
6	A new partner		
7	More sleep		
8	More sex		
9	A shorter commute		
10	More time with friends		
11	A new house		
12	A new job		
13	A new boss		
14	New work colleagues		
15	More exercise		
16	To be healthier		
17	To be slimmer		
18	To stop smoking		
19	More holidays		
20	A pet		

INTRODUCTION:
STUTTERING INTO HAPPINESS

Here's a confession that until recently I would have made only to my family and very close friends. I have a stammer (or stutter, if you prefer; they mean the same thing). It has probably been the single biggest blot on my landscape of happiness. It has been with me all my life and it has always affected me, despite my largely successful attempts to keep it hidden.

My mother took me to see a speech therapist when I was about seven years old and I was told that I would grow out of it. My stammer was especially awful when I was a teenager. I couldn't say my name. I hated using the phone. Any small speaking situation that nonstammerers take for granted brought on severe anxiety attacks before and during the event, and feelings of utter despair afterward.

The reason a stammer is such a problem is because it is the perfect attention-grabbing condition. It is the focus of a great deal of attention for the stammerer, and it draws attention to itself every time a speaking situation arises. As any stammerer will tell you, its frequency and severity are variable and so it takes a lot of what I shall call "attentional energy." If I had always stammered on every sixth word, say, I would not have attended to it anywhere near as much; and others would soon have become used to the pattern, too. Uncertainty grabs your attention, just as noises that occur at random (car horns, say) will attract your attention more than noises that are predictable (a ticking clock).

A stammer is also pretty difficult to explain, since the causes of stammering have not been fully established.[1] You generally pay more attention to stimuli that you can't explain; you will pay more attention to a pain in your leg, for example, if you do not know why it hurts compared to if you know it is because you fell off your bicycle a few days ago.[2]

Even those whose stammer is not too severe on the surface experience considerable anxiety below the surface, as they think about when their next disfluency will arise. My own disfluency typically manifests itself as "blocks," involuntary silent pauses in which I am unable to produce sounds and which, in those moments, feel like they last forever. Needless to say, there is a considerable fear of stammering. As if all that isn't enough, we stammerers also think that other people are paying a great deal of attention to our speech and that we are being judged harshly as a result. The only comforting thing was knowing that I would grow out of it. If only.

It took a disastrous seminar presentation as a final-year undergraduate to make me realize that my stammer was not going to simply disappear on its own. As a stammerer I had become a master at avoiding public speaking, and so that presentation was my first ever. Lots of people dread public speaking, of course, but this fear is magnified many times over in the minds of a stammerer. A year later, as a graduate student in York when I was twenty-two, I went to see a more enlightened speech therapist than the one my mother took me to, and she taught me controlled speech. This consisted of starting my sentences very softly, speaking slowly, and envisioning my words as seamlessly linked together. I was still a long way from being "fluent," but it did give me the confidence to start speaking publicly. I began increasingly to put myself into stressful speaking situations, to confront my fear, and found myself a lectureship.

Over time I became more willing to do public speaking events and worried about them less. I paid much less attention to the fear of speaking. I have dreaded many of these events but I genuinely cannot recall one that went as badly as I thought it might. Over the last couple of decades, I've become very proud of developing a general "fight" approach to my stammer, and I have actively sought out challenging but purposeful activities, like public speaking.

There have still been many specific instances of "flight," though, such as avoiding radio and television interviews; any live broadcast used to be completely off-limits. More important, my stammer continued to affect how I felt, resulting in considerable anxiety while speaking and in advance of important occasions when I felt my fluency mattered. So about six years ago I decided to attend a stammering conference in Croatia. On the plane ride home, I met a couple of speech therapists from the Michael Palin Centre in London. They kindly agreed to see me, although the center focuses on dealing with stammers in children.

This therapy was very different from my

previous experience. The focus was now on the attention I paid to stammering; hardly any of it was about my actual speech. I learned to pay much more attention to my current experiences, which mitigated the fear of how bad my speech might be and the worry about how bad it had just been. I also began paying attention to the internal feedback I received from speaking events, which was nearly always pretty good, so I could feed this information forward into my thoughts about future speaking events. Paying attention to how your behavior affects your feelings is critical to understanding what makes you happy and what does not.

I also realized that the attention I paid to my speech, and to my lack of fluency, was completely at odds with the attention paid to it by others. In fact, as I later learned when I "came out" as a stammerer, only a few people were actually aware of it. Most thought I simply spoke in an idiosyncratic way. Some of my current students who commented on earlier drafts of this book were surprised to know that someone whom they have seen speak in many different public fora had such concerns about his speech. Another important lesson was just how little it mattered even to those who knew me, how little they were judging me. My beliefs about myself were also at the heart of dealing with my stammer: it ceased to define who I was.

Once I stopped paying so much attention to my speech, it stopped bothering me as much. So changing behavior and enhancing happiness is as much about withdrawing attention from the negative as it is about attending to the positive. These days, my happiness, however you measure it, is hardly affected by my stammer. All in all, a reallocation of attention explains why I don't stammer anywhere near so much now, and why I don't really care when I do. Stammering less has helped, of course, but paying less attention to it matters much more. I am happier as a result.

What applies to my stammer applies to all the possible causes of your happiness and to all that you might do to be happier. Your happiness is determined by how you *allocate your attention.* What you attend to drives your behavior and it determines your happiness. Attention is the glue that holds your life together.

The professional catalyst for a focus on the allocation of attention comes from my training as an economist, which leads me to begin tackling any problem as an allocation issue. We see scarcity everywhere, and so the allocation of resources is critical to bringing about desirable outcomes. Your attentional resources are sometimes directed at the activities you are engaged in, and at other times you will be thinking about all sorts of things, like what to have for dinner, or you might simply be daydreaming. Attention devoted to one stimulus is, by definition, attention that is not devoted to another. When you are texting one friend, you are not paying attention to the other friend sitting next to you. It is no coincidence that we use the term "pay attention" in everyday language.

The scarcity of attentional resources means that you must consider how you can make and facilitate better decisions about what to pay attention to and in what ways. If you are not as happy as you could be, then you must be misallocating your attention. You will be the happiest you can be when you allocate your attention as best as you can.

The idea that you are what you attend to has been around for more than a century.[3] My interest in attention was sparked by working with Daniel Kahneman in Princeton. My own contribution here is to show how attention acts as a production process that converts stimuli into happiness.

Previous attempts to explain the causes of happiness have all mistakenly sought to relate inputs, such as income, directly to the final output of happiness. But my approach recasts the inputs as stimuli vying for your attention, with their effects on your happiness determined by how much they are attended to. So the effect of income on your happiness is determined not only by how much money you have but also by how much attention you pay it. The same inputs — money, marriage, sex, stammering, or whatever — can affect your happiness a lot or a little depending on how much attention you pay to them.

Some inputs, such as noise, naturally draw more attention to themselves than others, but you have some control over the impact they have on how you feel. I hope you agree with me when I say that this is pretty liberating.

A more humbling consideration is that much of what we attend to, and any resulting behavior, will be driven by unconscious and automatic processes. Indeed, the last couple of decades of research in behavioral science have taught us a simple yet very important lesson: much of what we do simply comes about, rather than being thought about. Whether or not you buy that big bar of chocolate depends largely on whether it is on display at the till and much less on any real, conscious decision to devour a giant candy bar. Life is full of examples like this. I'm not sure I know at what stage I normally put my seat belt on in the car. Do you? And do you go straight to the fridge when you get home from school or work, without really thinking about it?

We are all creatures of our environment. Consider data from over three million teenagers in California, which show that having a fast-food restaurant one-tenth of a mile from school increases the obesity rate among the children at that school by more than 5 percent. Similarly, for pregnant women, a fast-food restaurant within a half mile of their house leads to a 1.6 percent increase in the chance of gaining over forty-four pounds during their pregnancy.[4] Gaining weight has a lot to do with the opportunity to do so.

Let's go from eating to cheating. Much as we might like to think otherwise, when given the chance to, most of us will cheat at least a little bit, but not enough to interfere with a positive self-image of ourselves. Allow a group of students taking a general knowledge test to mark themselves and report their own scores, and they will report getting about four more questions right (out of fifty) than those who have the teacher check their paper. So not that many more right, then: that really would be cheating. Our propensity to cheat, just like our propensity to eat, has less to do with the type of person we are and more to do with the opportunity to do so.[5]

As you might more easily expect, my stammer is worse in some situations than in others. My most serious bouts of disfluency have all occurred in stressful situations and, as I think any stammerer will tell you, it is simply impossible to stammer, authentically, when we are on our own. My speech and how it affects me are influenced by who I am and also by my environment. Much of when and how my stammer manifests itself, though, and how I then respond to times of disfluency, feels completely random to me. If it has any coherence beneath the surface, I am unaware of it. So any attempts to understand human behavior and happiness must properly account for the effects of external context as well as internal cognition — for "contextology" as well as psychology.

This is a book in two integrated parts. Part 1 will "discover" happiness in a bit more detail. Elaborating on what I have just alluded to, it will show how happiness is caused by what we pay attention to. But before getting into what causes happiness, we must first define it. I'll show that the key to happiness is *finding pleasure and purpose in everyday life.* Building on the foundations of part 1, and informed by the latest evidence from behavioral science, part 2 provides you with some suggestions about how to "deliver" happiness for yourself and those you care about. The key here is to organize your life in ways so that you can go with the grain of your human nature and be happier without having to think too hard about it. This is *happiness by design.*

■ ■ ■ ■

PART 1
DEVELOPING
HAPPINESS

■ ■ ■ ■

Many books on happiness make prescriptions about what to do in order to be happier, without defining what happiness is in the first place. But the pursuit of happiness requires a definition of just what is being pursued, and so chapter 1 will define happiness for us as experiences of pleasure and purpose over time.

Using this definition, chapter 2 will present some new research, in which people report how happy they are as they go about their daily activities, and which supports the idea that some activities we get pleasure from, like watching TV, are different from those that bring us purpose, such as work. Chapter 3 sets out the best, and perhaps the only, way to really understand what causes happiness. Inputs like income and stammering don't directly cause the outcome of happiness — but the attention paid to them does. I'll introduce the notion of a *production process* of happiness, my blend of economics and psychology, which I hope will change the way we think about happiness and how to produce more of it. Chapter 4 considers three major attentional obstacles that stand in the way of us making decisions that are consistent with being happier.

1
WHAT IS HAPPINESS?

Your life goes well when you are happy. But what exactly is happiness? I'm not asking what happiness is affected by, but what it actually is. The different ways in which we define happiness affect what we can do to improve it. So a clear definition should be, but rarely is, a fundamental concern for any book on happiness. Having worked at the interface of economics, psychology, philosophy, and policy for two decades, I think I am well placed to make a strong case for the following definition: happiness is *experiences of pleasure and purpose over time*. This definition is novel, it's coherent, and it resonates with people in my research and in my life; and I hope it will with you, too. It is also measurable, which is vital if we are to advance our understanding of happiness. Now let's take a step back.

HAPPINESS AS EVALUATION

Happiness has not typically been measured in this experience-based way; rather, it has been assessed using evaluations of how well life is going overall. A personal anecdote illustrates the difference nicely. A few weeks ago, I went out for dinner with one of my best friends, whom I have known for a long time. She works for a prestigious media company and basically spent the whole evening describing how miserable she was at work; she variously moaned about her boss, her colleagues, and her commute. At the end of dinner, and without a hint of irony, she said, "Of course, I love working at MediaLand."

There is actually no real contradiction here: she is *experiencing* her work in one way and *evaluating* it in another way.[1] The distinction between experience and evaluation is rather like the difference between being filmed and having your photograph taken. My friend was describing the daily "film" of her job as miserable and the overall "snapshot" as quite satisfying in comparison.

We shall see that this is not only a common thing to do but it's also a common mistake to make about our happiness. Many of the assumptions we make about happiness and about ourselves have a lot to do with the fact that we generally pay more attention to what we think *should* make us happy rather than focusing on what actually does. My friend is not happy at work but her experiences have less influence on her behavior than do her evaluations. She loves the idea of working at MediaLand and this is what she acts upon. As a result, she is less happy, day to day, than she could be.

Satisfaction with particular aspects of life, such as work, health, and relationships, will often predict what we do — just as my friend's relatively positive evaluation of working at MediaLand means that she could stay put — but measures of satisfaction are still not very well placed to capture how we feel.[2] My friend is pretty miserable at work, and we should be taking that into account when we measure her happiness.

Most happiness surveys ask rather vague and abstract questions like "Overall, how satisfied are you with your life?" as well as about satisfaction with particular aspects of life. Of course, one question can never really get at all the complex aspects of happiness, but single questions can help us to approximate what makes most people happy or unhappy. The real problem with this question, however, is that overall life satisfaction is rarely considered in our daily lives; perhaps it is only ever really triggered in studies that measure it.[3] The word "satisfaction" is also problematic since it is open to many different interpretations, including "having just about enough," which does not really measure happiness at all. As such, the results tell us much more about what pops into your head when you answer these questions than they do about your experiences of happiness on a day-to-day basis. And it literally must be what "pops" in, because the time taken to answer what to me feels like a cognitively demanding question is around five seconds.[4]

This helps to explain why responses to life satisfaction questions seem to be affected by apparently irrelevant factors, such as whether or not you are asked about your political views before being asked a life satisfaction question, where the effect is nearly as large as becoming unemployed.[5] The order of the questions you're asked matters a lot, too. Your satisfaction with life is much more highly correlated with your marital satisfaction if the marriage question comes before the life satisfaction question instead of after it: being reminded about your relationship first makes it more important in determining your life satisfaction.[6]

You "pose" in a particular way when you have your photograph taken. Think of all the times you have posed for the camera in ways that do not reflect your current feelings. A camcorder is much better at showing how happy you are over time. So we need to move away from global snapshots of overall life satisfaction and instead focus more directly on our day-to-day feelings.

HAPPINESS AS FEELINGS

Your life therefore goes well when you *feel happy.* You experience a rich array of feelings in any one day, let alone over a lifetime. Psychologists often categorize feelings according to a two-by-two model — "positive and negative" as one category and "aroused and nonaroused" as the other.[7] Positive and "negative" speak for themselves; though I put negative in quotation marks because, as I shall discuss shortly, what we consider a negative feeling can sometimes be entirely appropriate with good consequences. You can think of aroused and nonaroused as feelings that are "awakened" or "sleepy," respectively. So joy is positive and aroused; contentment is positive and nonaroused; anxiety is negative and aroused; and sadness is negative and nonaroused — as shown:

Emotions	Nonaroused	Aroused
Positive	Content, calm	Joyful, excited
"Negative"	Sad, depressed	Anxious, angry

We would expect the distinction between positive and negative to affect happiness, and the distinction between aroused and nonaroused matters, too. In contrast to life satisfaction data, data from the Gallup World Poll (a survey of the happiness of adults in 132 countries around the world) show that richer people in any country do not always feel happier than poorer ones. And beyond about $75,000 a year in the United States, more money does not buy any more happiness *at all* for the average US citizen earning above this amount.[8] Being richer might make you *think* you are happier but it does not necessarily make you *feel* any happier.

The idea that your feelings are what matter to your life originated with the work of Jeremy Bentham, an eighteenth-century philosopher and radical who believed in the decriminalization of homosexuality and equal rights for women. Bentham was a child prodigy and attended the University of Oxford at the age of twelve to study law. He soon became disillusioned with the legal system and instead devoted his life to campaigning for reform. He is well known to visitors of University College London, where he sits embalmed at the entrance to the university. As requested in his will,

Bentham's body was dissected as part of a public anatomy lecture and the skeleton and head were preserved and stored in a wooden cabinet with the skeleton dressed in Bentham's clothes. His head is actually a wax head, because the mummification process left him looking a little odd. It does have his real hair, though.[9]

Bentham argued that pleasure is the only thing that is good for you, and pain the only bad. Some scholars have moved away from using pleasure and pain because of the association with bodily pleasures and pains, preferring instead terms such as enjoyment and suffering.[10] According to my broader interpretation, pleasure and pain can also refer to the many other adjectives that describe positive and negative feelings: joy, excitement, and fun on the one hand and anger, anxiety, stress, and worry on the other. So when I use the words "pleasure" and "pain" in this book, I do so as umbrella terms or shorthand for a whole raft of feelings, recognizing also that we can simultaneously feel and display a complex mix of emotions.[11]

What you feel is determined by what happens to you but also by the kind of person you are. I am nearly always in an aroused emotional state, most of the time feeling happy but sometimes feeling anxious. I rarely feel content or sad. I quite like it this way and my wife, Les, and my friends tell me they do, too (though I guess they would have left me by now if not). You might be similar to me, or you might be different; calmer, perhaps.

Overall, each of us can be categorized according to the preponderance of different types of feelings. The happy ones among us have more positive feelings than negative ones. Using Bentham's language, they generally feel pleasure and not that much pain. So, the more frequent and more intense are your various feelings of pleasure, the happier you are. But are there other feelings that might matter besides categories of pleasure and pain?

THE PLEASURE-PURPOSE PRINCIPLE

Yes, there is another important category of feelings that matter to you, and these are the feelings of *purpose* and *pointlessness* you feel. I will use these adjectives as shorthand for a range of positive and negative feelings, such as fulfillment, meaning, and worthwhileness on the one hand and boredom and futility on the other. These feelings affect your happiness in ways that must be properly accounted for. You only have to think about working or studying to know that these activities can feel quite purposeful some of the time — and quite pointless at other times. These good and bad feelings matter to you every bit as much as do feelings of pleasure and pain.

Feeling It
Now, calling purpose a feeling suggests that it is an emotion that can be placed on a comparable footing with more recognized emotions like joy, anxiety, and anger. But I have a more general interpretation in mind here; namely, what I call *feelings as sentiments.* I do not mean sentimental in the tears-in-your-eyes sense; rather, sentimental in the sense of a rich array of feelings. In my definition, a sentiment is a feeling that covers the kinds of emotional pleasures and pains that psychologists generally have in mind but it additionally includes feelings about the degree to which an experience is purposeful. The adjectives for feelings of purpose are distinct from those used for pleasure. Purpose is a simpler construct than pleasure because it's largely nonaroused, so either it's good (purposeful) or bad (pointless).

Writing this book is a great example of doing something that feels purposeful. It feels purposeful while I am doing it; just as having a beer with my mates feels pleasurable. Helping a friend move house is another example. Lugging boxes and furniture up and down three flights of stairs all day isn't particularly pleasant but it does feel purposeful at the time you are sweating on the stairs. Or perhaps watching that moving documentary, which may not be exactly fun but keeps you engrossed throughout. I'm sure you can think of plenty of your own examples.

There are also times when you feel the opposite — pointlessness, futility, or a lack of purpose. That work assignment where you are convinced nothing will ever come of it, which feels painful as well as pointless. Or that romantic comedy you watched last night, which was actually quite pleasurable but did not feel at all purposeful.[12] I bet you don't have to try too hard to think of these sorts of examples.

It is surprising to me that happiness has not really been considered in this way before. There has certainly been much discussion in the academic literature about day-to-day experiences of pleasure, but purpose is not usually considered in this experience-based way. Insofar as it has been considered, it has typically been tapped into by studies that ask us general questions about whether life overall has direction, meaning, or purpose.[13]

Just like life satisfaction questions, these kinds of questions capture overall *evaluations* of purpose when life as a whole is reflected upon and not the day-to-day *experiences* of purpose, which are what really matter to how you feel. As an example, new fathers report more purpose in their lives than their childless peers, and the effect is much less pronounced for new mothers.[14] These results are interesting but they could simply be explained by responses being driven by what is prominent at the time of assessment. New fathers might pay more attention to the general fact that they have just had a kid as compared to new mothers, who might also be thinking about the housework (which they still do much more of). A more accurate and useful measure would consider whether new mothers and fathers also report different amounts of purpose in the daily activities of their lives.

As I sit here now, typing these words, I *feel* pretty good. But most of that good feeling is not an emotional reaction to what I am writing but rather that the words, and my attempt to convey their meaning to you, generate a feeling of purpose. I am sure that you feel similarly as you go about your daily life. You might spend time tending to your garden, and this might feel purposeful in addition to — and separate from — any emotional reaction you have to looking after your roses. Or you might have a job that feels rewarding; it might even be less fun than your last job but it makes you feel happier overall.

So I am much more interested in the meaning of moments than I am in constructions of the meaning of life. There is pleasure (or pain) and purpose (or pointlessness) in all that you do and feel. They are separate components that make up your overall happiness from an experience.

That our happiness includes both pleasure and purpose is also reflected in what people like you tell me. Few scholars have studied what people think about happiness in their own lives, or what data governments could use to inform decisions about how we spend money on public services, and so with the support of the Office for National Statistics in the UK, Rob Metcalfe and I designed an online survey to help fill that gap. We need to have a healthy degree of skepticism about what people tell us in surveys because the responses are heavily influenced by the wording of the questions, but, when asked about happiness in their own lives and in the context of informing public policy, about as many participants were in favor of a focus on "happiness and sadness on a day-to-day basis" as were in favor of focusing on "the degree to which you consider the things you do to be worthwhile."[15] In other words, both pleasure and purpose matter to us (although admittedly this is a rather evaluative way of describing purpose).

To be truly happy, then, you need to feel both pleasure and purpose. You can be just as happy or sad as I am but with very different combinations of pleasure and purpose. And you may require each to different degrees at different times. But you do need to feel both. I call this the pleasure-purpose principle — the PPP.

As well as explaining human motivation to seek out pleasure and purpose and avoid pain and pointlessness, the PPP can also help explain why some generally negative emotions can in fact sometimes be positive if they serve a purpose. Anger, for example, helps us to avoid bad situations and seek out good ones, and it can elicit a "positive" reaction by directing us toward rather than away from conflict resolution.[16] In particular, anger has the propensity to discourage selfishness and to encourage cooperative behavior.[17] So you don't want to experience good sentiments all of the time. Life can be cruel, and people can be, too, so you sometimes need to get angry. But we can also get angry unnecessarily, of course; such as when we get stressed by small annoyances.

The PPP might also help us answer a hugely important question, which actually got me thinking about purpose in the first place: why would any of us ever choose to have children? I mean *really choose* to, rather than because of a biological imperative to reproduce? A big part of the answer to this question must be because we would expect to be happier as a result. What do the data tell us? Well mostly, that, at best, children are neutral in their impact on happiness.[18]

Now, it could still be the case that many of those who have kids might have been much less happy if they remained childless and also that some of those without kids would have been happier with them. To truly show the effect of kids on happiness, we would need to know what otherwise might have been the case for each individual, and this is impossible to establish. This highlights the fact that we need to be very careful about making any claims about the causal effects of life events on happiness when people, to some degree at least, self-select into the groups whose happiness we are comparing.

It should come as no great surprise that having children does not improve happiness, though. You need only to have a desire for having sex, which sometimes results in pregnancy, and then to emotionally connect to a baby that looks like you when it is born, which means that you are then much less likely to abandon your kids. What happens to your happiness thereafter is then of little consequence.

So when I first started thinking about having kids of my own about a decade ago, the happiness-informed decision could well have been to remain childless, right? Perhaps, but the data at that time were based largely on evaluations of life satisfaction and partly on experiences of pleasure alone. I had the strong sense that some of what I would do as a parent might feel purposeful, such as helping my kids put their shoes on or learn to read. I did not expect such activities to be that pleasurable, and certainly not as much fun as a night out with my mates, but I did think that reading a story to my kids, or later listening to them read to me, would feel purposeful at the time of doing so.

Armed with the strong intuition that having children could potentially make me happier by adding more purpose to my already pleasurable life — or at least *differently happy* by changing the balance of pleasure and purpose in my life — I decided to take the plunge and have kids. Les and I now have a daughter, Poppy, who is six, and a son, Stanley, who is five. They bring us a bit of pleasure, a lot of misery, and a massive dose of purpose. I would say that they have definitely made me differently happy as the balance of pleasure and purpose has changed in my life. They might even have made me happier overall, as the relative shift from pleasure to purpose quite suits me as I get older. In the next chapter, I'll discuss studies that I've since conducted which show that time spent with children is about average in terms of its impact on pleasure but that it is one of the more purposeful ways of using your time.

Now, I am certainly not suggesting that you rush out (or, more precisely, stay in) and have kids: much of what you do can feel purposeful without it having to involve children. All I am saying is that a happy life is one that contains lots of positive sentiments of pleasure and of purpose. Equally, a miserable life contains a preponderance of negative sentiments of pain (anger, worry, stress) and pointlessness (boredom, futility).

Creating a definition of happiness is a complex endeavor, but the PPP helps us cut through various other definitions by incorporating a rich array of sentiments into the daily experiences of life. Getting angry from time to time, working long hours, and having children may no longer be such crazy things to do. But they might be if you sacrifice a lot of pleasure for a little more purpose: that is, if your own balance between pleasure and purpose is out of kilter.

Balancing It

You are unlikely to have thought explicitly about your balance of pleasure and purpose before now. To begin considering it here, think about the kinds of programs you typically watch on TV (or books you read if you don't watch TV). Would you say that you generally sit down in front of programs that you would describe as pleasurable, or those that you would describe as purposeful? Or perhaps you watch a balance between the two. To help you to visualize where you are located on the "swing-o-meter" of pleasure and purpose, take a look at the pendulum:

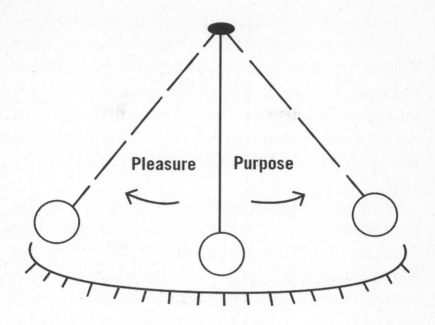

Now that you have warmed up by thinking about TV, think about yourself in general. Are you more of a "pleasure machine," experiencing lots more pleasure than purpose? Or are you more of a "purpose engine," experiencing lots more purpose than pleasure? Or are you one of the "balanced folk," with a mix? Where would you locate yourself now? Is this where you would like to be?

How and in what ways your own happiness should swing back and forth between pleasure and purpose is for you to decide, just as you should decide what you watch on TV. What floats your boat may not be what keeps mine bobbing along. Our preferences may differ. Watching *The X-Files* might make you happy while I prefer *The X Factor.* Allowing different things to affect you in different ways has been missing from a lot of the "one size fits all" books on happiness. You need to work out what works for *you.*

Whatever your reactions, however, it is the frequency and intensity of your feelings (sentiments) that ultimately matter. You are happiest when you have a balance between pleasure and purpose that works best for you. They will not necessarily always be in the same proportion as one another, and it will probably be different from the balance I have in my life. Moreover, each of us requires different combinations of pleasure and purpose at different times in the day and in our lives.

Having said all of this, it is possible for me to make a general claim: if you have a lot more pleasure in your life than purpose, then you should spend a bit more time doing something that is purposeful. And equally, if you have a lot more purpose than you have pleasure, then you should spend more time engaging in pleasure. This claim is based on the *law of diminishing marginal returns* (in our case, to happiness), a concept that is very close to any economist's heart.

To illustrate, imagine two goods, beer and pizza, and assume you like both. The first beer goes down smoothly, and the first slice of pizza tastes really nice. The next beer is good but not quite as good as the first one, and the next slice of pizza is nice but not as nice as the first. So if you have had four beers, you would probably be willing to give up the fifth beer for a first slice of pizza. If instead you have had four slices of pizza, you would probably be willing to give up the fifth slice for a first beer.

The same logic applies to other goods and aspects of life, and also to pleasure and purpose. Without data on the precise trade-offs, consider a sample of two: my friends Mig and Lisa. Mig is my best friend and he lives in Ibiza. He works as little as is required, enjoys parties, and laughs a lot. I have had some of the best times of my life in Ibiza, thanks largely to being with Mig. He calls me Professor Happy and being with him makes me happy. Lisa has a passion for using behavioral science to improve people's lives and she takes her work very seriously. She is a very intense person and only smiles on special occasions. Mig has lots of pleasure whereas Lisa has lots of purpose.

Mig would be happier if he found something purposeful to do (in exchange for some of his fun stuff) and Lisa would be happier if she had a little more fun (in exchange for some of her time spent feeling purposeful). Mig and Lisa have both confessed to me that they think they would be happier with a different combination of feelings of pleasure and purpose in their lives. But neither has acted upon their recognition of this. It is one thing to know and quite another to do, and I will show how you can achieve changes like this later in the book.

In order to say a little more about how people weigh up pleasure and purpose, Tali Sharot, Ivo Vlaev, and I recently conducted a small study involving twenty students who were asked to rate a series of daily activities (such as taking a friend's dog for a walk, reading for work or school, watching TV, listening to music, and so on) according to the pleasure and purpose they would feel during these activities. They were then presented with a series of eighty choices between two activities and asked which one they would prefer to engage in when they got a couple of hours of free time one day soon. The results show that ratings for both pleasure and purpose can be used to predict people's subsequent choices about how to spend their time, but with more weight given to the ratings of pleasure.[19] One possible explanation for this is that free time is more likely to be used for fun than for fulfillment. Our follow-up study will address this issue, and we also plan to look at brain activity when people are experiencing pleasure and purpose.

The PPP Over Time

Day to day, moment to moment, you feel sentiments of pleasure, purpose, pain, and pointlessness. You are happier when you experience more of the positive sentiments — and when you experience them for longer. So happiness is ultimately about the pleasure-purpose principle *over time*.

Time is a truly scarce resource. You can beg, borrow, and steal money but a minute spent has gone for good. Each day, you have a time bank account with 1,440 minutes in it. Each day that account goes back to zero again, with no borrowing or saving. Put bluntly but accurately, you are getting ever closer to death. There are surprisingly few researchers who think about happiness in terms of your time use. But the scarcity of time means that any sensible definition and measure of happiness must consider the duration of your experiences of pleasure and purpose as well as their intensity.

Ultimately, we should all be seeking to use our time in ways that bring us the greatest overall pleasure and purpose for as long as possible. Just as you cannot recover time that is lost, you cannot recover happiness that is lost. Staying in a boring job or an annoying relationship simply prolongs the misery and any future happiness is unlikely to fully compensate for this loss. *Lost happiness is lost forever.*

I should say at this point that more sleep is not necessarily a waste of time. A colleague of mine thought that a consequence of thinking about happiness over time was that happiness levels would go up when waking hours go up because you have more time to be happy. But you would then also have more time to be tired and miserable, too. Happiness is not only about the quantity of time (though that matters) but also about its quality. As someone who does not sleep too well, I would be happier overall during my waking hours if one more of my hours overall were spent sleeping.

So you are happier when you feel better — and for longer. In fact, strictly speaking, you are happier when you feel better for *what feels like* longer. It is our perceptions

58

of duration that govern our experiences. I'm sure you're aware that time seems to pass much more quickly for some activities than for others. As Einstein said: "When a man sits with a pretty girl for an hour, it seems like a minute. But let him sit on a hot stove for a minute — then it's longer than any hour. That's relativity!"[20] If you are in pain, time may feel as if it is passing quite slowly and the same applies to feelings of pointlessness, which seem to drag on and on.[21] Calculating the happiness from different activities using real time is only an approximation of the value of the real experience.

In making decisions now that affect us in the future, we generally care about today far more than we care about tomorrow, and we care about tomorrow more than the day after — but there is very little difference between how we view a year's time versus a year and a day.[22] So we have a strong preference for the present, which explains why some of us (and I include myself in this) are quite impulsive and impatient.

My own recent research, conducted in collaboration with David Bradford and Matteo Galizzi, confirms that we "warp" time in much the same way we have long been known to warp noise, heat, and light.[23]

If I doubled the volume of the TV from 50 decibels to 100 decibels, you would think that the sound had increased by less than a factor of two. So differences feel smaller the more extreme they get. Similarly, if I doubled, from today, the duration I asked you to consider from a week to two weeks, it would feel like the time had increased by less than a factor of two. Let's do the time warp again here:

Imagine a day exactly a week from now. On the line below, the leftmost end of the line represents "very short," and the rightmost end of the line represents "very long." Please place a mark on the line to indicate how long you consider the duration to be between today and a week from now.

Very short _____ Very long

Now imagine a day four weeks from now. On the line below, please place a mark to indicate how long you consider the duration to be between today and four weeks from now.

Very short _____ Very long

If you are anything like the participants in

our studies, then the perceived distance between now and one week from now is about the same as the perceived distance between one week from now and four weeks from now. In other words, as seen from today, the first week feels about as far away as do the three weeks after that, even though the latter is obviously three times as long in real time.

There is no doubt that how impulsive you are and how you perceive time will greatly affect your behavior. But whatever your preferences, your sentiments of pleasure and purpose are always experienced *in the moment*. It is the full flow of sentiments that matters to your happiness, and they are what should be used to judge your behavior.

I accept that you should sometimes be willing to give up a bit of happy time now for more happiness later. An unhappy marriage can be the impetus for divorce, for example, and especially so when one partner is significantly less happy than the other, even in the first year of marriage and especially over time if the gap widens.[24] The good news is that divorce, in Britain at least, has been shown to improve the happiness of the divorcees and their adult children (aged eighteen to thirty) after the knot is broken.[25] You might be made less happy in the short term by reducing how much you smoke but become happier in the long term when you reap the health and happiness benefits of having done so.[26]

So it can be good to be unhappy if you will reap the benefits at a later point, and it's important to consider this temporal dimension to your happiness. As I write this sentence, my family and I are halfway through an eight-week stint in a rented two-bedroom flat so that our new house can be renovated. We expect that our lower happiness from living in cramped conditions for eight weeks will be more than compensated by living in a renovated house for at least eight years. The only way we can make this judgment is by considering experiences of happiness over time.

When economists and others talk about delayed gratification, they are implicitly referring to sacrificing pleasure now for pleasure later. When happiness is defined as experiences of both pleasure and purpose, the circumstances under which it is sacrificed for the pursuit of achievement are potentially much more limited. So the less pleasurable things that you do should at least feel purposeful. Serious athletes provide a good example for they give up a lot of the fun in their lives in order to make it to painful early-morning training sessions. This could be seen as delayed gratification, but I believe that these athletes experience purposeful gratification from training. Just as there is pain from the lactic acid in their muscles, they feel sentiments of purpose too. My research and my experiences tell me that life is less about trading off happiness now for happiness later (and vice versa) and more about trading off pleasure and purpose at different rates at different times.

THE PPP FOR LIFE

Whether or not anything is worth doing depends on your experiences of pleasure and purpose. This includes good and bad sentiments in anticipation of an event that is yet to happen and the good and bad memories of past experiences. There is nothing that exists outside of the here and now: your anticipations and memories are all part of your current feelings. A focus on pleasure and purpose over time allows us to say whether or not a decision is or was rational in a substantive sense according to its overall consequences for happiness.

This is important for a wide range of audiences. It matters to individuals deciding whether it is worth staying in all weekend to devour a DVD box set, and it also represents a new way of thinking for policy makers who are deciding whether they should influence people's decision to devour a KFC bucket. The effects of DVDs and KFCs need to be assessed according to their consequences for happiness, and not on the basis of any other judgments, moral or otherwise, about the "goodness" of these activities.

As an example, consider staying up late (drinking, perhaps, though I won't assume so). You will often regret having done so the next morning when you feel tired. And sometimes you will be right, in an experience-of-happiness sense, to say that the pain of the tiredness outweighs the pleasure of the late night. But sometimes you will be wrong — perhaps the night's pleasure more than makes up for the morning's pain. Importantly, there might also be the memories of the night before to draw from as future pleasures. When thinking about how to be happier, you must keep in mind that your memories of the past are important experiences of happiness *in the present*. Happiness includes good memories of good experiences.

Many economists view you as the perfect judge of your happiness now and projected into the future. From this perspective, you must be better off from staying up late whenever that is what you decided to do, fully aware of all the future consequences of your behavior. They make the same point about everything else, too, since it enables them to look only at what you do. So if you eat lots of cakes and become fat, then that's what you wanted and so you are better off than if you were prevented, or nudged away, from doing so. But it is naïve to say that your preferences *before the event* are all that count since you can sometimes have preferences *after the event,* when you may wish that you had behaved differently. I think we can all agree that we've each had times in our lives when we've said, "I really wish I had not done that."

At the other extreme from the economists are the public policy experts, who argue that regrets after the event should count over all else. But this is also naïve. You can regret lots of things when you experience the adverse consequences of your behavior but that is not to say that you would have wanted to behave any differently before that. There is pleasure in eating cakes. There can be purpose in skydiving even if there is some associated risk of death or serious injury.

In any case, regrets are far from straightforward. We are more likely to regret not doing something than having done it, especially if we are presented with an opportunity to make a big life change.[27] And regrets have been shown to be sensitive to the time frame over which the retrospection takes place. When researchers looked at the regrets of college students in relation to their recent winter breaks and at the regrets of college graduates looking back at the winter breaks they had forty years earlier, the college students regretted not working harder (purposeful activities) while the alumni regretted not partying harder (pleasurable activities) all those years before.[28] Instead of worrying about immediate or more distant regrets, better to focus on consuming a good balance of pleasure and purpose *now*. A good balance of pleasure and purpose is also likely to have the positive by-product of you having fewer regrets.

So whether staying up late, eating cakes, skydiving, or anything else is good or bad should not be judged according to forward-looking preferences or backward-looking regrets but rather directly on the experiences of happiness over time; over your lifetime, in fact. It's all the happiness you experience over all of your life that matters to you (even if you will necessarily pay attention to the happiness over much shorter time frames).

Everything that happens in your life, in principle, can be subject to empirical enquiry into consequences. Your experiences of happiness give you an account by which you can judge whether every single behavior eventually resolves itself as being, on balance, a good or a bad decision. It is difficult in practice to know how different decisions will pan out in the fullness of time but that does not negate the fact that, in principle, the lifetime approach to happiness is the correct analysis. How much more or less pleasure and purpose you feel from one set of experiences compared to another depends on what you might otherwise be feeling instead. Again, you cannot possibly think about the benefits foregone or to be gained from every activity but, by definition, doing one thing means that you lose the happiness from doing something else.

Some philosophers say that you can only really judge a life from its deathbed, as you reflect upon your successes and failures.[29] To quote Bertrand Russell, "I feel as if one would only discover on one's deathbed what one ought to have lived for."[30] But no moment should be privileged simply because it is that moment, and that includes your deathbed. I'm sure many of us care about how we will look back on our lives on our deathbed, but the value of our lives comes from the experiences of pleasure and purpose over our lifetimes and not from a judgment we might make at an arbitrarily chosen moment in time.

You don't have to completely sign up to this exposition of happiness. Much of what I have to say later in this book applies to other definitions of happiness, such as those that rely on evaluations of life satisfaction, although it does influence some specific observations, such as thinking about how you can make better use of your time. My definition of happiness also influences my discussion of the empirical evidence on happiness, since I am most interested in understanding experiences of pleasure and purpose over time. These data on happiness are the focus of the next chapter.

2
WHAT DO WE
KNOW ABOUT HAPPINESS?

For reasons alluded to in the introduction, and which will become even clearer in the next chapter, I would ideally like to find out *what you are paying attention to* in a given moment and relate this to how happy you feel. It is difficult to ask you "What are you attending to right now?" and so most attempts to measure happiness over time have done so by asking "What are you doing right now?" The inferences made from such data will assume that your happiness comes from these activities (such as working or watching television), when you might, in fact, be thinking about a whole host of other things as you "listen" to your boss or "watch" *The X Factor*. On average, though, and across large enough samples, measures of happiness focused on activities will probably provide a reliable approximation of where attention is generally directed.

I should also add a few words of caution

about the interpretation of happiness data. Our understanding of the *correlation* between happiness and a range of factors has come a very long way over the past couple of decades, but we do not know as much as we would like to about the degree to which those factors truly *cause* happiness. There are two main obstacles that prevent us from making the leap from correlation to causation: selection effects and reverse causality. Take the effects of volunteering as an example. It's possible that those choosing to volunteer are those most likely to benefit from it, which means that we may not be able to generalize the happiness effects of volunteering to a wider population. Also, those with greater happiness may be those most likely to volunteer in the first place, and so part of any correlation will be picking up the reverse causality from happiness to volunteering. Telling the chicken from the egg in happiness research is quite a challenge.

Having said all of this, it is likely that any happiness ratings for an activity will eventually be determined by the attention paid to it, even if the initial impetus for the activity was driven to some degree by initial happiness. You might be in a great or awful mood and decide to do some chores, but eventually tidying the house will affect how you feel. And, in any case, we can still learn a lot from who the happy ones among us are and what they do.

EXPERIENCE SAMPLING

What, then, does the empirical evidence tell us about experiences of pleasure and purpose in our lives? There have been some experience-sampling studies, which typically send reminders to people's phones at random times during the day to obtain reports of how they are feeling. Such studies are quite intrusive and most people would rather not hear the beep on their mobile phone while in the throes of passion. Also, simply being asked to think about how happy you are feeling in the moment could affect your response.[1] Experience-sampling studies can also be pretty expensive and time-consuming. As a result, they are usually conducted on samples that are convenient (such as students and iPhone users) and not very representative of the general population, so the transferability of the results to other samples of people is questionable. Most important, the studies, consistent with most research on happiness, rarely consider purpose.

The most serious effort to account for the duration of feelings throughout the day, alongside their type and intensity, involves using the day reconstruction method (DRM), which was designed by Daniel Kahneman and colleagues. It asks people to divide the previous day into a series of episodes (commuting, having lunch, watching TV, and so on) and then to rate how they felt during those episodes (joy, sadness, anxiety, and so on).[2]

The DRM is a huge step forward in the measurement of happiness because it is not as invasive as experience sampling and it can capture the amount of time spent engaged in different activities. But it misses out on feelings of purpose. So I conducted my own DRM-type study in 2006 that asked about how worthwhile activities felt in addition to how pleasurable they felt.[3] As in the original DRM, pleasure was measured by asking participants to indicate how much they felt each of the following during each episode: happy, nervous/anxious, sad/depressed, content/relaxed, frustrated, impatient for it to end. To assess purpose, three adjectives were added — focused, engaged, competent/able — as well as three statements: "I feel the activities in this episode . . .": were worthwhile and meaningful; were useful to other people; helped me achieve important goals. The response scale for all questions ranged from 0 (not at all) to 6 (very strongly).

To get a feel for this kind of empirical research, imagine yourself in a simplified version of this study. Think back to one episode yesterday morning, and use it to answer the questions in the table below, describing what you were doing, who you were with, and how much overall pleasure and purpose that activity brought you on a 0 to 6 scale. Do the same for an activity in the evening.

Episode	What were you doing?	Who were you with?	Pleasure (0–6)	Purpose (0–6)
From yesterday morning				
From yesterday evening				

I worked on this project with Mat White, who was based in Germany at the time, and so the sample was recruited via an Internet panel run from a German university. Of the 625 participants, 61 percent were female, and ages ranged from sixteen to eighty, with an average age of thirty-six. The graphs on pages 75 and 76 show a day in the life of one of our German participants. She is thirty-eight years old; has a husband, a pet, and no children; and her household income is between €80,000 and €100,000. From the first graph showing pleasure alone, she is happiest during her lunch break and when watching TV. From the second graph, which adds purpose into the mix, there is less of a difference between her happiness at work and while watching TV and her lunch break is now not so good because, for her, it is less purposeful than most other activities.

We then looked at the pleasure and purpose ratings for each of the main activities for all the participants in the study. Each day the participants spent an average of about seven hours sleeping, three and a half hours working (only half the sample worked on their designated diary-writing day), two and a half hours watching TV, two hours with kids, two hours eating, an hour doing housework, a half hour commuting, and ten minutes volunteering (only 5 percent of the sample volunteered). The remaining five hours or so were made up of other activities like praying, having sex, playing sports, and shopping.

Each activity has its own combination of pleasure and purpose. The graph on page 78 summarizes the average ratings. Activi-

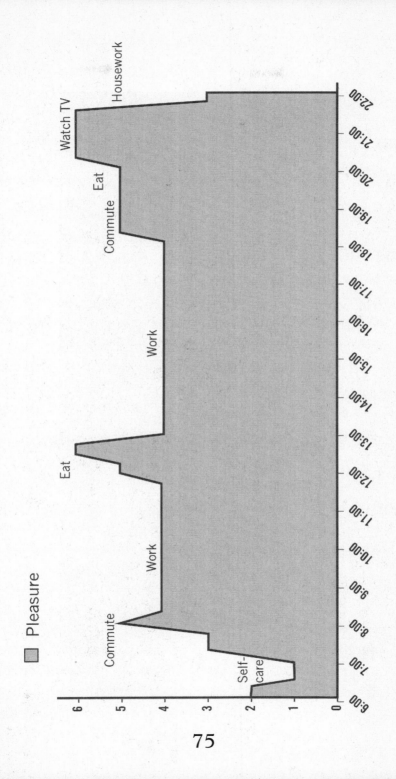

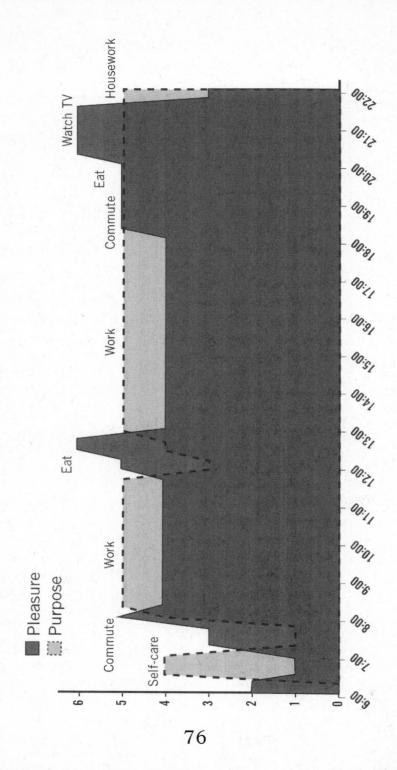

ties become more pleasurable as we move from the bottom to the top of the graph and activities become more purposeful as we move from left to right. If all activities contained the same amount of pleasure and purpose, they would lie on the diagonal line. So if they are to the left of the diagonal line, they contain more pleasure than purpose, and if they are to the right, more purpose than pleasure. Watching TV, eating, and commuting are therefore more pleasurable than purposeful, and volunteering, working, time with kids, and doing housework are more purposeful than pleasurable. Watching TV is the most pleasurable activity and it is also the least purposeful; and working is the second most purposeful activity (behind volunteering) and it is also the least pleasurable. Watching TV and working occupy a lot of time, so it might be that people are achieving some sort of balance between pleasure and purpose.

My main point here, though, is that if we ranked activities by their pleasure and then by their purpose, we would get different rankings. That is, we would make different inferences about what makes people happy. Only by looking at pleasure and purpose together can we really see just how happy we are made by what we do.

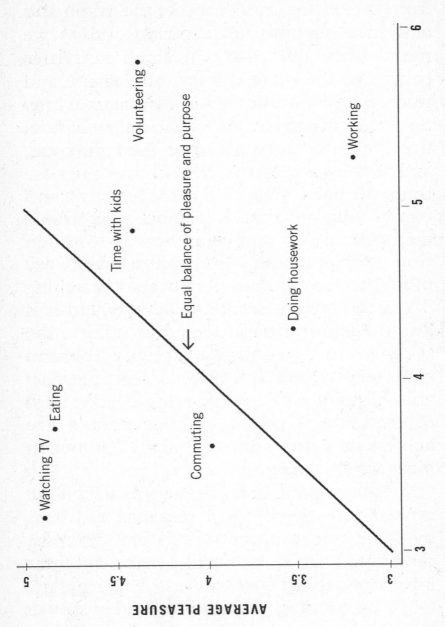

AVERAGE PURPOSE

AVERAGE PLEASURE

Watching TV • Eating

Time with kids

Volunteering •

Equal balance of pleasure and purpose

Commuting

Doing housework

• Working

78

Let us concentrate on working and watching TV for the moment. About 20 percent of the sample did both on the day they were surveyed. So we can look at the relative pleasure and purpose they got from each of these activities. This then allows us to say something speculative about the pleasure machines and purpose engines in the sample. We begin by subtracting each person's purpose rating from their pleasure rating for each activity. If the number is positive, then they get more pleasure than purpose from the activity, if the number is negative they get more purpose than pleasure, and zero would mean an equal amount of each.

The results are summarized in the graph on page 81. We would generally expect most people to get more purpose from work and more pleasure from TV. These are the people represented by the dots in the top left quadrant of the graph and these are colloquially labeled "balanced folk." About 60 percent of the sample are located here. Those who get more pleasure than purpose for both work and TV are in the top right quadrant of the graph and so they are labeled "pleasure machines." They make up about 10 percent of the sample. Those who get more purpose than pleasure for both activities are in the bottom left quadrant and so they are labeled "purpose engines." They make up about 30 percent of the sample. Nobody got more pleasure than purpose from working and more purpose than pleasure from watching TV. So it would seem from this analysis that most people in our study get some kind of balance of pleasure and purpose from the two activities that many of us spend quite a lot of time engaged in.

One general consideration that shows up clearly in this study is the effect of spending time with people you like. In these and other data, being with people is good for feeling good, even at work.[4] Being with others is particularly pleasurable during the most pleasurable activities, eating and watching TV. Being with others is especially purposeful when commuting and doing housework.

In terms of background characteristics, men experience greater pleasure over the day but women experience greater happiness overall when purpose is added. Those who care for sick or elderly family members compared to those who do not, those who earn €60,000 to €80,000 compared to all other income groups, and those who are married as opposed to single are all less

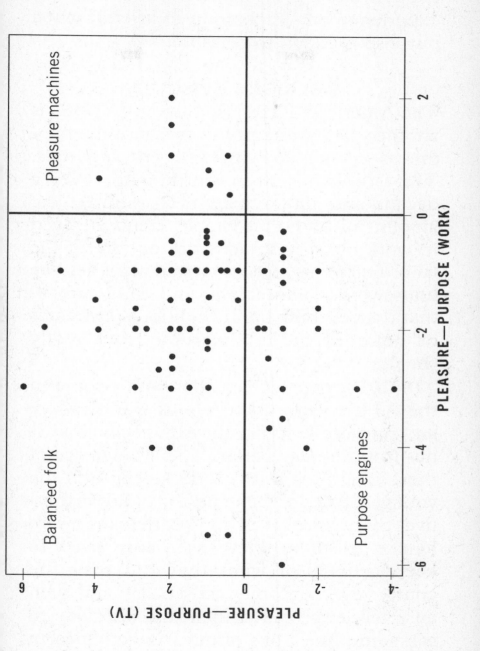

happy from a pleasure standpoint but they experience greater happiness overall when purpose is added to pleasure.

AMERICAN EPISODES

The American Time Use Survey (ATUS) is another, larger attempt to measure the happiness associated with different activities. This study has been running for over a decade and allows analysts to estimate the amount of time that people spend engaged in work but also in activities outside of the labor market — that is, unpaid activities like housework, volunteering, and child care — that do not show up in traditional estimates of national productivity but that really should.

In 2010, the thirteen thousand people in the ATUS were asked about the pleasure and purpose they felt during specific activities from the day before. The average age of those interviewed was forty-seven, with the youngest being fifteen and the oldest eighty-five. Sixty percent of the participants were female. All those interviewed were asked to keep a diary of what they did over the course of a randomly chosen day and then an interviewer called them the next day to ask some questions about the activities in their diary.

One of the questions was: "From 0 to 6, where a 0 means you were not happy at all and a 6 means you were very happy, how happy did you feel during this time?" Another was: "From 0 to 6, how meaningful did you consider to be what you were doing? A 0 means it was not meaningful at all to you and a 6 means it was very meaningful to you." The first question is of course representative of my "pleasure" category of feelings and the second concerns "purpose." With this distinction in mind, Laura Kudrna and I have been analyzing the ATUS.

Each day, the overall sample spent an average of about eight and a half hours sleeping, three hours working (again, only about 60 percent worked on that day), two and a half hours watching television, one hour doing housework, one hour eating, an hour with kids, a half hour commuting, ten minutes volunteering, and ten minutes doing homework. The remaining six hours or so were made up of using the computer, reading, sports and recreation, practicing religion, shopping, caring for pets, talking on the phone, socializing, and other miscellaneous activities.

The amount of time spent on various activities differs across groups. Men spend about an hour longer working than women, and they also spend about an hour more watching TV; and women spend about an hour longer doing housework than men. These gender differences are consistent with the typical household divisions of labor found in time use surveys.[5] Married people work for about forty-five minutes more than those who are single, widowed, or divorced; and people who are not married spend about a half hour more sleeping. There are also differences in time use by age. The average amount of time people spend working is roughly the same, at around four hours a day during working age, then dropping to around an hour in the sixties and seventies. The amount of time devoted to housework increases with age, but it is difficult to say whether this is an effect that reflects generational differences in housework or age-related changes in the time it takes to do chores.[6] TV watching also increases with age, from around two hours a day for those in their twenties to nearly four hours a day for those in their fifties and sixties.

Then we looked at the average pleasure and purpose ratings for each of the main activities described above. Each activity obviously has its own combination of pleasure and purpose. The graph on page 86 summarizes the average pleasure and purpose ratings in the ATUS data, where you'll see that the results are pretty similar to those for the German DRM data. So watching TV, eating, and commuting again have relatively more pleasure than purpose, and time with kids, volunteering, working, and doing homework are more purposeful than pleasurable. Doing housework is about equal in pleasure and purpose whereas in the German DRM data it was more purposeful than pleasurable. Again, if we ranked activities by their pleasure and then by their purpose, we would make different inferences about what makes people happy, and so we need to consider both.

We also find in these data that people generally experience more pleasure and purpose from their activities when they do them with others. The ATUS results show that interacting with someone else is worth about an additional 0.4 points on the pleasure scale and about 0.6 points on the purpose scale. The table on page 87 shows how much more we enjoy most activities when we do them with other people. There are a few fascinating exceptions, however; where we appear to be made unhappier when we do an activity with someone else. Commuting seems to be less pleasurable

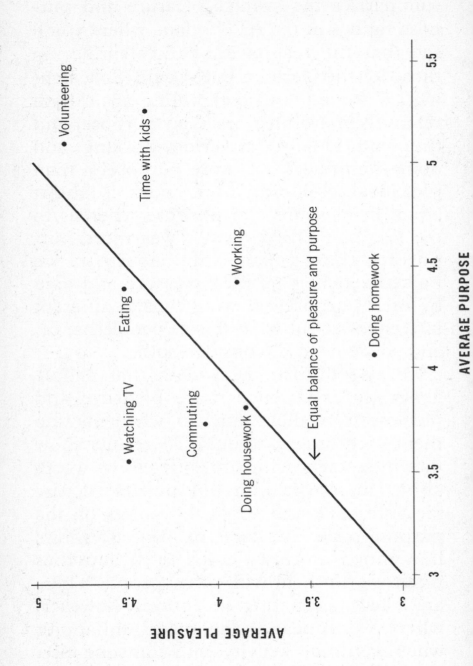

when done with someone else — perhaps being in control of the radio and not having a backseat driver increases the joy of the ride. Homework is much less purposeful when engaged in with someone else, which makes sense if solitude allows people to get more done. We have to be alert to the "chicken and egg" problem as we look through this table, though; that is, people may choose to be alone when they are in a particular mood.

| Activity | Difference when interacting with someone else | |
	Pleasure	Purpose
Volunteering	+0.67	+1.49
Eating	+0.06	0.00
Doing housework	+0.02	+0.53
Working	-0.05	+0.06
Commuting	-0.13	+0.50
Watching TV	+0.22	+0.12
Homework	+0.02	−1.55

We next looked at which types of people bring us more pleasure and purpose as we go about our daily activities. The purpose of time with kids increases when done with relatives. Volunteering is both more purposeful and more pleasurable when done with pretty much anybody else. Eating is more pleasurable when done with relatives and commuting is more purposeful when engaged in with coworkers. Housework is more purposeful when done with household children. Work is more pleasurable with family and friends. Watching TV is more pleasurable and purposeful with other people's kids. Homework is made much less purposeful when engaged in with siblings. Apologies for the quite long list of facts here, but I hope you will agree with me when I say that these results all make intuitive sense and therefore add to the confidence we can have in these data.

These data also allow us to consider some interesting differences in the ratings of different groups of people. The following graph illustrates that there are very small differences in pleasure or purpose by age — but that the purpose ratings of those aged fifteen to twenty-three are significantly lower than the purpose ratings of other age groups — and also significantly lower than their own pleasure ratings. If we looked only at pleasure, we would conclude that there are no age effects in these data, but consideration of purpose tells a different story.

When we look at differences by people across activities, some interesting patterns emerge. Men experience more pleasure from time with children than women but

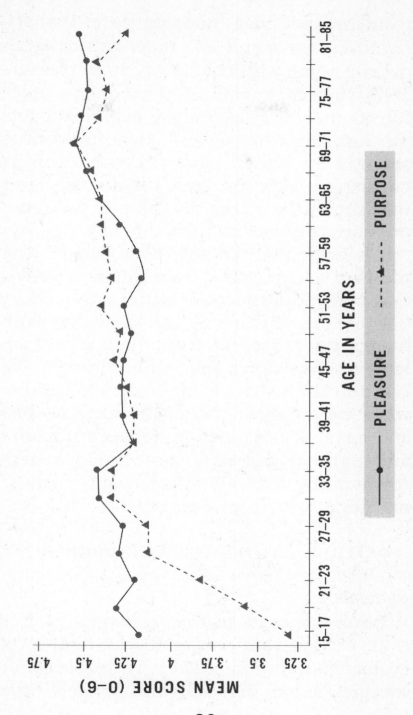

women experience more purpose. Perhaps because men spend less time with children overall, being with children is more pleasurable, whereas for women, it's more purposeful. As income rises, people experience less purpose from housework. If housework is seen as an added time pressure, this is consistent with research I'll discuss later that shows the richer people get, the more pressure they feel on their time.[7]

It is great that we now have data on the pleasure and purpose from different activities, and the distinction matters. By adding purpose into the mix we can show that work brings happiness in ways that would be ignored if we considered only pleasure. We can also show that we are generally happier when we are interacting with other people, and again the distinction between pleasure and purpose provides some nuance here (commuting with other people adds purpose but not pleasure, for example).

OTHER EVIDENCE ON HAPPINESS

Evaluations
When it comes to measuring happiness, it is a lot cheaper and easier to ask high-level evaluative questions than it is to ask about specific feelings and activities. While I have

voiced my concerns about these questions, happiness snapshots are better than no record at all of our happiness and we have more information on them than for any other measure. As a result, some of the evidence I cite in later chapters will refer to life satisfaction and so it is worth briefly considering some of the evidence.

Imagine yourself as a participant in one of the surveys. On a scale from 0 (not at all) to 10 (completely), overall how satisfied are you with your life nowadays?

_____ out of 10.

Probably the best international data on life satisfaction come from two studies carried out in the UK and Germany. In each data set, for about the past twenty years, the same ten thousand or so people have been asked about their life satisfaction alongside lots of other questions about themselves and their lives. These are called longitudinal data because we have multiple observations on the same people over time. Economists like me generally prefer longitudinal data because they allow us to see how each individual's happiness changes in response to good or bad life events. A few years ago, I led a comprehensive review of this literature with Tessa Peasgood and Mat White, gathering up papers that had looked at the variables associated with reports of life satisfaction, focusing on large longitudinal data sets like the ones from the UK and Germany.

Our conclusions were that life satisfaction ratings are higher for those who:

a. are wealthier (especially when compared to people who are like them)
b. are young or old (being in your forties and fifties is a bad time for life satisfaction)
c. are healthier
d. have lots of social contact
e. are married (or at least cohabiting)
f. are a little more educated (having a degree is good but you probably shouldn't get a PhD if you want to maximize your life satisfaction)
g. are religious (it doesn't matter which religion)
h. have a job
i. commute a short distance to work[8]

Since our review, some further details have been added to some of these effects. Money appears to matter a lot when you are poor, but the impact on life satisfaction of each additional dollar shrinks — though never to zero, as it appears to do for daily mood.[9] We need to be careful here, though, because income does not only directly affect life satisfaction; it also indirectly affects happiness through its impact upon other inputs that affect life satisfaction. Richer people are generally more likely to have more friends, get married, be in better health, and so on, all of which improve life satisfaction. So rather than isolating the effect of income, which economists tend to do, we need to sprinkle its effects across all the other inputs into life satisfaction. When this sprinkling takes place, the effect of income on life satisfaction is much greater than found previously in the literature because we are picking up its indirect effects as well as the direct effects that come from having a bigger bank balance.[10]

It has been suggested that the U-shaped relationship between life satisfaction and age (with happiness lowest in middle age) might be because of expectations: as young people get older, they expect to be more satisfied with their lives than turns out to be the case, but once they get through their fifties, they expect to be less satisfied than they end up.[11] Having children delays the onset of the downward move on the U by two decades but this is due to differences in income and education among people with and without children rather than the children per se.[12] It would also appear to be the case that life satisfaction takes another dip again once you are lucky enough to reach seventy-five.[13] There is some evidence that those who say they are at the top point on a life satisfaction scale, such as "10 out of 10," are likely to be older (as well as poorer, less healthy, and less educated) than those who say they are "9 out of 10."[14] Such findings can lead us to further question just what the term "satisfaction" is getting at.

Context seems to matter, too. As a nice example, in an analysis of data from forty-three European and Anglo-Saxon countries, personal religiosity is associated with higher life satisfaction in countries where religiosity is higher on average as well. So the happiness benefits from religion stem in large part from the benefits that come from being part of a group.[15]

Our ratings of life satisfaction are also affected by "internal" attributes, like personality and genes. Sociable people (high in extroversion) tend to be the most satisfied with their lives, and anxious people (high in neuroticism) tend to be the least satisfied.[16] It is important to keep in mind, though, that personality is not entirely fixed and can change over time.[17] The effect of genes, in particular, has led some to believe that we each have a set point of happiness that we fluctuate around but always return to. But this is not supported by evidence, because some events, like unemployment and disability, can permanently lower satisfaction with life.[18] And for some people, marriage can have long-lasting positive effects.[19] In the next chapter, I'll consider in more detail the evidence on what we get used to and what we do not.

The ONS Four

There are also some exciting new data that, in time, will enable us to make more confident claims about the associations between different measures. The Office for National Statistics (ONS) in the UK, which gathers a range of data about economic growth and about how well life is going in other ways, is now trying to monitor national happiness in a number of ways.

The ONS asked Richard Layard and me, ably abetted by Rob Metcalfe, to make recommendations about which questions to ask.[20] The questions were intended to be added to existing surveys that already ask lots of questions about income, work, education, health, etc., and so they needed to be questions that could be answered quite quickly. It was not possible, therefore, to add detailed questions on the flow of happiness over time but the ONS did eventually agree to include four "headline questions" about happiness. This meant that we could ask some general questions that broadly covered pleasure and purpose, though in a more evaluative way than I would have ideally preferred.

As a result, the ONS surveys are now asking nearly two hundred thousand people per year across the UK about their happiness, using four main questions:

1. Overall, how satisfied are you with your life nowadays?
2. Overall, to what extent do you feel the things you do in your life are worthwhile?
3. Overall, how happy did you feel yesterday?
4. Overall, how anxious did you feel yesterday?

All responses are on a 0 to 10 scale where 0 represents "not at all" and 10 means "completely." You have already had a go at the first question, so please take a few moments to answer the others:

Worthwhileness =_____
Happiness yesterday =_____
Anxiety yesterday =_____

Thanks to analysis performed by Kate Laffan, you can see how you compare to the UK general population, whose average scores were as follows:

1. Life satisfaction = 7.4
2. Worthwhileness = 7.7
3. Happiness yesterday = 7.3
4. Anxiety yesterday = 3.1

I must stress that the averages, despite appearances, are quite different. The 0.3-point difference between life satisfaction and worthwhileness, for example, is slightly more than the impact on life satisfaction of being widowed.[21] These differences justify asking more than one question in happiness surveys.

There are similarities in how age affects responses to the four questions: there is a general "misery of middle age" confirmed in all cases. Those aged forty-five to forty-nine report the lowest life satisfaction, worthwhileness, and happiness and those aged fifty to fifty-four report the highest anxiety.

There are also some interesting differences in the responses across different groups. Women are happier on all three positive measures but they also report more anxiety. This finding is broadly in line with other research looking at gender differences, although the gap between the life satisfaction ratings of men and women appears to have been narrowing over the last few decades.[22] Happiness also appears to vary across ethnicities in the UK, with people in the Black, Arab, Bangladeshi, Pakistani, and Indian ethnic groups reporting significantly lower scores on all measures than those in the White group. Overall, a white man is, on average, slightly happier than a woman from an ethnic minority.

Some intriguing associations come up when we look at marital status (remember that we need to be cautious about inferring anything causal). Those who are married or in a civil partnership (the latter was restricted to same-sex couples in the UK at the time of the survey) report higher happiness on all the three positive measures than those who are divorced, separated, or widowed. Being in a civil partnership has a bigger effect on the positive measures than being married but no effect on anxiety. Those who are married and in civil partnerships are happier than those who are cohabiting. So there seems to be some extra happiness benefit from putting a ring on it, as Beyoncé might say. Interestingly, though, being in a civil partnership is associated with higher scores on all measures in London but has no effect in Northern Ireland. Perhaps Londoners are generally more tolerant of gay and lesbian couples than people in Northern Ireland.

As previously discussed, unemployment has a big negative impact on life satisfaction. At the other end of the spectrum, working long hours might not be good for how people feel and think about their lives, either: those working more than forty-eight hours per week are less happy. Despite the fact that European Union law states that employers cannot force employees to work more than forty-eight hours per week, many "choose" to do so. This would be all well and good if these figures reflected a real life choice and these longer working hours brought more happiness. Without good causal data we do not know, but further findings in the Organisation for Economic Co-operation and Development's (OECD) "How's Life?" report in 2011 suggest otherwise: the study found that three-quarters of people in European countries are not satisfied with their work/life balance, with too much "work" and not enough "life."[23]

Before moving on, I would like to raise a word of caution in comparing the results across different studies — and sometimes even within studies. When the first ONS data were released in 2012, George Kavetsos and I noticed that the questions were asked either during face-to-face interviews or over the telephone, and so we looked to see whether the mode of administration made a difference to reports of happiness. There was a difference — but in which direction? If you are anything like me, you would think that there is an inclination to appear happy when someone is sitting opposite you and so the participants interviewed face-to-face would report being happier than their telephone survey counterparts. You know what's coming — we found the exact opposite: the telephone folk were happier.[24] We don't have a robust scientific interpretation of why this occurs, but when I discussed our results with Daniel Kahneman he suggested that people can't lie to your face whereas they can inflate how happy they really are on the phone. More research is needed but in addition to knowing what questions people have been asked in happiness surveys, we need to know how they have been asked.

THE MEASURE MATTERS

We are gathering more happiness data at a good rate and we are learning lessons all the time, particularly about the pleasure and purpose associated with different activities. We still know much more about how people evaluate their lives than about how people feel in the experience of their lives, though. For some factors associated with happiness, the effect is similar for evaluations and experiences: people who are tall, for example, report more positive life evaluations and better emotional experiences. Some of this effect is because taller people tend to be better educated and earn more money, which is often attributed to the fact that taller people may have received good nutrition and care during childhood, thus enabling them to reach their full cognitive and physical potential in adulthood.[25] It could also be because taller people are perceived to be smarter and stronger than shorter people, which has knock-on effects throughout life — in much the same way that more attractive people are more likely to be hired after a job interview.[26]

Overall, though, the circumstances of your life (income, marital status, age, etc.) matter much more to your evaluating self, and what you do matters more to your experiencing self. Consider unemployment. We know that people who are unemployed are less satisfied with their lives than people who are employed. We also know that people who are unemployed are sadder when doing many of the same activities that employed people do, such as shopping, traveling, and socializing. Despite this, being out of work does not have much effect on DRM responses because time in work is not particularly pleasurable.[27] Our own German DRM data show that work is purposeful, though.

Or consider marriage. Our review of the literature showed a positive effect on life satisfaction. But if we look at how they use their time, married women are no happier than single ones. It also looks as if married women benefit more from intimate time: Les enjoys watching TV with me, mostly because she enjoys our shared rants about what we are watching. But the lucky single folk among you have more free time, which it seems you use pretty well. This is all on average, of course, and it is consistent with my observation that the happiest couples are those who spend a fair amount of time apart as well as together, thus benefiting from "shared" time and "free" time; they also have less time to get on each other's nerves.

Overall, when researchers and commentators make claims about what affects happiness, they are often not as clear as they should be that the associations depend greatly on the ways in which happiness is measured. It has been claimed that happiness suffers a midlife crisis, and with good reason, if you think back to the U shape of happiness across the life span, where being in your forties and fifties is a bad time for life satisfaction, and which we replicated in the German DRM data. Not only that, but some intriguing recent evidence suggests that happiness is U shaped in age among great apes, too.[28]

But let's not be so hasty. Reports of daily pleasure don't change much with age in the ATUS data, and purpose in the German DRM data has more of an inverted U shape, peaking just when life satisfaction troughs (in the late forties). Other research has found that empathy also has an inverse U-shaped relationship with age (perhaps we need to be more empathetic with kids around).[29] Stress, worry, and anger appear to decrease with age.[30] Other more general negative sentiments like boredom, as mentioned earlier, as well as shame and guilt, become less frequent until about sixty years of age, when their frequency stops declining any further.[31] Intriguingly, Laura Kudrna and I have also found that reports of the tiredness associated with daily activities also decreases with age in the ATUS data.[32]

Yet when we combine all of the happiness measures in ATUS — tired, pain, stress, happy, sad, and meaning — the familiar U shape found in evaluative measures is also evident here. It looks a bit different though: from the teens to about thirty, our experiences get better before they start to decline with the downward move on the U. In the ONS data, however, there is no increase from the teens to the thirties, and the U shape is of the generally observed kind. Despite our best efforts to quickly pick up experiences through happiness and anxiety the day prior, these responses will be generated by reflecting on yesterday and so, in hindsight, it is not surprising that the responses are more like evaluations. We should therefore do even more now to measure experience-based happiness directly, either through experiencing sampling, which asks people how they feel at random times of the day, or through efforts like the DRM or the ATUS study, which in both cases reminds people what they were doing at specific times during the day, thus reducing the tendency for them to generate responses based on overall evaluations.

To reiterate, the conclusions we reach about the factors associated with happiness depend greatly on the measure of happiness used, and much more than most scholars have typically accounted for. Despite declining levels of life satisfaction, people's feelings appear to improve from their teens to age thirty. They might be feeling increasingly good as they approach thirty, until they're reminded that they're reaching thirty. So much depends on what we pay attention to — in fact, everything depends on what we pay attention to, as we shall now see.

3
WHAT CAUSES HAPPINESS?

There have been many attempts to describe the causes of happiness, and many reasons put forward for why we might not be as happy as we could be. As I noted in the introduction, all explanations have sought to directly relate inputs (the various determinants of happiness, such as income and health) to outputs (happiness measured in particular ways, such as by life satisfaction). The research and policy questions have been framed along the lines of "What is the effect of health on happiness?" I have always felt that these discussions are incomplete and rather piecemeal. The academic economist in me has been searching for a more complete explanation, and ideally one that does not needlessly complicate matters.[1] I think I have found one.

FROM WIDGETS TO HAPPINESS

To an economist, if any output is not being maximized, it means that the resources devoted to its production are not being used as well (efficiently) as they could be. If you are not maximizing the output of widgets, you could produce more if the *production process* were more efficient; that is, if the staff and machinery used to produce widgets were better allocated. Notice that the production process converts inputs into outputs: inputs are not directly related to outputs. You could possibly produce more widgets if you had more staff and machinery but you might not if the additional resources were used so inefficiently as to have no effect on output. The production of widgets depends critically on the efficiency of the production process.

Analogously, there is a production process that converts income, health, etc., into happiness. What, then, is the production process for happiness? One immediate response, at least when thinking about happiness as the flow of pleasure and purpose over time, might have something to do with how you use your time. You take income, health, etc., and convert them into happiness by allocating your time to different activities. But time is not spent just doing — it is also spent thinking. In fact, much of your time is spent paying attention to stimuli that have very little to do with what you are seemingly engaged in. I have been distracted many times during the course of writing this difficult paragraph, for example; I am aware of having thought about whether to have another coffee quite a few times. And I'm guessing you have had the odd distraction reading it, too.

The production process for happiness is therefore how you *allocate your attention*. The inputs into your happiness are the plethora of stimuli vying for your attention. These are then converted into happiness by the attention that you pay to them. A focus on attention is the "missing link" in the chain between inputs and outputs. The same life events and circumstances can affect your happiness a lot or a little depending on how much attention you pay to them. Two people who in every other way are identical can be very differently happy, depending on how they convert inputs into the output of happiness.

You therefore need to consider how you can make and facilitate better decisions about what to pay attention to, and in what ways. You might have many demands on your attention as you read this book. Perhaps you can hear the kids playing outside or the television in the next room, or you might feel the urge to check your phone for new messages or to make a cup of tea. All these stimuli need to be dealt with somehow.

Inputs → the production process → outputs

Various stimuli, e.g., this book, kids, bank balance, health status → the allocation of attention → happiness

Thankfully (for most of you, I'm sure), this is about as formal as my exposition of the production processes will get. The point here isn't to give you a literal model of how inputs are converted into outputs. Rather, I am seeking to describe the production process in a way that has intuitive appeal and that allows us to develop a narrative that facilitates a better understanding of the causes of happiness and what you can do to become happier.

Just as a company seeks to combine its various inputs in the most effective ways, you are seeking to process all the stimuli vying for your attention in ways that bring about as much as happiness as possible. And just as with the production of widgets, you might be able to produce more happiness with more inputs, but you can definitely produce more of it if you allocate your attention more effectively. These insights bring together the production process of economics with the role of attention in psychology. Interestingly (to an academic economist, at least), attention does not appear in any economics textbooks.

Rationing Attention

Your attention, like everything else in life, is a scarce resource. You must ration it, since attention devoted to one thing is, by definition, attention that is not devoted to another. Attend to one thing, and you pay by not being able to attend to something else. The concept of scarcity lies at the heart of economics — it is actually what defines the dismal science, as the discipline is fondly known. The scarcity of attentional resources lies at the heart of my investigations into happiness.

The key to being happier is to pay more attention to what makes you happy and less attention to what does not. Notice this is not the same as paying attention to happiness itself. A company will monitor its output when it redesigns its production process but once it finds an efficient process, it will not change the process unless there are changes in external conditions (such as the relative prices of the inputs). When there is no incentive to change things, the production process is said to be in *equilibrium*. You are searching for equilibrium, too, so that you don't have to monitor your happiness directly until you or the world around you changes.

Economists are beginning to use attention to explain economic decisions.[2] As a nice example, if shoppers were to pay full attention to the price they paid for goods and services, we would predict that $4.00 CDs could be advertised on eBay as $0.01 plus $3.99 shipping or $4.00 plus no shipping and generate the same sales. But in reality, shoppers pay much more attention to the sale price and much less to the shipping cost, and so sellers make more sales in the former condition.[3] The inherent scarcity of attention has also caught on in the business world; it's described as the "attention economy," where obtaining the attention of customers and employees who are constantly bombarded by information and technology is an essential element of commercial success.[4]

As well as being aware of how best to allocate your attention, you need also to consider how to effectively manage your attentional energy. Just as a productive company does not work its workforce and machinery into the ground, you should not work yourself into attentional exhaustion.[5] Once you feel that you are in equilibrium, you can rest your attentional energy for a while.

In order to help myself focus my attention on this book and prevent exhaustion as I strove to finish it, I set up an autoreply on my e-mail account, which said: "Hi. I am prioritizing working on my blockbuster during July and August, and so I am dealing with only the most urgent of other matters. Thanks for your understanding. See you, Paul." It is also worth noting that this message helped to manage other people's expectations about where my attention would be directed during this time.

Paying attention can literally change your brain. Drivers of London's black cabs have to pass a very difficult test that requires them to know and be able to navigate twenty-five thousand different city streets. Only half of the prospective cabbies who take this test pass it. Those that do pass have larger hippocampi — the part of the brain that corresponds with spatial processing — than those who fail. Yet it isn't that the drivers started out with better spatial processing; instead, as they studied for the test, their hippocampi became larger as they learned more.[6]

The brain is a highly complex and sophisticated processing system, with billions of neurons and trillions of synaptic connections, and you can learn to pay more attention to some stimuli. But you can only ever process a limited amount of information at any one time. As a nice example of the scarcity of attentional energy, consider the contestants on a quiz show called *Britain's Brightest*. The quiz culminates by asking contestants a series of tricky trivia questions. Participants have to answer as many as they can in forty seconds — the even trickier bit is that they get to decide when they think the forty seconds are up. They can stop the clock at any time, but they lose more and more points the longer they take to answer beyond forty seconds. It turns out that many contestants take so much time that they lose more points by doing so than they gain by providing the answers they're thinking so long about. And they do this for the simple reason that they cannot attend fully to answering the questions and to the time passing. When they focus on the former, the latter quite literally runs away with them.

The Missing Gorilla

Daniel Simons and Christopher Chabris at Harvard University conducted one of the most famous experiments on attention with the help of an "invisible gorilla." They made a short film of two teams of their students, dressed in either black or white, who passed a basketball back and forth between themselves. They then asked students from around campus to watch the video and count how many passes the players dressed in white made. After the experiment, the participants were asked if they had seen anything unusual or odd during the video, or if they'd seen anyone other than the players. More than half of the participants had failed to notice a large furry gorilla walking directly through the teams passing the basketball back and forth; they were shocked when they rewatched the video to find out that they had not noticed something that was now very obvious. Because the participants were paying attention to counting the number of passes the players made, they did not attend to the gorilla at all.[7] I did this task when I was at Princeton before I knew about the results and did not notice the gorilla, and I was just as shocked as the Harvard students to find out that I had missed it completely.

Radiologists trained in the art of detecting a different kind of invisible gorilla — cancerous tumors — also failed to notice a small picture of a gorilla when it was placed in the upper corner of a CT lung scan. These specialists, trained in seeing the unusual, missed out on the extraordinarily unusual. They still did better than nonspecialists, though: 20 percent of radiologists said they saw the gorilla in the scan compared to no one from a general public sample.[8]

Now, gorillas may not often cross your path, but here they are simply standing in for anything out of the ordinary that many people should notice but fail to. These experiments illustrate powerfully that when you attend to one aspect of your environment you do not attend to another. This can lead to *situational blindness,* whereby you are so focused on one aspect of your environment that you fail to notice the bigger picture. This is most frequently discussed in the aviation and medical sectors to describe the causes of errors made by pilots and surgeons when they miss crucial information in their environment.[9]

In 2005, Elaine Bromiley was undergoing

a routine operation on her nasal passages at a UK hospital when she suffered unusual complications that stopped her breathing. The medics involved in treating her were so overly focused on attempting to clear her airway that they did not perform emergency surgery to open it, which would have saved her life. This mistake occurred even with the appropriate medical specialists and equipment in the room.[10] Elaine Bromiley's husband, Martin Bromiley, a commercial pilot, investigated the circumstances of her death and concluded that the procedures used by the airline industry to respond to emergencies could also be applied to medicine to reduce human error.

Pilots have relied on routine checklists to improve their *situational awareness* for quite a while. The checklists contain some quite simple information but serve to ensure that the cabin crew have a complete picture of the factors associated with airline safety. Thanks to the efforts of Martin Bromiley and some pretty compelling and robust evidence that medical checklists literally save lives, they're now increasingly used in hospitals around the world. They contain some glaringly obvious but sometimes overlooked items such as checking the patient's name.

Situational awareness is an issue in any environment, not just the operating theater and cockpit. Research shows that drivers who use adaptive cruise control (which adjusts the speed of your car according to the speed of the car in front of you) report being less situationally aware, which may increase the likelihood of accidents when unexpected events occur on the road.[11] Given this, it seems likely that all of us can be blinded from the obvious in understanding the causes of our happiness. Nothing is ever that obvious.

ABOVE AND BELOW THE SURFACE

The foregoing discussion suggests that you might automatically pay more attention to some stimuli than to others. It was actually recognized 150 years ago that a great deal of perception, memory, and behavior occurs without conscious deliberation or will.[12] We therefore need to distinguish between two types of attention. *Conscious attention* is when you are in some way aware of where your attention is being directed and *unconscious attention* is when you are unaware of what you are attending to. Unconscious attention encompasses the thought processes that occur while conscious attention is directed elsewhere.[13]

Understanding the distinction is critical if you are to give yourself the best shot of being happier for longer; and ultimately in being so without exhausting yourself through the effort of trying to be happier. Some of the time, you are aware of what you are paying attention to, and much of the time, you are not.

As with the intuition behind the production process of attention, my aim isn't to be literal here. We don't really allocate unconscious attention in any meaningful way — it just gets allocated without us having to make any real decision about what is attended to. But, as we shall see, you can consciously select the environments that your unconscious attention can roam in. Although you can't consciously dictate how your dog runs around a field, you can choose which park you take it to. We are a lot like dogs in how we react to situational triggers.

System 1 and System 2

To get a better sense of the distinction between conscious and unconscious attention we need to go back a bit in time. The first stage of humankind, in terms of our evolution, is thought to be *Ardipithecus ramidus,* a four-foot-tall tree-dweller who lived about four and a half million years ago. He's dead now but, to some extent, his brain lives on in all of us. We are Ard-wired, if you will. Much of how our brains work today owes a lot to our ancestors.

In more recent times, there has been an emerging consensus in behavioral science that we are all driven much more by the automatic processes of "system 1" — the hardwired bit of our brain — than by the deliberative reasoning of "system 2," which is the Spock-like bit of our brain. The word "system" is used here as shorthand for *two processing system*s.[14] According to my classification, unconscious attention is all system 1. There aren't really two separate processing systems in the brain; it's much more complex than this, with significant overlaps between brain regions. But it is a useful distinction for illustrating the different influences of context and cognition.

All of us have an automatic system 1 that is wired in pretty much the same way. It has not evolved differently in an East End boy and a West End girl. You may have a deliberative system 2 that is quite different from mine because of the cultural and other forces that shape us, and this will result in us behaving quite differently some of the time. But, even then, our system 1 is still reacting in a similar way. And as we've learned, context will dominate much of the time, making it likely that you'll act just like this East End boy.

System 1 is always active and is constantly being primed in ways we're unaware of. The literature on this is ever expanding. Take fast food, which has become a modern symbol for time efficiency and instant gratification.[15] When we think about fast food, we feel and act more impatiently: show us pictures of restaurants like McDonald's and KFC so quickly that we are not even consciously aware of having seen them, and we'll subsequently read a paragraph about the city of Toronto fifteen seconds faster than people who have simply seen blank squares. Ask us to critique the design of fast-food logos rather than those of inexpensive diners and we can't wait to get paid: we are more likely to prefer $3.00 right then than to wait a week and receive more money (anywhere from $3.05 to $7.00).[16]

In fighting matches at the 2004 Olympics (in boxing, tae kwon do, Greco-Roman wrestling, and freestyle wrestling), competitors were randomly assigned blue or red uniforms. If the color of uniform were unrelated to performance and the judges' assessments, there should have been a

120

similar amount of winners wearing blue or red. But those wearing blue won about one-third of the time and those wearing red won about two-thirds of the time.[17] Remarkably, then, competitors were twice as likely to win if they were lucky enough to be given red at the start of the contest. Red is an aggressive, sexual color that "beats up" the creativity of blue, not only in the performance, but also in how the judges then assess the performance.

When wine shoppers pass by a display of French and German wines with French accordion music playing in the background, they're more likely to pick up a French bottle. Play a German song by a brass Bierkeller band, and they're more likely to pick up the German brand. Indeed, a study looking at just this showed that 70 percent of the bottles sold in the store reflected the music playing in the background. But when asked, only 14 percent of the shoppers said that the music was what influenced their purchase.[18]

The sharp rise in our understanding of unconscious processes has led to many books on the subject and opened up a wealth of new possibilities.[19] One prospect I find amazing is encrypting computers with passcodes that are embedded in the unconscious mind but that are not accessible by conscious thought.[20] The research evidence has even led some to question whether conscious thought has any influence on behavior at all.[21] This might be an overstatement, but the causal role of conscious thought has certainly been overstated.[22]

One thing is for sure. Our brains are lazy and want to conserve attentional energy. Looking to automate behaviors, where it can, means that many decisions that start out as system 2 end up as system 1. Have you ever gone the wrong way to a meeting that is not at your office because you are used to going to your office? Or have you ever gone back home to check that you have locked the house properly even though you had locked up without realizing it? I have done these two things within the last week. And both came about as a result of my brain wanting to create a habit and conserve energy. A habit is a behavioral pattern enacted automatically in response to a situation where the behavior has been previously performed repeatedly and consistently.[23] Why waste attentional energy thinking about how to get to work or whether to lock the house when you can automatically do both in the same ways every day?

Sports stars are able to shut out various

distractions completely in order to focus only on the task at hand. They have to get themselves "in the zone" until being there becomes automatic for them. In a similar way, art historians are better able to spot a fake work of art when they transfer their wealth of knowledge and wisdom from system 2 to system 1, and thus make what appears to be a snap judgment.[24] Ideally, much of what you must initially concentrate on to improve your happiness similarly becomes automatic in time.

The last thing that experts who have transferred from "slow" to "fast" thinking should want to happen is to start thinking consciously again. For stars in sports like weight lifting, golf, and snooker, thinking consciously about the task can lead to "choking" — freezing up and failing because of the pressure of the situation. In a weight-lifting competition, you would be more likely to lift a given weight if you were ranked tenth after the first round than if you were ranked first.[25] The guy ranked first is the one to aim at; he knows it, and he often chokes as a result. Decisions can move from system 2 to system 1 and back again over time.

A Quick Task
The main message from this section and the evidence introduced is that the world is

a complex place and your brain tries to make it easier for you by devising simplifying strategies to help you cope. We can see this for ourselves with things like the "Stroop task."[26] This is a popular psychological exercise that was developed by John Ridley Stroop in Tennessee in 1935 as part of his PhD dissertation. Stroop was one of the first to see how putting colors and words together affects the time taken to process and respond to them, although there were certainly other researchers working on similar topics around that time.[27] I've adapted the exercise to black-and-white print but it works just the same.

Step 1: Name the colors of each of the boxes (black, white, or gray) as quickly as you can.

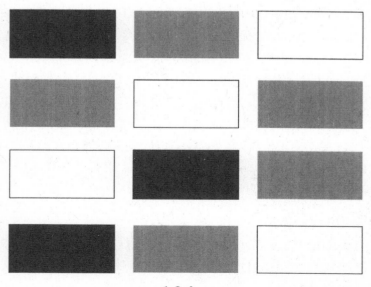

Step 2: Name the colors inside the letters of each word as quickly as you can.

BLACK GRAY WHITE

GRAY WHITE GRAY

WHITE BLACK GRAY

BLACK GRAY WHITE

It takes most of us longer to name the colors in the second step than in the first. In step 1, you can just rely on system 1, which automatically names the colors by association with their display. In step 2, your system 1 wants to automatically read the words as written instead of their color and so it takes your system 2 a bit of time to override this automatic tendency. By the way, as a nice example of the importance of context, the time taken on accurately completing step 2 of this exercise will be reduced when you have a full bladder: your system 1 is partly overridden by the urge to wee.[28]

BEHAVIORAL SPILLOVERS
So far, we have been implicitly considering each behavior or attentional process, and

their effects on happiness, in isolation. But no action or thought sits in a vacuum: there are often significant *spillover effects* from one context to the next. So you need to consider not only what you do and feel now but also what effect your current actions and feelings might have on what you do and feel next. These spillovers are brought about by the allocation of conscious and unconscious attention.

Like Ripples on a Pond

I first thought about spillover effects when I was working with the UK government to consider behavior change policies. I was presented with some evidence that enlarging the front compartment of a supermarket cart leads to increased sales of fruit and vegetables. The policy wonk that told me was very excited. I was excited to know if these increased sales led to increased consumption of fruit and veg. "What do you mean?" he said. Well, I have never seen a Mars bar rot in the fridge but, as the comedian Eddie Izzard can tell you better than I can, it is never the right time to eat a pear. So these extra sales of fruit and veg might simply mean more waste.

Okay, let's assume that at least some of it does get eaten. My next question was,

"Does the consumption of more fruit and veg lead to healthier lives or does it simply give people license to eat more Mars bars?" Remarkably, we do not know the answer to this question. But after you have read the next few paragraphs, you might well conclude (as I have) that the increased consumption of fruit and veg that has taken place in recent years, in the UK at least, has probably led to weight gain and not weight loss, as people (unconsciously) reward themselves with a piece of cake for having eaten an apple. To inform research, policy, and our own choices, we should ideally capture all the ripples of behavior when a pebble of behavior change intervention is thrown into the pond.

Promoting, Permitting, and Purging

Inspired by the lack of evidence on such a basic question, Matteo Galizzi and I have developed a conceptual frame within which a broad range of spillovers can be systematically interpreted. We begin by assuming that two different behaviors take place sequentially and are linked, at a conscious or unconscious level, by some underlying motivation, such as the desire to lose weight (which is ultimately motivated by a desire to be happier). The first behavior leads to another subsequent behavior, which, so far as the motivation is concerned, can either work in the same direction as the first or push back against it. So you might start exercising to lose weight. This could lead to another behavior that also leads to weight loss, such as eating healthily. We refer to this as a *promoting* spillover. This is shown in box 1 in the table on next page.

But it might instead lead to another behavior, one that increases weight gain, such as eating more. This will happen if we reward ourselves with something "naughty" when we have just done something "nice." We refer to this as a *permitting* spillover and it is shown in box 2. There is then a third class of spillovers, which we call *purging,* where the second behavior is motivated out of a (conscious or unconscious) desire to undo some of the damage caused by the first behavior. So you might eat healthily because you did not exercise, as shown in box 3. Finally, there is box 4, where the initial inability to exercise promotes the subsequent desire to say "what the heck" and to eat less healthily.

To conduct a controlled test of the impact of exercise on eating, Matteo and I asked students at the London School of Economics to step onto and off a wooden box for

		Second Behavior	
		Eat healthily	Eat less healthily
First behavior	A workout after work	**1. PROMOTING** I worked hard at the gym, let's keep up the good work	**2. PERMITTING** I worked hard at the gym, I deserve a big slice of cake
	Sofa-sitting after work	**3. PURGING** I've been lazy today, best not eat so much tonight	**4. PROMOTING** I've been lazy today, so, what the heck, let's have a big slice of cake

two minutes. We randomized the students into one of four different groups: (1) paid ten pence per step; (2) paid two pence per step; (3) simply encouraged to keep going by the researcher at fifteen-second intervals in the two minutes; and (4) a control group that was asked to perform the task without further incentive. Those being offered the cash exercised more: about 105 steps in groups 1 and 2 compared to 90 steps in groups 3 and 4. Those being paid ten pence, or who were being encouraged to exercise, were more satisfied with their performance: about a whole point difference on a ten-point scale. All groups were remarkably accurate at estimating how many calories they'd burned off in the task: between 20 and 30.

Here's the best bit. We then offered our participants a buffet lunch of sandwiches and snacks, again on an individual basis. Unbeknownst to them, we watched what they ate. More precisely, after each student left, Matteo rummaged around in the bins (in his sharp Italian suit) to look at the waste sandwich boxes and chocolate wrappers and potato chip bags. Those who thought they had done well on the exercise task (thus, those in the ten-pence and encouragement groups) ate, on average, about 320 calories compared to the 240 calories eaten by those who did not think they had done so well (those in the two-pence and control groups).[29]

So the conclusion we can draw here is that the more satisfied we are with our effort in a "calories-out" exercise task, the more we feel that we can reward ourselves with a "calories-in" lunch. Doing a little bit of exercise in order to lose weight will lead to weight gain if you put more calories past your lips than you burn off your hips. This is precisely what happens for many people, and it is the main reason why weight-loss programs predicated on exercise alone don't work very well.

Indeed, it has been shown that more exercise at one time leads to more rest at another. In a study of two hundred children from three schools, participants wore accelerometers to test whether the schools' different fitness programs had an effect on how active the children were. It turned out that children who were more active at school rested when they were at home, and vice versa.[30] Similar results were found in another study looking at the effect of walking versus driving to school.[31] Because food is now more plentiful than it was for our ancestors, these behaviors are a carryover from a time when we needed to conserve energy.

Moral Licensing and Cleansing

Results like those from our study are strongly supportive of a permitting spill-over. They're also consistent with a concept in psychology called *moral licensing*. Think of yourself as being in possession of a moral bank account. When you have a positive balance, you will license yourself to use up some of the credits. Moral licensing was originally documented in the context of discriminatory behavior. Participants who, in an easy hypothetical hiring situation, chose to appoint a manifestly better black candidate for a job, thus had the chance to establish they were not racist and were then more likely to make prejudiced choices in a subsequent harder hiring decision.[32] Similarly, participants who said they were endorsing Barack Obama instead of John McCain in the 2008 US presidential election were then more likely to make a prejudiced choice in a subsequent hiring task, or to allocate more money to a charity fighting poverty in a white rather than in an African American neighborhood.[33]

Conversely, when you're in deficit in your moral bank account, you'll need to stock up

132

on credits through *moral cleansing.* The evidence supports this. In a neat experiment, participants were asked to recall in detail either an ethical or an unethical deed from their past and describe their feelings. They were all then asked to rate the desirability of various products, including neutral items, such as juices and chocolate bars, and cleansing products, such as shower soap and disinfectant. Those who had recalled the unethical deed were much more likely to choose a cleansing product.[34] The recollection of doing a bad thing prompts the need literally to cleanse oneself — and again in largely unconscious ways.

THE SHIFTING SANDS OF ATTENTION

The foregoing discussion highlights the temporal nature of your behavior and, consequently, your happiness. There is also a dynamic nature to the impact of many changes in life. Let us now consider the importance of attention in explaining how we adjust the impact of changes in our lives.

Getting Over It

One of the main lessons from happiness research is that the impacts of many life changes fade quite quickly. There is lots of *adaptation* — lots of getting used to change. Adaptation is explained by the withdrawal of attention to inputs as their impact on happiness diminishes.[35] The novelty of a new stimulus attracts your attention, but when you get used to it you stop focusing so much attention on it. When this happens, your attention is freed up to find something new to attract it. A new king of attention soon replaces an old one. The King is dead. Long live the King.

Many events are unpredictable and their impacts on happiness are hard to figure out because we cannot always plan and measure happiness before the event happens, but sometimes we get lucky and the data are already there. The September 11 attacks are among the most prominent recent example of an event whose timing was unpredictable, but they also happened to take place in the same month as most of the interviews in the large UK longitudinal study discussed in chapter 2. This study surveys about ten thousand people every year and in addition to life satisfaction (which unfortunately was missing as a variable in 2001) it also asks about mental health, using a standard assessment measure. Some people had been asked about their mental health before the September 11 attacks happened and some asked afterward, so it allowed us to see what difference the event made by looking at the mental health of different people at different times from the event. In this way, we could see whether the negative impact of the September 11 attacks on mental health in the UK wore off over time.[36]

It turns out that there was a significant effect in 2001 during September, which then fell over the next couple of months to completely disappear by December. An initially attention-grabbing phenomenon ceases to remain so over time. Note that we were not looking at the effects of 9/11 by asking people to think about those effects, for if we had done that, we would have got very different results: the attacks will always feel very important to those who are being asked to think about them directly. The term "focusing effect" has been used for occasions where something matters because it is being attended to.[37] The way to avoid focusing effects is to ask people how happy they are first and then find out other relevant things about them (such as when they were interviewed, in this case). I'll discuss how focusing effects influence your happiness and behavior in greater detail in the next chapter.

Thankfully, most other changes in life are

less dramatic than terrorist attacks. Together with David Bradford, I have also looked at the existing life satisfaction data to see what happens to people as they gain weight. They get less happy, right? Well, no, not really. Life satisfaction is hardly affected by weight gain. The theoretical model we developed posits that you can do one of two things to stay happy when you gain weight: the first is to expend effort in losing weight, and the second is to expend effort in playing down the importance of weight gain in your life. Our data analyses support the second explanation. As people put on weight, they shift the focus of their attention away from parts of their lives that are associated with weight, like health, toward aspects where their weight is less important, like work.[38]

This shift in attention explains some of the behaviors we observe; many of us gain weight but do not lose it. The effort needed to lose weight may be greater than the effort required to shift the attention you give to your health and weight.

There's some evidence that obesity can have a small but significant effect on life satisfaction but it does not have anywhere near as much of an effect as other problems in life. Notwithstanding some issues in how best to analyze the data, based on ratings of life satisfaction in the UK, we can tentatively suggest that your body mass index (BMI) would have to increase by at least 30 BMI points (which would be very extreme, since obesity is defined as a BMI of 30) to have about the same negative effect upon your satisfaction levels as a marital breakdown.[39] The longer-term consequences of obesity, such as diabetes, would have a big impact on happiness, of course, but the more immediate impact of a breakup explains why many people care more about their relationships with other people than the one they have with food. Of course, obesity does not occur overnight, and so there is a gradual adaptation to weighing more.

There is also now some genetic evidence to show that gaining weight may not necessarily make you any less happy. The same gene that is associated with a predisposition to obesity, the FTO gene, is actually associated with a reduced risk of major depressive disorders.[40] The impact may also depend on cultural norms and socioeconomic factors.[41] In some countries, such as Russia, getting fatter is actually good for life satisfaction because it acts as a signal of affluence. In the United States, those in high-status jobs are most adversely affected by being overweight, probably because of the stigma attached to it in those cohorts.[42]

While we each may initially react quite differently to an event, we all have a built-in ability to detect and neutralize challenges to our happiness. This has been called our *psychological immune system.*[43] Just as your body adjusts to getting into hot water, so your mind adjusts to change: the psychological reaction to changes in stimuli is analogous to the physiological reaction to changes in temperature. And your psychological immune system works a little like your physical immune system, which kicks in when faced with a threat, such as when someone nearby coughs or sneezes.[44] This highlights the fact that many adaptation processes take place automatically and unconsciously; we simply get used to some changes without thinking about whether or not we really want to.

In one of the most interesting studies in this area, students were asked to predict how much worse their mood would be if they were rejected for a job: their average estimate was two points lower than their current mood on a ten-point scale. In sharp contrast, the actual effect of being rejected was only 0.4 points on the same ten-point scale. Even that effect was fleeting: ten minutes after the rejection, their happiness levels had returned to normal. By the way, there was no real job offer — such is the fun that psychologists often have at their students' expense.

If your partner dumps you, give it a few months and you'll generally look back on your partner as having been unsuitable. Chances are that you will then meet someone who makes you happier than that loser did. This is not to say that the pain of the breakup is any less real, just that you can take some comfort from it not lasting. You can also take comfort from the fact that you will make sense of the relationship and the breakup in ways that enable you to move on to bigger and better things. You are good at making sense of most life events in ways that enable you to move on. It is better to have loved and lost than to have spent your life with a psychopath, as one of my (single) colleagues says. What doesn't kill you makes you stronger — and often happier, too, eventually.

On the flip side, your psychological immune system seems to neutralize the impact of many good things, too, and so the positive happiness effects of a pay raise, a marriage, or a new job won't last for very long for most people, either.[45] As we shall see more clearly in part 2, this is where the allocation and reallocation of your attention is crucial: we shall consider ways in which you can prolong pleasure and purpose and nip pain and pointlessness in the bud.

Not Getting Over It

We will obviously adapt to some changes more quickly than to others, to a pay raise faster than to marriage, for example. Further, the impact of some inputs on the production of happiness does not appear to wane over time. Unemployment, as I mentioned, has lasting negative effects (even if we allow for the fact that less happy people are more likely to lose their jobs in the first place). This is not so surprising, is it? One of the first questions someone new asks you is "What do you do for a living?"

To underline the importance of attention, even in the context of a generally attention-grabbing event like unemployment, we have compared the impact on life satisfaction of unemployment on those who mentioned unemployment as a major life event with the impact on those who did not mention it as an important event when completing the survey. Unemployment hurts a lot, whether or not it is mentioned as a major life event, but it hurts twice as much for those who report the loss of a job as having been a major life event in the last year compared to those who have lost their job but did not mention it as being a major life event.[46]

You may also become increasingly *sensitized* to some changes. That is, you pay more, not less, attention to some stimuli as time passes. Sadly, these are usually bad things, like noise, especially when the noise is unpredictable in its timing. The evidence shows that we don't generally withdraw attention from traffic noise because cars do not go by at regular intervals.[47] As disheartening evidence of this, children in urban areas who live in noisy, lower floors of apartment buildings have lower reading scores than those on quieter, higher floors where traffic noise doesn't reach to the same extent.[48] This result persists after the authors account for the educational level of the parents and also note that the apartments on each floor cost about the same, so it is not as if the poorer kids are living on lower floors.

Losing your sense of smell, which might even be considered to have its upsides in some instances, has a significant downside: you lose your sense of taste, too. This can lead you into a poor diet and reduce the functioning of your physical immune system.[49] There is hardly any adaptation to not being able to smell and yet I suspect that many of us would think that we would get used to it quite quickly. We make a lot of mistakes about what will grab our attention and for how long, as we shall see in the next chapter.

Resolving Uncertainty

There is an intuitively appealing model of adaptation called the AREA model. Events in life are *attention*-grabbing to begin with. You then *react* and, if you can *explain* the event, you will withdraw attention and *adapt* to it.[50] Much of this process will occur automatically without conscious effort. Most of the time you can explain things and you will adapt as the impact of the stimulus wears off. A pay raise is generally quickly explained — you're a good and loyal worker, right? And so you stop paying attention to it. Indeed, you are such a good worker that your pay raise should perhaps have been larger, right?

Sometimes, though, you will keep reacting if you are lacking that all-important explanation. As I mentioned before, if physical pain has an explanation, such as when the ache in your leg is due to a sports injury, then you will withdraw attention from the pain and adapt to it, but if it remains unex-

142

plained, it continues to draw attention to itself. Recall from the introduction that a stammer is difficult to explain, and so it draws attention to itself over and above any effect it might have on specific speaking situations.

If you are able to resolve the uncertainty surrounding a situation, you will be better able to explain the consequences that ensue. This sounds obvious, but the implications aren't: we have data that show that cancer patients report *lower* life satisfaction rates when they are in remission.[51] My interpretation is that the "certainty" of death allows a person to put his or her house into order, and remission casts uncertainty on that purpose.

A similar story can be told for genetic testing. In a study looking at testing for Huntington's disease — an inherited genetic disorder that affects muscle coordination and generally leads to psychiatric problems and early death — those who were told that they had a decreased risk of the disease reported better mental health over the year of the study following testing than those who were told their risk was unchanged.[52] So far, so obvious. But those who were told that they had an *increased* risk also reported better mental health than the group whose risk was unchanged. The unchanged-risk group arguably still faced the same uncertainty as before, whereas the other two groups benefited from the uncertainty being reduced, even if it was in a "bad" way.

These examples show how the resolution of uncertainty about bad life events is potentially good for your happiness. Your attention is diverted away from worrying about what might or might not happen (and all the possible stresses and strains that those scenarios might involve) toward dealing with a future that can be better planned and managed. This goes a long way toward explaining why people's life satisfaction takes a massive drop close to the time of separation but then bounces back upon divorce.[53] Divorce provides closure by resolving the uncertainty of whether you will get back together again — and it also sorts out the finances, too. Resolving the uncertainty surrounding a situation like divorce forces an explanation, and thus its impact as an input into the production process of happiness wanes.

What applies to pain might not apply to pleasure, however. Perhaps you have stored a bottle of wine for years or stretched out the time you spent planning your holiday in order to enjoy the pleasure of anticipation as well as consumption.[54] If you could have a kiss from your favorite movie star, you might prefer to wait a few days rather than to receive it immediately.[55] Or, if you're like English soccer fans, perhaps you're more inclined to watch a game when you're unsure about who will win the match.[56] We often seek out uncertainty for pleasure.

Changing Purpose
Unfortunately, we don't know very much about the effects of change on experiences of purpose, so please allow me to use a selective sample and example: me and my weight training. I first walked into a gym about thirteen years ago, weighing 145 pounds and with a twenty-nine-inch waist. I now weigh 215 pounds and have a thirty-two-inch waist. From the first time I lifted a dumbbell, weight training has been a pleasurable activity for me. Over time, it has additionally become a purposeful one, as I began to treat my diet and exercise program as a project. I find it interesting to see what happens to my size and strength as I vary my workouts and eat different combinations of carbs, fats, and proteins. I am proud of the gains I have made, particularly as I am naturally very skinny and I find it incredibly hard to gain weight (I am an exemplar ecto-

morph). You might have comparable projects in your life, such as reading or gardening, which over time have become both pleasurable and purposeful.

Most of the activities and projects we stick with will end up being both pleasurable and purposeful in time — even if they started out principally motivated by one category of sentiments or if the relative weights of pleasure and purpose continue to change over time. Pleasure and purpose will often go hand in hand over time even if they are traded off against one another at any one moment in time. In the language of economics, pleasure and purpose are complements over time even if they are substitutes at any one moment in time. So my weight training is now both pleasurable and purposeful (these sentiments are complements over time) even though it started out as relatively more pleasurable and became relatively more purposeful (these sentiments are substitutes at each moment in time).

Adaptation to purpose will result in boredom and futility, so you are more likely to stop engaging in such activities. In general, the impact of purposeful inputs will probably wane less because many activities that you continue with will become more purposeful over time. Context matters and this will not be true all of the time. But it remains important to think of pleasure and purpose as separate, but interrelated, components of happiness.

ATTENDING TO HAPPINESS

Attention holds together our lives — as well as this book. It converts stimuli into happiness and it drives our behavior. We are often unaware of the effects of attention on our happiness and our behavior, just as many people are unaware that background music affects their choice of wine. Yet this precious and scarce resource is responsible for all of what we do and how we feel. Attention explains why we adapt to weight gain and not to noise and stammering. It also explains why we might not be as happy as we could be.

4
WHY AREN'T WE HAPPIER?

We have seen that our brain, particularly
our automatic system 1, tries to help us out
in a complex world, but its efforts to simplify
things can sometimes be silly strategies so
far as making decisions that make us happier are concerned.

The brain is of course truly wondrous but
it's much more interesting, to me at least,
to look at where it makes mistakes. We have
evolved to be attractive mates and to sur-
vive, but aspects of ourselves might also
simply be evolutionary mistakes — and it's
almost impossible to tell the difference,
especially because societies develop so
quickly. Given how much more complex the
world is now compared to the one faced by
our tree-dwelling ancestors, it is remarkable
how well we function. Equally, it is unre-
markable that we are prone to misallocating
our attention. We do so by making conscious
mistakes and unconscious errors that mean

we aren't as happy as we could be.

When you are attending to what you think will make you happy in the future, you are making predictions about what the production process will look like: what you will attend to, in what ways, and for how long. We need to understand the attentional obstacles to being happier if we are to consider ways in which we can be happier. This chapter addresses what I categorize as the three main attentional problems: *mistaken desires; mistaken projections;* and *mistaken beliefs.* Let's consider each in turn.

MISTAKEN DESIRES

On the face of it, we ought to desire what makes us happy. In a thorough attempt to see if what we desire is consistent with maximizing happiness, nearly three thousand people from various sources — patients in a doctor's waiting room in Denver; a telephone survey; and the student population at Cornell University — were asked which of two scenarios would bring them the greatest happiness, and which of the two they would choose. The choices were consistent with happiness 83 percent of the time. The other 17 percent of the time, the choice was different from the one thought to maximize happiness. For example, if someone said they would choose a better-paying job requiring them to sleep less, their choice would have been inconsistent with happiness maximization if they had also said more sleep would bring them more happiness than a better paying job.[1]

Now, you could say that this shows happiness does not always dominate, but I suspect that much of the 17 percent could be explained by assumptions about happiness in the long run (e.g., from taking a higher-paying job that makes you miserable in the short run but gives you a nice nest egg for later). Moreover, in further analysis, predicted sense of purpose was an important driver of people's choices and so some of the results in the original study may have been because the authors didn't include purpose in their original conceptualization of happiness.[2]

Nonetheless, there are many scholars who believe that attending to certain goals, such as achievement, bring happiness in themselves and others who maintain that there are objectives, such as authenticity, that transcend happiness. I consider these to be mistaken desires, for the reasons outlined below.

Achievement

We have a desire to achieve, and some argue that this brings happiness in itself. There is no doubt that achieving a goal, which makes our evaluative self happy, can feel pretty good in itself: in video game players, achieving goals releases dopamine, which is the pleasure-producing neurotransmitter in our brains.[3] But even if the goal is achieved, these are only fleeting moments, and so the process of attempting to get there should be a pleasurable and/or purposeful one, too.

It is also true that the desire to achieve can bring happiness later on — but only for those who do achieve. Some great studies have looked at the desires people expressed when they were students and then the difference between desires and achievements twenty or so years later. Those who as students were motivated by making money turned out to be greatly affected by whether or not they became wealthy later in their lives. If they did, they were satisfied with their lives, but many did not make as much as they would have liked to, so they were not that satisfied. The message from this research is that if you care a lot about money, you better make sure you get it. If you do not become rich, then being motivated by money will, unsurprisingly, lead to disappointment.[4]

Consider the story of the fisherman and the businessman, a narrative highlighting the paradoxes in our relentless drive for achievement.

There was once a businessman who was sitting by the beach in a small Brazilian village. As he sat, he saw a Brazilian fisherman rowing a small boat toward the shore having caught quite a few big fish. The businessman was impressed and asked the fisherman, "How long does it take you to catch so many fish?" The fisherman replied, "Oh, just a short while." "Then why don't you stay longer at sea and catch even more?" The businessman was astonished. "This is enough to feed my whole family," the fisherman said. The businessman then asked, "So, what do you do for the rest of the day?" The fisherman replied, "Well, I usually wake up early in the morning, go out to sea and catch a few fish, then go back and play with my kids. In the afternoon, I take a nap with my wife, and [when] evening comes, I join my buddies in the village for a drink — we play guitar, sing and dance throughout the night."

The businessman offered a suggestion

to the fisherman. "I am a PhD in business management. I could help you to become a more successful person. From now on, you should spend more time at sea and try to catch as many fish as possible. When you have saved enough money, you could buy a bigger boat and catch even more fish. Soon you will be able to afford to buy more boats, set up your own company, your own production plant for canned food and distribution network. By then, you will have moved out of this village and to São Paulo, where you can set up an HQ to manage your other branches."

The fisherman continues, "And after that?" The businessman laughs heartily. "After that, you can live like a king in your own house, and when the time is right, you can go public and float your shares in the Stock Exchange, and you will be rich." The fisherman asks, "And after that?" The businessman says, "After that, you can finally retire, you can move to a house by the fishing village, wake up early in the morning, catch a few fish, then return home to play with [your] kids, have a nice afternoon nap with your wife, and when evening comes, you can join your buddies for a drink, play the guitar, sing and dance throughout the night!" The fisherman was puzzled. "Isn't that what I am doing now?"[5]

Much of what the fisherman is meant to aspire to he has now. The consequences of this tale could, in fact, turn out to be worse than circular, as the fisherman loses friends on the way up and out. He could also develop doubts about his sense of identity. This is one reason why many of the scholarship kids from poor backgrounds are not as happy as their equally high-achieving peers from wealthier backgrounds.[6] This sense of identity (or rather a lack of it) resonates with my own experiences of moving from a lower-working-class background to an upper-middle-class occupation. While one part of me quite enjoys not belonging to either group, another part dislikes not knowing where I belong.

Be especially alert to the fact that a desire for achievement may help in achieving a narrow set of goals but at the expense of the more important goal of happiness. It is good being motivated to be successful at work but not at the cost of health and personal relationships. Sometimes we can get so wrapped up in things that the attainment of a goal becomes all that matters. Some people will make extreme sacrifices to achieve them — like the many climbers

154

who have died on Everest because they are obsessed with getting to the top. In these cases, the attainment of their goals comes at too great a price for happiness.[7]

On occasion, achieving more objectively might result in feeling worse subjectively. What would you say if I asked whether you'd be happier with a silver medal or a bronze one? If you are anything like athletes at the 1992 Summer Olympic Games in Barcelona, it might well be that a bronze would make you happier. Observers rated the immediate reactions of the athletes on a 1 to 10 scale of agony to ecstasy. The results showed that bronze medal winners were considered to be happier than silver medal winners. While a silver medal winner is gutted that they just missed out on gold, a bronze medal winner is simply pleased to be on the podium.[8] Of course, it's an open question whether or not bronze medal winners remain happier than silver medal winners over time. Unfortunately, we do not have data for the months after the event that would enable us to know this.

Here's a story David Bradford told me to illustrate that second place can hurt for quite some time — and that this feeling can even sit alongside a general sense of success. A relative of his played for the NFL team the Buffalo Bills for eight years back in the 1990s. He was one of the best players in his position in the entire NFL and made the Pro Bowl four years in a row. While he was on the Bills, the team had great success — well, sort of. They made the playoffs most years, and actually won their Divisional Championship and played in the Super Bowl four years in a row. But they lost all of those matches (twice by missing a field goal kick by no more than a few feet). David's relative got four NFC Divisional Championship rings (the NFL equivalent to a silver medal). He hated to see those rings because they reminded him that his team lost the Super Bowl — not that his team had done better than every other team bar one. He kept them in a closet in the back of his house and wouldn't show them to anyone, no matter how many times he was asked. The interesting point from an attentional perspective is that he talks very fondly indeed about his NFL career when he is not forced to pay attention to the Super Bowl. So whatever you achieve, try to pay attention to the good bits.

It is certainly true that pursuing a goal (as well as cutting down on cigarettes, alcohol, chocolate, porn, or Facebook) can be a challenge in the short term and may make you feel less happy for a while. We stick with goals like this because we think they'll make us happier in the long run. Sometimes the gain may not be worth the pain, but you always think it will be at the outset. It would simply be masochistic for you to make a decision that you knew *for sure* would make you more miserable overall. So you must be alert to what you are sacrificing as well as how you are benefiting from fulfilling your ambitions. Remember that future happiness cannot really compensate for misery now: lost happiness is lost forever. So you need to be pretty confident that any current sacrifices of happiness you make in order to fulfill some ambition or other will actually be worth it in the long run.

As elsewhere, we need more research and better evidence on the full costs and benefits of different decisions and life courses. We do know people are happier with their lives over time if they are satisfied with aspects of their jobs like their boss, pay, and daily tasks, which suggests it is most important that the job is a good fit for the individual rather than the type of job per se.[9] This might help explain why the happiest workers in the UK are florists and the least happy are bankers (see the table on page 159 for more details).[10] Of course, the florists could have started out happier than the bankers before any of them started work. We need more happiness data on the same people over time so that we can see how their happiness changes in response to their jobs.

Even without good causal evidence, I am pretty confident that I am happier — but certainly not richer — as an academic than I would have been as a banker. I would have been happier as a builder than as a banker, too, but my clients would not have been: I have no practical skills whatsoever. I am willing to bet that my kids would also be happier as builders than as bankers, since they would more directly see the tangible fruits of their labor. As such, and notwithstanding the fact that my kids may have inherited my inability to do any form of DIY at all, I would much rather that they be builders than bankers.

In any event, I am sure to remind my kids that I am blessed to have a job that brings me some pleasure and lots of purpose, pays pretty well, and does not involve getting my hands dirty or risking death. And I will remind them that, whatever else they may achieve in their lives, their greatest achievement of all will be their happiness.

I actually think that, deep down, other parents tend to agree with me, when at first

Profession	Percentage agreeing that they are happy
Florists and gardeners	87
Hairdressers and beauticians	79
Plumbers and water workers	76
Marketers and PR people	75
Scientists and researchers	69
Leisure and tourism workers	67
Construction workers	66
Doctors and dentists	65
Lawyers	64
Nurses	62
Architects	62
Child care and youth workers	60
Teachers	59
Accountants	58
Car workers and mechanics	57
Electricians	55
Caterers	55
HR and personnel staff	54
IT and telecom workers	48
Bankers	44

it might appear that they do not. Many of the middle-class parents I come across in Brighton are seemingly obsessed with their kids achieving as much as possible at school. There are many potential reasons for this, but I'm pretty sure that the main reason why parents care about achievement in quite narrow terms is because they see achievement as a route to happiness. They think that if their kids excel at school, they will later go to a good university and land a well-paid job, and that all of this will make their kids happy. They may have mistaken desires for their kids' achievements but it would be sadistic for them to want something for their kids that they knew *for sure* would make them unhappy.

Authenticity

You might continue to maintain that it is perfectly rational to have some evaluative desires that you know might make you feel less happy. You may have "higher-order" desires for morality, freedom, truth, knowledge, aesthetics, beauty, and the preservation of species of birds and animals, which may not be based solely on the consequences for your happiness (or, importantly, for the happiness of those you care about). But it strikes me as rather odd, to put it mildly, to desire something that will *never show up* in better sentiments of pleasure or purpose.

Consider an example that philosophers are fond of: your partner is cheating on you. Assume for simplicity that no one else knows about it. You would like to know, right — even if it made you miserable? Of course you would, and so, the argument runs, the truth must matter more to you than "deluded happiness." But you probably think that you will eventually be happier from finding out — that clearing the air will lead to greater happiness *in the end,* whatever you decide to do about the affair. And so it is the consequences for happiness of the truth that matter, not the truth in itself.

Now consider perhaps the most famous critique of happiness, developed by Robert Nozick, a philosopher who came to prominence in the 1970s. He asks you to imagine being connected up to what he calls an "experience machine." Every neurotransmitter in your brain would be connected to a system that could simulate the happiest life for you. You could have a fabulous career, fantastic kids, and a great partner, all without any pain or suffering. In a straight choice, which life would you choose:

your "real life" with all of its associated pain and suffering or an "artificial life" with greater happiness created by the experience machine? Nozick suggests that most of us would choose the former.[11] As with the cheating partner, the authenticity of real life seems to be of value to us beyond simply feeling good.

But I think most philosophers, with a few notable exceptions like Roger Crisp, have been too quick to jump to this conclusion. In both examples above, you know what the alternative scenario is. You cannot think about not knowing about an affair without first thinking about knowing about it. You can't unknow what you know. So the cat is already out of the bag when you do the thought experiment. I would probably also be persuaded to choose reality over being a brain in a vat if I was aware of being a brain in a vat. But if the thought experiment were taken literally, your life right now could be one big experience machine — and you wouldn't know. And since you would never know, it makes most sense to live the life with the greatest happiness in it.

Many of the conclusions reached by philosophers are based on thought experiments that I don't think stand up to scrutiny. By making them the focus of attention, they ensure that concerns for the truth, etc., are bound to be considered important. And they do so in a contrived way — how can you truly imagine not knowing your wife is cheating when you are told she is, or being a brain in a vat when you know you could otherwise be a "real" person?

In my own work, I have asked survey participants whether or not they would take a pill to improve their happiness. Only one-quarter of participants said they would be willing to do so; the remaining three-quarters objected in various ways to "un-natural" enhancements of happiness and to a "quick fix."[12] These are interesting responses, especially given the widespread use, and acceptability, of drugs to treat depression. It is possible that improving happiness is seen as less acceptable than treating misery. So in the survey that estab-lished that pleasure and purpose matter to people, Rob Metcalfe and I also asked people whether they agreed that govern-ment policy should seek to (a) improve hap-piness and (b) reduce misery. There was more support for the second statement. Such findings have important implications for how happiness (and depression and misery) are discussed in the popular press and in policy circles.[13] Policy makers wishing to promote the use of happiness measures might instead refer to them as measures of misery. While empirical studies like this can fuel interesting discussions, we are still left having to make judgments about what ultimately matters in life.

Desires in Themselves

Many economists and philosophers will maintain that getting more of what you want is what really counts in life. This is why economists spend so much time talking about income: all else equal, more money means that you can buy more of what you want. It is not the income in itself that makes you better off but, rather, the increase in choice that means you can satisfy more of your desires.[14] You could choose to buy more stuff or you could decide to work a little less, or maybe both.

But why would you want more possessions or more leisure time unless you imagined (correctly or otherwise) that you would be happier as a result? If something won't ever show up at all in your happiness or in the happiness of those you care about (which can sometimes include strangers), I cannot see where its value can reside.

Let me give an example to illustrate (and a chance to get something off my chest, if

I'm being totally honest). I like to read, and, as I hope you can tell, I read loads of academic papers and nonfiction books. But over the years, many people have told me that I should read novels. I have never read a novel in my life (unless you count *Of Mice and Men* at school — we were also supposed to read *The Mayor of Casterbridge* but have you seen how long that is?). Let's suppose that I listen to these people and that I develop a taste for literature and that I then devote time to reading other stories. I have developed a new preference, and it is being satisfied. So that would be enough for many economists and philosophers to say that I was better off, especially as reading novels is likely to be seen by them as a preference worth having.

But what if I was not made any happier from reading novels? Developing a new preference that is now satisfied isn't important in itself. It only makes me better off if it makes me or those I care about happier than we were before I started reading. I make no grand claims for the significance of anything — a job, a spouse, a house, *The Mayor of Casterbridge* — beyond its effect on happiness. Everything except happiness requires some justification or other: it is just obvious that happiness matters.[15]

Now, other considerations, such as achievement or authenticity, are clearly important. But they are only important because of their *instrumental value;* that is, they matter only insofar as they produce more happiness. They may generally promote more happiness but we should not be slaves to them. It would be masochistic and sadistic of me to tell the truth about something if I knew *for sure* that I would create only misery for myself and others. We've all heard of pathological liars. Telling the truth in such circumstances would be an example of being pathologically honest. We need to judge each behavior on its specific consequences for happiness and not on the basis of whether or not it accords to a generally good rule.

Once we accept that the experience of happiness (for yourself and others) is the final arbiter of the rightness of what you do, we can move away from making moral judgments based on ill-conceived ideas about what is right and wrong. We can instead use factual assessments of the consequences for pleasure and purpose to judge the goodness of what we and others do (including policy makers) and to guide our views about how society ought to be organized.[16]

So experiences of pleasure and purpose

are all that matter in the end. *Hedonism* is the school of thought that holds that pleasure is the only thing that matters in the end. By adding *sentiments* of purpose to pleasure, I define my position as *sentimental hedonism.* I am a sentimental hedonist and I think that, deep down, we all are.

If you remain convinced that concerns beyond happiness are not mistaken desires, you should still care greatly about happiness because it is the best way to bring about those other outcomes. There have been many studies to show, using causal methods, that those who experience better emotions live longer, are in better health, recover from viruses more quickly, take less time off work, are more successful in their careers, are generally more productive, and have happier marriages.[17] In a study of siblings, kids who have a sunnier disposition are more likely to get a degree, get hired, and get promoted.[18] Good emotions also foster original thinking and improve our ability to resolve conflicts.[19] Furthermore, those of us who are seen to be in a good mood are thought of as more attractive, which means getting better grades at school and more money at work.[20]

So much for pleasure. What about the effects of purpose? Although there are fewer studies, the effects seem to be just as important. Engaging in meaningful and purposeful activities promotes better health, social integration, and daily functioning.[21] Some of the activities linked to successful aging that people consider purposeful are golfing and exercise.[22] Moreover, a lack of purpose at work, unsurprisingly, has been shown to result in lower productivity and increased absenteeism.[23] Students who feel bored during their free time are more likely to drop out before graduation from high school.[24] And at home, couples who report boredom during their marriage now are less likely to be satisfied with it nine years later on.[25] Happiness really does matter, however you look at it.

MISTAKEN PROJECTIONS

We frequently make mistakes about how much something will make us happy, even when we are convinced that happiness is all there is. We make mistakes about our future happiness when we pay undue attention to (a) the effects of a change; (b) the differences between two options; (c) current feelings; or (d) unrepresentative snapshots of past experiences.

Focusing Effects

How much happier would you be if you won a load of money? A lot happier, right? Well, only if you spent a great deal of time thinking about how much happier you are with all that cash. In a different respect, if you were to ask Midwesterners and Californians who they think is happiest, they will both say Californians. How could they not be, given how much nicer the weather is, right? Well, the weather actually only really affects happiness when we think about it — and we don't think about it that much. So, in fact, Midwesterners are just as happy as Californians, but both groups pay too much attention to the impact of the weather when thinking about who is happiest.[26]

When you think about the impact of anything, good or bad, you are basically asking yourself how much it matters when you are paying attention to it, and so you think it matters a lot — and typically a lot more than it will actually matter when you experience it in your life, where your attention will flit around rather than remaining focused on it. This is the *focusing effect* in action. The fortune cookie maxim here is, "Nothing is quite as important as you think it is while you're thinking about it."[27]

Here are a couple of questions for you (if

you have a car, that is; apologies if not). First, how much pleasure do you get from driving your car, on a scale from 0 to 10? Second, how much did you enjoy your last drive, on the same scale? When PhD and MBA students from the Ross School of Business were asked similar questions, along with questions about the car so that researchers could estimate its market value, there was a high correlation between answers to the first question and market value. So, this question taken at face value would tell us that a more expensive car brings more pleasure. But there was no correlation at all between answers to the second question and market value. So a more expensive car had no effect on the enjoyment of the last drive but it did predict higher levels of reported pleasure from driving it.[28]

The difference is explained by attention. When you are asked how much pleasure you get from driving your car, you start thinking about how much pleasure you get from driving your car. You think about the car itself — and the nicer the car, the more pleasure you get from thinking about driving it. But the actual experience of driving is very different, and when doing so you rarely think about the car itself — rather, you are focusing on the idiot in front of you, or arguing with your husband or wife, and thinking about all those other things that have nothing to do with the car that you drive.

Together with Alan Williams, who was an inspirational professor of health economics at the University of York, I spent a good part of my early academic life asking people to think, hypothetically, about the impact that different states of health would have on their lives. As part of a study we conducted in the early to mid 1990s, three thousand members of the UK general public were asked for their judgments about the relative severity of different imagined health states so that policy makers could make better decisions about which treatments were doing the most good. Participants were asked to imagine being in a poor state of health, such as having problems with walking about, and then to think about how many years of life they would be willing to give up to have those problems removed. This is called the time trade-off method.[29] The more years of life people are willing to sacrifice, the more severe the state is seen to be. If I were to give up half of my remaining life to avoid a health problem, then that problem would have to be pretty serious. By asking questions about a whole range of possible health states, it is possible to see which ones people care most about treating.

My most cited academic paper came out of this research and has had a considerable impact on how the UK National Health Service values the benefit from new drugs and therapies.[30] Basically, it puts the time trade-off values from the general public alongside the costs of different treatments and interventions to assess which ones represent the best value for money.[31] The UK Home Office uses a similar approach, based on my work, to value the impact of being a victim of crime.[32]

While this work has benefited my career, I wish that it had not had such a policy impact, because I can now see the serious forecasting errors made by people asked to imagine future conditions. Working with Daniel Kahneman at Princeton helped me to crystallize these concerns.[33] Fundamentally, we are not especially good at knowing how different conditions will affect us when they drift in and out of our attention in the day-to-day experiences of life. People in the United States say they are willing to give up about 15 percent of their life expectancy to avoid problems with walking and about the same to avoid moderate anxiety or depression.[34] Yet my own recent research shows that the latter has about ten times as much of an impact on our happiness as the former.[35]

Things don't get much better if we ask only those with experience of the specific health problems. People with problems walking who are asked to imagine having their walking restrictions alleviated will inevitably imagine actively paying lots of attention to walking freely, which they will eventually take for granted.[36]

So, in appraising the impact of health and other policy interventions, I think it would be much better to look at the impact of conditions on the happiness of those affected, properly accounting for any adaptation or sensitization processes. And the general public lends some support to the idea that happiness matters: George Kavetsos, Aki Tsuchiya, and I have recently added life satisfaction levels to the description of the health states and found that scenarios including high levels of satisfaction increase the likelihood of preferring to live for longer in poor health.[37]

Adam Smith, the founding father of economics, recognized the pervasiveness of focusing effects: "The great source of both the misery and disorders of human life seems to arise from over-rating the difference between one permanent situation and another."[38] You think that something will greatly affect your happiness because you are focusing attention on it.

Rob Metcalfe and I have even shown that what you are asked in a previous survey can affect what you attend to in a current one.[39] We took advantage of the fact that the 2008 Champions League Final was between two English soccer clubs, Manchester United and Chelsea. Both sets of supporters predicted that they would be much more affected by the outcome of the event than they in fact were, which had been shown before for other events. But we also found that Chelsea fans (whose team lost the final) were less happy after the event when they had been asked to predict their happiness before the event than those Chelsea fans surveyed only after the event. So, after the event, those who were also asked about their happiness before the final were being reminded of the defeat that had happened between the surveys, whereas the happiness responses of those asked only after the event were not contaminated in this way — and showed that losing the final (even on penalties to English rivals) did not affect them that much at all after a couple of days.

It is very hard to predict how much something will matter when you are not paying attention to it. It is not surprising, then, that we are all prone to make mistakes about what will continue to grab our attention and what will not.

Many Choices; One Experience

Typically in your day-to-day life, you are not just making predictions about how one thing will affect you, but you are making a choice between two or more options. In so doing, you are prone to mistaking the relative impact of those choices. And again the problem lies in where your attention is directed — in this case, what is attention grabbing in the choice itself as compared to attention grabbing in the consequences of that choice. *Distinction bias* is the tendency to view two options as more dissimilar when evaluating them simultaneously than when evaluating them separately.[40] So whenever you are making a choice — about which ice cream to buy, say, or which job to take — you tend to look at what is different about the options instead of paying attention to how you will actually experience your final decision.

My friend's kitchen sink is really quite a sight to be seen. She bought a beautiful chrome faucet after jointly evaluating dozens at a really expensive hardware store. She didn't realize until after the installation that it was much larger in proportion to her sink than it really should have been. This enormous kitchen faucet has been an annoyance to her but a great source of amusement for her family and friends, as we all experience the consequences of her distinction bias when she bought that ridiculous tap.

Consider deciding whether or not you should buy that house you just looked at. This choice involves a joint evaluation of your current house against the new one. The new one is bigger, so you go for it. But its bigness relative to your current house will soon not matter that much once you move in (unless your kids didn't have their own bedrooms and now do). The size of any house is constant and not especially interesting from an attentional point of view. In your experience of the new house, you are much more likely to be affected by the noise outside at night; a stimulus that will continue to grab your attention on a regular basis. You'll quickly adapt to the space for the boxes but not to the noise of the foxes.

Feelings Focused

Buying a house is a nice example of a further element of mistaken projections; namely, our proclivity to allow how we feel now to affect how we imagine feeling in the future. *I simply love that house, so how could I not love living there?* *Projection bias* is what behavioral scientists call the scenario when we mistakenly use our current feelings to project how we will feel in the future.[41]

One of the classic studies in this research area found that men are more likely to call a woman who gives him her phone number immediately after having crossed a suspension bridge compared to ten minutes after crossing it.[42] The men project their aroused feelings in the moment to their future feelings about how they would feel on a date with the woman.

Since then, there have been many demonstrations of projection bias. Students' choices about which university to attend are influenced by the weather on the day they visit campus with, surprisingly, cloudier days predicting a greater likelihood of enrollment.[43] The purchase of winter clothes depends on the weather on the day of purchase, with more clothes being purchased on colder days and then subsequently returned.[44] And you have almost certainly noticed that if you shop for next week's food while you are hungry, you are likely to buy more than you intended.[45] What's interesting about this example is that so few of us seem to learn from our past mistakes. We keep falling into the trap of buying more food when we are hungry. It's as if we are hardwired to mess up, which is not surprising since our ancestors were nearly always hungry, and they did not have the luxury of knowing they could just run to the supermarket.

Your future feelings will ebb and flow in ways that your current feelings do not appear to account for. Take the extreme but resonant case of 168 terminally ill cancer patients (who were no longer seeking treatment) voluntarily admitted to the Riverview Health Centre Palliative Care Unit in Winnipeg, Canada, from 1993 to 1995. Their will to live was shown to vary by about sixty points on a hundred-point scale from "complete will to live" to "no will to live" over the course of a month, and by about thirty points over twelve hours. These huge differences can be explained by how the patients felt at the moment that they were asked the question.[46]

In less stark scenarios, think about how

your feelings now guide your decisions. Do you always say yes when asked out, and then wonder why you're so bored on dates? Does an early Sunday brunch with your friends sound like a good idea on Friday night but not from the comfort of your bed come Sunday morning? Did you wind up enjoying going out for an evening bike ride even though it was hard to pull yourself away from the TV? Implicit in many of your decisions is the assumption that your current sentiments of pleasure and purpose, or misery and futility, will carry over.

Having said this, there are also occasions when our behavior is driven by our *anticipation* of future feelings, which may be different to how we feel now.[47] As an example, consider our reluctance to swap lottery tickets with others even if we are offered money to do so. We don't want to swap because we anticipate the feelings of regret that will ensue if we traded away the winning ticket.[48]

But we're often wrong about how much regret we will feel. Commuters who have just missed their trains feel less disappointed than other people predict they themselves would feel if they had just done so. And participants who can win a prize by correctly guessing the cost of common supermarket items, like gum and detergent, regret missing out on the right answers less than others expect they would if they were in their shoes.[49] Overall, then, we are prone to mispredict our future feelings.

Misremembering

Not only do we make poor projections into the future, but we are also prone to misremembering the fullness of a past experience. Take a second to recall your last holiday. How much did you enjoy it? Would you go back again? If you are anything like other people, two factors will explain your answers: the peak moment of pleasure or pain and the final moment of pleasure or pain. This is known as the *peak-end effect.*[50] Further, your overall assessment of an experience doesn't even pay that much attention to how long it lasted. This is known as *duration neglect.*[51]

Your memories, even the most recent ones, are etched with extremity and recency at the expense of duration. They are imperfect guides to the flow of past experiences but they do determine how you feel about the past and, crucially, they drive your future behavior. Think about your favorite films. You'd be hard-pressed to tell me how long each one lasted, but you'll certainly remember your favorite scene and most likely the final one, too. That's why screen-writers or playwrights will often spend a great deal of time making the last scene full of sparks and emotion. The whole film might be rubbish, but if the finale is genuinely good and memorable you'll most likely recall the whole film as having been good. The overall happiness you get from the film is what you experience while watching it and what you draw from as memories of the experience afterward. In other words, overall happiness comes from all the sentiments you experience as a result of it.

The takeaway from this is that the duration of an event *might be* less important than how the event ended *if* the ending plays a prominent part in your future recollections of the event. Some of the best nights out may have been short but ended very sweetly, and these may be the ones you recall most later on. So how the event ended might be more important than how long the event lasted if you draw more on your memories of the ending of the event than on your memories of the rest of it — which we often do, of course.

Consider the experiences of those attending a performance at the New York Philharmonic on January 10, 2012. In the final mo-

ments of the eighty-two-minute performance (of Mahler's Symphony no. 9), an
alarm on an audience member's iPhone
went off. Despite the beauty of the previous
eighty-one minutes of the performance,
many audience members later recalled how
their whole experience had been ruined.[52]
But can that be correct? After all, only the
final minute was ruined. But it was also the
most important minute — the peak and the
end.

In principle, it is possible to say whether,
on balance, an overall experience was good
or bad by accounting for how much the bad
memory of the experience plays into future
experiences. Memories of the past are
experiences in the present. Just how often
will those who were at the New York Philharmonic think about their ruined night
out? If the pain of their memories exceeds
the pleasure they experienced during the
first eighty-one minutes, then it was overall
a bad experience. If not, it was overall good.

The critical point that I want to emphasize
here, and which was first made in chapter
1, is that you simply cannot know if an
experience was, on balance, a net benefit or
a net cost to your overall happiness without
considering the frequency and intensity of
future experiences of the memory of it.

We often recall experiences as having been "spoiled" because bad aspects of it continue to loom large. From an evolutionary standpoint, this makes perfect sense. Almost getting attacked by a lion when out for a stroll in a new area means that you are less likely to stroll in that area again, no matter how nice the flowers look and smell. But, as so often, context matters. Speaking personally, the memories of many great nights out have stayed with me far longer than those from bad nights.

It is possible that you recall peak moments of pleasure and pain differently, and probably more intensely, than peak moments of purpose and pointlessness, although there might be some important differences between us as individuals (dependent, for example, upon the degree to which we can be categorized as pleasure machines or purpose engines). I have already stated that writing this book has felt purposeful and nothing can change that experience. But my memory of the experience may well be influenced by how successful it is. The more copies it sells, the more likely I will be to recall the experience as having been a purposeful one. And these memories will probably greatly influence any future decision about writing another book.

Whatever your own precise focus, however, you're unlikely to remember the past in ways that are consistent with the facts. What this means is that your inaccurate memories may steer you toward decisions that are not consistent with the future maximization of your happiness, and away from the need to establish the appropriate balance between pleasure and purpose in your life. Because of one exciting moment you might choose to repeat a holiday where you were bored most of the time or, perhaps more importantly, because of one awful moment you might choose to quit a job where the majority of your experiences are decent. Job satisfaction is actually an excellent predictor of quit rates, and in the large data sets from Germany and the UK, peak and end job satisfaction are a better predictor of quitting than overall job satisfaction ratings.[53]

You might want to consider a time when you've been wrong in predicting your happiness in the past and what you focused on in your prediction that turned out to be different from the experience. As an example, last Christmas, Les and I took the kids to see Mig in Ibiza. The words "Mig" and "Ibiza" primed me to focus my attention on the prospect of having a good time. But a place that shuts down for the winter is not a good place for a family holiday with two kids who require constant stimulation (or three kids, from Les's perspective). We spent a lot of money on flights and a villa and had a pretty lousy time despite Mig's best efforts to find things for the kids to do. Les says she did warn me that this might happen and I'm sure she is right.

MISTAKEN BELIEFS

We also make mistakes about who we are and how we would like to be that sometimes get in the way of us being happier. We are often wrong about (a) the kind of people we are and why we do what we do; (b) the expectations we have; and (c) the benefits of accepting who we are.

Delusion

You and a friend have just had an argument. She is furious that you weren't civil. You think she's overreacting. There's no record of what was said. Who's right? You both are, because there is no objective truth, only your subjective interpretations. You explain your behavior to form stories about yourself that are consistent with your beliefs. You believe you are a respectful person, and she believes you're wrong.

We are actually quite stubborn about what we believe to be true and so it is hard for us to change our minds. Indeed, how many times in the last few years have you genuinely changed your mind about something significant you believe? Not that often, I suspect. We think we have good, logical reasons for our beliefs but, in reality, our beliefs typically come first and then we attend to reasons that support them. If we really based our beliefs on evidence, we would change our minds much more often as better evidence became available. Instead, we search for information and evidence to support what we believe and ignore information that does not. This is called *confirmation bias.*[54]

As a relevant example for me, reviewers of academic journal papers are more likely to publish articles that conform to their own theoretical perspective.[55] If the evidence does not quite fit what we believe to be true, we will dismiss it or find ways of explaining how that evidence would actually fit our beliefs if only it were gathered or interpreted "properly."

In a related way, if there is a discrepancy between our beliefs and our behavior, we will seek to explain away the difference. If you believe that you are a good cook and you cook a bad meal, you can attribute it to poor-quality ingredients, a malfunctioning oven, or the pressure you were under to prepare it in time for your friends' arrival. So long as you can apportion responsibility for your behavior to sources other than yourself — to the context, other people, and so on — you can continue to see yourself as a good cook. In this way, you can hold a belief about yourself that continually remains at odds with your behavior. Every bad meal has an explanation.

Our tendency to attribute our behavior to our context or to blame others for it is directly in contrast to how we tend to judge others' actions. When it comes to other people, we are far more likely to attribute the bad meal to their inability to cook rather than to other causes. This is called the *fundamental attribution error.*[56] When explaining other people's behavior, we overestimate the effect of their underlying disposition and underestimate the effect of context. This is a central concept in psychological research and there have been thousands of articles published on the topic, many on its implications for how we judge people who are different from us.[57]

Everything is relative, though, and we still do not appreciate quite how much we are influenced by context. We delude ourselves that we make choices that are driven by system 2 and we ignore the influence of system 1. This is hardly surprising, given that we don't have conscious access to the automatic and unconscious drivers of our behavior. But we do have access to the behaviors themselves. So we could work out how we acted previously in a given situation and that will be a very good guide to how we will act the next time we are in that situation — and a much better guide than any intention to behave differently.[58] Indeed, intentions explain, at most, only about a quarter of the variation in changes in health behaviors, such as exercise, leaving three-quarters to be explained by factors associated with the specific contexts that trigger an action — such as whether you have a nice outdoor area to exercise in or a gym at your office.[59]

Mistaken beliefs about our immunity to context can get us into serious trouble. Much as some of us might like to think otherwise, most men, and quite a lot of women, too, would cheat on their partners in the "right" context; drunken nights out with attractive friends that end up back at their place, for example. If you consider yourself to be immune to context, you will be much more likely to "find yourself" in those situations where you simply will not be able to help yourself. Only by recognizing the role of context, and insofar as you do not want to cheat, you can try to avoid situations that make it more likely.

While we really must all learn to accept that we are creatures of our environment, there still remains happiness in a bit of self-delusion. Very few of us are as good a cook as we think we are — or as attractive, intelligent, or funny. And this is all fine. Who really wants to have the truth pointed out to them? And even this assumes that there is an "objective truth" out there in the first place, which there rarely is. Most things are relative, including your culinary skills, which are probably fantastic compared to my kids' and pretty unimaginative compared to Heston Blumenthal's. As we have seen, the truth, insofar as one exists, is an overrated concept in the experiences of our lives.

There's a limit to how much we can delude ourselves, however, and sometimes the discordance between our beliefs and our behavior will be hard to explain and the gap can make us unhappy. When this occurs, it's easier for us to change what we think about a particular behavior than to change the behavior itself. Indeed, behavioral science has taught us that our behavior drives our attitudes every bit as much as, or even more than, the other way around. If we are not satisfied with our work or social lives, for example, we'll often simply just deem them less important than other aspects of our lives with which we are more satisfied.[60]

It is well established that you will feel uncomfortable when there is a discrepancy between what you think and what you do. This is known as *cognitive dissonance.*[61] In such circumstances, it is much simpler to bring your attitudes in line with your behavior than vice versa. The theory of cognitive dissonance was originally developed in the 1950s by Leon Festinger. This social psychologist conducted a classic experiment where he asked participants to turn pegs in a tray, a very dull task. These participants were then instructed to convince other people to do the same task and were paid either $1 or $20 to do so. Those who were paid less liked the task more than those who were paid more. Why? Well, getting paid $20 gave the participants a good reason for what they did: "I did it for the money." Being paid $1 required a different justification to bring their attitudes in line with their behavior: "I didn't do it for the money; I did it for the joy."[62]

Cognitive dissonance is pervasive. It explains why children like certain toys less after they play with other toys, why gamblers at a racetrack think that their horse is more likely to win after they have placed their bet than before, and why people who have been unfaithful to their partners are prone to trivializing their affairs.[63] It also applies to politics. In twenty years (1976–96) of US election data, the attitudes of young people were more polarized in the group that were just old enough to vote as compared to those who were just too young; that is, the act of voting in the just-old-enough group drove their attitudes toward the candidate.[64]

Cognitive dissonance also explains the claim that "you can't help who you fall in love with," which is really only ever said when a relationship has turned sour. The word "love" is used as a way to bring attitudes in line with staying in the relationship. Narratives to explain behavior can have dangerous consequences, such as when abused spouses stay with their abusers because they love them.[65] Decisions about relationships, like all other decisions in life, should be based on their consequences for experiences of pleasure and purpose over time, and not by narratives surrounding them.

Cognitive dissonance can also be used to explain assumptions about your optimal balance of pleasure and purpose. My friends Mig and Lisa tell themselves that pleasure and purpose, respectively, are all that matter because that makes their beliefs consistent with their ongoing behavior. The state of cognitive dissonance is unpleasant, so this is a way for them to protect their happiness. They could each be even happier, however, if they adjusted the activities in their lives and what they pay attention to in order to find a better balance of pleasure and purpose.

Expecting Too Much

Another facet of who you are (and particularly your evaluating self) is the *expectations* you have, which can be established very early on in life. Grace Lordan and I are currently analyzing the data from a large longitudinal survey in the UK to show that, from childhood to adulthood, current income relative to previous income is a significant predictor of life satisfaction and mental health, whether people move up or down.[66] There is also evidence, again using reports of life satisfaction and mental health, that the gains from increases in income can be completely offset if your expectations about gains in income rise faster than does income itself.[67] Expectations are also central to experiences of purpose in life, as well as to the lack of it. Those who experience the most purpose at work have jobs that fit with their expectations about how they see themselves.[68] On the other hand, if you are expecting something to be particularly interesting and it doesn't meet your expectations, you will be bored.

So, in general, it is better for your happiness if you have modest expectations. Take having a party. Those with high expectations about and big plans for the millennium celebrations were less happy on the night than those with low expectations and not much planned.[69] And you know that about nights out on the town: the best ones tend to be unplanned. In the end, expecting to be very happy is probably a surefire way of not being so.

Modest expectations will also mean that you can avoid *false-hope syndrome,* whereby we stick with crazy expectations way past the point at which we should have reined them in.[70] False hope springs from optimism, but having modest expectations need not be incompatible with optimism. Optimism research teaches us that we should expect the best and have a contingency plan for the worst.[71] It doesn't mean we always need to expect the very best or ignore the worst when it occurs. When facing an uncertain future, the rose-colored glasses of optimism serve us just fine, as long as we can take them off from time to time for a dose of realism. Although figuring out what are and are not sensible expectations is difficult, you should at least experience pleasure and purpose as you work toward a goal you have set. As we will see later, there are some effective ways to obtain this feedback from yourself — and from others — in order to know what to stick with and what to abandon.

Other times, however, we try hard to force our behavior to be more like that of the people we want to be. Self-improvement is important, but it needs to be conducive to your happiness. If an ambition will not make you or those you care about any happier, then there really is no point in striving to be someone else. You should carefully consider your reasons for the ideal self you construct and then select goals and ambitions that are sensible and conducive to your happiness.

Accepting Too Little

Whatever else you do, don't be too hard on yourself, because trying to *force* yourself to be different never really works. One of the most effective ways to get others to do as you would like is to make them feel that they are doing it voluntarily.[72] If they feel coerced, they are much more likely to resist. What applies to conversations with other people also applies to the conversations we have with ourselves. Try as hard as you can to stop yourself from thinking about a white bear and you won't be able to stop yourself from thinking about it — in fact, even more thoughts of the darn bear will pop into your head when you are allowed to think about it once more.[73]

In general, we need to learn to accept much more about ourselves than we do, thus integrating our evaluations with our actual experiences. Nonacceptance is seen as an internalization of feelings of shame, which then results in a range of other negative emotions that get in the way of behavior change.[74] Ignore the fact that you are a lousy cook and you'll just keep your dinner guests away, wondering why nobody ever takes you up on your invitation for a home-cooked meal. Effective behavior change can only really come about after you accept what you already do. Accept that you are a lousy cook and you might be motivated to get some lessons. And even if you don't, accepting that you are an imperfect, fallible, and mortal creature will mean that you are happier in your own skin. This was certainly true for my stammer, especially when I accepted that there was no need to be ashamed by it.

The serenity affirmation Alcoholics Anonymous uses says: "Grant us the serenity to accept the things we cannot change, courage to change the things we can, and wisdom to know the difference."[75] Separating the wheat from the chaff of your ideal self — knowing which ideals to hold and which ones to fold — is a real challenge. Ultimately, you need to consider the various ways in which your thoughts about yourself are helping and hindering you in the pursuit of happiness.

Making mistakes along the way is absolutely fine, so long as you learn from them. There are good and bad mistakes. Good ones are those that you learn from and that you do not attempt to hide, especially from yourself.[76] Bad ones are those that you keep repeating. As Einstein is famously attributed with saying, the definition of insanity is doing the same thing over and over again and expecting different results.

Following Shakespeare's *Macbeth,* it has often been said that someone has been the "architect of his own destruction."[77] I have certainly been my own worst enemy at various times over the years, and I'm sure you have thought or done things that made you wonder what the hell you were thinking — perhaps even at the moment of doing them. It seems to be human nature that we often spend far too much of our time thinking about how other people have wronged us, when we should really be paying a bit more attention to the harm we do to ourselves. If you think one of your friends has been mean to you, perhaps stop and ask yourself why you allow him to be. In fact, first off, perhaps consider whether he really was being mean at all. Nobody's perfect, and to be happy in any relationship, you can either accept the other person, flaws and all, or walk away. You live with yourself forever, of course, and this means accepting yourself as both imperfect and able to change.

REALLOCATING ATTENTION

The fundamental reason why most of us aren't as happy as we could be is that we allocate attention in ways that are often at odds with experiencing as much pleasure and purpose as we could. It's not surprising that we aren't as happy as we could be when we allow our evaluative self to attend to mistaken desires about what should motivate us and make us happy. It's no wonder that we make choices that are incompatible with our future experiences of happiness when our attention is focused on what's in front of us right now rather than on what will be in front of us once we have made a decision. And it's actually quite easy to be miserable when our beliefs and behavior conflict, when we set lofty expectations about ourselves, or when we can't even accept ourselves in the first place.

So if the misallocation of attention is our fundamental problem, the reallocation of attention must be the fundamental solution. You need a more efficient production process to become happier. Fortunately, behavioral science provides you with some help in understanding some of the reasons why you might not be allocating your attention as well as you could. Better still, it provides illuminating insights into how you can reorient your attention to "deliver happiness," as we shall now see in part 2.

■ ■ ■ ■

PART 2
DELIVERING
HAPPINESS

■ ■ ■ ■

The ways in which you can reallocate your attention to be happier are best understood from three separate but related perspectives: deciding, designing, and doing. Chapter 5 shows how you can mitigate the attentional obstacles to happiness by deciding to pay attention to what makes you happy, including decisions ranging from which job to take to what to do this evening. Chapter 6 considers how you can design your surroundings so as to become happier without having to think too hard about it, such as when you set a particular home page on your computer. Chapter 7 will show that, as a rule, we are all happier when we give activities, like talking to friends, our full attention. The most effective ways to be happier will involve joining up these various components, and so chapter 8 illustrates how to bring together deciding, designing, and doing to address, separately, two behaviors that I hope will resonate with many readers: how to procrastinate less and how to help others more. Even if they don't directly apply to you, there will be general lessons that can be applied to other behaviors you might wish to change. But let's first get into the details of the "three Ds."

5
DECIDING HAPPINESS

We'll now turn our focus toward the perspective of *deciding* the production process, concentrating on how to mitigate mistaken desires, projections, and beliefs. A major part of the solution to these problems is right under your nose: it lies in the experiences of pleasure and purpose you have, and in the judgments that those close to you make about your happiness. You need to be careful not to overthink things, though.

PAY ATTENTION TO YOUR OWN FEEDBACK

Do you ever think about what brings you the most pleasure and purpose in your experiences? One important and useful way to deal with the various mistakes you might make about your happiness is to pay attention to direct *feedback* about what brings you pleasure and/or purpose and what does not, and then to use this information in your anticipation of future happiness. This section is therefore all about how you can find out which inputs into your happiness production process bring you pleasure and/or purpose and which ones do not. You are seeking to establish equilibrium so that you can stop monitoring your production process, reallocating attention thereafter only when you have good reason to (such as when the inputs, or their impacts, change).

Making Happiness Salient

Your happiness is the most important feedback you can get from your behavior, but it is not always the most salient. Something is *salient* if it is noticeable and relevant. When I hear people talking in a foreign language, it's noticeable but I quickly zone out because I do not understand what is being said. When I hear someone with a regional accent, it is noticeable (especially among senior government officials in the UK) and I can usually make out what they are saying, and so it is salient: both noticeable and relevant.

Our happiness is sometimes not very salient, and we need to do what we can to make it more so. Imagine playing a piano and not being able to hear what it sounds like. Many activities in life are like playing a piano that you do not hear; you're experiencing pleasure or purpose but you are not appropriately attending to the experience. You can tune in by better attending to inputs and noticing how you feel. Once you do this and learn what the songs from the activities of your life sound like, you can feed this information into your predictions of how the piano will sound the next time you play it.

Tuning into salient feedback is critical in everything that you decide to do. Nowhere is this more important than in understanding adaptation processes. Imagine that someone dented your car and drove off. You might react immediately by getting it fixed because looking at the dent makes you feel miserable. But you might leave it a week or two and see if you still feel the same. If you do, get it fixed; but if the dent does not bother you anymore, you could leave it until some other idiot crashes into you or until you want to sell the car. Monitoring the effects of any event beyond its initial impact will serve to show you what you get used to and what you do not.

This kind of information can be especially useful if you are trying to give up something. Smokers' physical cravings peak at around three days after quitting and last for about three to four weeks; for caffeine, physical withdrawal symptoms peak after about thirty-six hours and subside after about one week.[1] Knowing these kinds of facts, especially when they are generated by your own direct feedback, can help you make better-informed decisions about what to do and when.

In situations where you are facing some painful uncertainties, it will almost certainly be better to turn them into adaptable realities. Do you have an unopened bill that's bothering you? Then open it. You will have to do something about it eventually and, when you do, its impact on your happiness will wane. Resolve the misery-making uncertainty and get quickly to the adaptation process by confronting the uncertainty head-on. Monitoring the feedback of resolving painful uncertainties will show just how quickly you do generally get over things.

You can trust your own experiences more than your desires. You might think that being the next Lady Gaga will make you happy and attempt to achieve it but then find that all your experiences along the way are miserable ones. It's uncertain what your experiences of fame would be like if you were to attain it and so if you aren't experiencing pleasure and purpose along the way, you are giving up happiness now that might not lead to more happiness later. Keep your eye on the happiness prize by tuning into the feedback from your experiences.

You can also trust your own experiences more than your projections. Whatever you choose to do, you will only ever experience your choices, not the other options involved in the decisions, and so you won't spend anywhere near as much time thinking about what might have been as you think you will. You'll open the bill and not wonder what it would have been like if you hadn't.

We often think about small decisions more than we need to and about big decisions much less than is optimal for our happiness, such as spending days looking at what colors to paint the walls but only a couple of hours visiting the house we buy. We also agonize over decisions with highly uncertain outcomes more than those with more certain ones, such as which class to take as compared to what notebook to take to class. When it comes to the small and uncertain, getting feedback from the consequences of our decisions will show that our experiences of pleasure and purpose are rarely as affected as we imagine they will be.

And you can trust your own experiences

more than your beliefs. If you can get yourself to behave in ways that produce more pleasure or purpose, you will then construct an attitude that is consistent with this kind of action, thus reinforcing the behavior. Actions do speak louder than words. And you may recall that past behavior is a much better guide to future behavior than our intentions are.

Imagine that losing weight would make you happier. You might remember an indication in chapter 3 that it may not, unless you get really sick, but let's assume here that you would be happier from losing weight. There is nothing more salient about your weight than . . . what you weigh. So get a reliable scale and stand on it twice a week at the same time of day (because you weigh less in the morning than the evening). Getting feedback about what you really weigh might just help you to put some of your feed back. I weigh myself every other day, but I admit this might be a bit over the top. Although I have been trying to gain weight rather than lose it, I am convinced that frequent salient feedback can in itself have an effect on your behavior. There is evidence from other areas to support this claim. Pedometers, which monitor the number of steps you take, increase walking.[2] People who self-monitor their blood pressure are better able to reduce it.[3]

When it comes to diet, if we are asked to estimate how much we eat, many of us gauge our daily caloric intake as being much lower than it really is — even when our body weight might suggest something quite different. Over six hundred diners at a fast-food restaurant estimated that their meals contained an average of about 120 calories less than they actually did.[4] So the suggestion to write down all the calories in what you eat and drink to help you lose weight is a good one.[5] Once you have a better idea of what you're eating, you can stop monitoring until you change what you typically eat, just as you can stop monitoring your happiness feedback once you know what makes you happy. You will only need to begin monitoring again if the inputs into your happiness production process, or their effects, change, such as if you start eating different meals.

We can see from chapter 2 that, on average, eating is a quite a pleasurable activity. There is now evidence, though, that obese people get less pleasure from food, which may explain why they need to eat more of it. In one study, a group of overweight and obese women had their brains scanned while they were drinking milk shakes at the beginning and end of a six-month period. Relative to the women who did not gain weight over this period, the women who gained weight showed less activation in the regions of the brain that produce dopamine, which, as you may recall, is the neurotransmitter in our brain associated with reward and feelings of pleasure.[6] Whether getting less pleasure from food is a cause or a consequence of weight gain doesn't really matter because people who are overweight get less pleasure from food, regardless of the cause. Taking this into account, the latest weight-loss pill actually aims to increase the pleasure effects of food so that people feel the need to eat less.

In general, attending to the pleasure from food can be good for your waistline. When you are not paying attention to the food, the feedback for your happiness is less salient, and eating is less pleasurable, so you eat more to get more pleasure. Ideally, attending to your food will help you eat more slowly, enjoy the food more, and consequently eat less of it. People eating at McDonald's in Paris take about twenty minutes longer to eat their food than diners at McDonald's in Philadelphia.[7] This study did not look at overall calorie consumption, but other data confirm that the French typically eat less than do Americans.

We've also learned that it's generally good for us to be with other people. Remember that doing so increased the pleasure people experienced from eating in both the German DRM and the ATUS data. But if you want to lose weight, paying attention to people means that you might be distracted from paying attention to what you are eating. As evidence of this, we will generally eat more when we are around other people.[8] We tend to want to keep eating if we are around others, whereas if we are alone, our desire to eat again lessens after eating.[9]

This highlights the importance of being alert to context. As we shall consider in more detail in the next chapter, most of the time it's more effective to design your environment in ways that automatically shift your attention so that you don't have to think too hard about the behavior that follows, but sometimes, as with eating, you may deliberately want your attention drawn to what you are doing. If *mindless eating* is the problem, then paying attention to what you eat through salient feedback will be a big part of the solution.[10] The main point of salient feedback is to help you make decisions about the inputs into your production process of happiness. Feedback itself is often not enough to change your behavior and improve your happiness, however, and we shall see later that a well-designed environment is also critical to being happier.

You should certainly not lose sight of the salience of pleasure and of how making pleasure even more salient might be good for you. So find ways to laugh more and remind yourself how happy it makes you feel. And you don't have to do too much to get results. Studies show that smiling can cause happiness as well as be a consequence of it because the conscious decision to smile unconsciously makes you happier as a result.[11] And so you will quickly, and quite automatically, feel better. Even a false smile, such as one contrived by holding a pen sideways between your teeth, can make you feel happier.[12] Others might know you are faking it, but you still feel happier.[13]

It's also important to find ways to make purpose more salient. Children's behavior and performance in school can be improved with challenging tasks.[14] So find ways to challenge yourself in some of what you do. It has also been found that applying a variety of different skills at work is linked to higher experiences of meaningfulness on the job.[15] Find ways to vary the skills you use. Our attention is attracted to what's new, remember, so using varied skills focuses our attention on them, thus making purpose more salient.

It is vital that pleasure and purpose are kept salient whenever you use feedback to decide whether an activity or a goal is, in fact, contributing toward your happiness. In general, you should not give up too much happiness for too long (clinging to the mistaken belief that you will be able to recoup the loss at some point later on in life). Don't put off until tomorrow happiness that can be experienced today. If you are planning to lose weight, or whatever, to be happier, take the steps to start doing it now. Quite apart from any future happiness from being thinner or fitter, you can feel purpose *now* alongside the pain of the interval training on the treadmill. Remind yourself of this whenever you can; for example, by putting gym visits in your diary as "purpose trips." Making salient the current impact on your happiness of any behavior is important, especially when you are trying to change what you do (rather than simply how you think). Desires, projections, and beliefs are often about the expected impact on future happiness of future events, but to kick-start a behavior change now, you need to make salient the benefits of doing so now as well, because you care less about future benefits.

You might think of saving more money for the future as a trade-off between a beautiful pair of boots now and an expensive custom-made walking frame later on. Well, this could work to some degree but I bet the boots would win. The benefits of saving for your retirement come not only from *being* secure in your old age but also from *feeling* secure about your old age now. So in place of the new shoes now you get a cool walking frame later on *and* the comfort of knowing the walking frame will be on its way. The boots are no longer such a clear winner.

Your happiness bears the consequences of your behavior, and so continuing with any behavior requires positive feedback — and it needs it now. If an activity makes you feel happy and you are aware of that, you are more likely to carry on doing it. On the flip side, if another activity, such as overeating, does not make you feel miserable now, you have less incentive to do anything about it. This is especially true for pleasure and often for purpose, too, although purposeful activities do require more attentional effort and it's easier to get sidetracked when engaged in them.

Attend to your current experiences of exercising rather than what you think the future benefits will be, because health only weakly motivates behavior now, if at all.[16] It is generally a mistake for any encouragement of "healthy" behaviors to be based on what might happen in the uncertain and distant future. Instead, focus on how exercising makes you feel now. I am certain that my own exercise has very little to do with concerns for being healthy. I may experience some health benefits in a couple of decades' time, but I may also have some joint problems from heavy training. Either way, it is all very uncertain and twenty years is a long way off. My ability to keep weight training — my "stickability" — is simply sticking with an activity that brings happiness in the current moment, rather than in the future. It's the pleasure-purpose feedback you get while you are engaged in an activity that matters most.

In much the same way that happiness data can be used to guide policy decisions by showing the relative impact of different allocation decisions, such as treating physical health or mental health, your own happiness data can be used to guide your own allocation decisions. You might think that putting in all those hours at the office to get promoted is worth the sacrifice of your home life but the feedback for your happiness might tell another story. Keeping your eye on the ultimate prize of sentiments of pleasure and purpose might rein in some of your more excessive desires, in and out of work.

Reconstructing Time

"But how can I do all this?" you might sensibly ask. To aid salience, you could consider writing a diary for your happiness by completing a day reconstruction method (DRM) exercise, along the lines of what we discussed in chapter 2. You can find a DRM to complete in the box on the next page. I appreciate that this looks a little onerous, but I think it will be helpful to do it at least once to bring your time use to your attention. You shouldn't be overly concerned if you can't remember every detail of your activities or precisely when each one started and finished. It is not intended to be a test with right and wrong answers but a way for you to place a happiness lens over how you use your time. Simply having this information to shape your perspective could affect your behavior in ways you might not be able

Fill out this day reconstruction method diary for yesterday to help you get feedback on your happiness. Include activities that have a natural start and stop time, such as when you changed tasks or locations.

Episode	Time it began	Time it ended	What were you doing?	Who were you with?	Pleasure (0–10)	Purpose (0–10)
1						
2						
3						
4						
5						
6						
7						
8						
9						
10						

to predict or indeed even be aware of.

The DRM can help to draw your attention to whether you might have developed mistaken desires that are reflected in how you use your time. Perhaps you have a desire to know more than anyone else about what started out as your favorite TV show but, upon reaching season 17, you discover it isn't that good anymore. Your evaluative self continues to think it's a good show, because it still ought to be good given the cast and writers, but your experiencing self is giving you direct feedback that is quite different. So you can use the DRM to contrast your evaluations with direct evidence on whether and how you might have adapted to the pleasure or purpose of an activity you have been engaged in for a while.

Or you might have a mistaken desire, for achievement say, which may not be consistent with the maximization of your happiness. Maybe you spend too long at work, or looking for another job on the Internet. A DRM will also enable you to see more clearly how much time you fritter away unnecessarily. Some companies offer software that makes tracking your productivity easier by logging how much time you spend on various websites, documents, and programs, producing a chart that draws your attention to important facts like your Facebook-spreadsheet ratio.

Information of this kind can also be helpful in overcoming mistaken projections. To illustrate, imagine the following choice that many Londoners face: you can take the tube to work or hop on a bus. The tube ride takes thirty minutes and it involves changing trains and riding with your head wedged against the doors because it is so busy. The single bus ride takes forty minutes, but it's a calmer and quieter trip. The time taken is likely to matter most in a joint evaluation of these options and so you will probably take the tube. But you could use the DRM to tell whether the ten-minute time difference between taking the tube and the bus to work will really matter to you in a happiness sense. If the bus ride is more pleasant and you tend to spend the first hour or so at work a little less stressed, then you might take the bus to lift your mood, at least from time to time. Indeed, you might find that it's the variety itself from switching back and forth between the tube and the bus that makes you feel happier.

A DRM can also prevent your feelings now from guiding your decisions about the future. Just as a grocery list can prevent you from buying too much on an empty stomach, a DRM can keep you from making plans for a Sunday morning that would be better spent in bed (avoided when you notice a lot of low happiness ratings on weekend days with early plans).

DRM-type data on your own experiences of pleasure and purpose can also help you avoid mistaken beliefs about how you use your time and what brings you happiness. You obviously have to devote time to the necessities — earning money, household duties, personal care, sleep, and so on — but you have a great deal of choice over how you use your *discretionary time:* what you have left over each week once the necessities of life have been dealt with.[17]

How much time do you spend doing things that are decided upon *for* you? And how much time do you spend doing things that are decided upon *by* you?

You probably have more control of your time than you think you do. Each of us in our way thinks that we are really busy and just don't have the time for various activities. I consider myself to be pretty busy but I somehow find time to go to the gym four times a week. It's a question of priorities. When we say we don't have time to exercise, we really mean that we don't prioritize using our time in that way. The barriers to using our discretionary time differently emanate much more from failing to accept that we are not *making* the time and less from genuinely not *having* the time, except among people who work long hours just to make ends meet of course. I sent the final draft of this book to a dozen very busy colleagues and, with one exception (you know who you are), they all found the time to provide detailed comments.

You also need to have sensible expectations about your time use, and the DRM can help here, too. If your commute is two hours long perhaps it isn't sensible to expect that you will have time in the evening to go to the gym, meet up with a friend, cook dinner, watch your favorite TV show, and also get enough sleep to show up rested for work the next day. The DRM will bring the consequences for your happiness from these activities to your attention. It might also force you to consider whether that two-hour commute, every day, is really worth it or, in the very least, whether you might be able to work from home once in a while.

You might well find that how you use your discretionary time could matter more than how much of it you have.[18] If you recorded a DRM for a few days while on holiday, you would be able to see which aspects of the holiday really made you happy and which did not, rather than being unduly influenced by what you think should make you happy about the trip. This will allow you to plan future holidays more effectively. You can also find out how you are trading off pleasure and purpose within and between activities by looking at the relative balance throughout your days.

Reconstructing the context of events will help you better remember them and give you more accurate feedback about their impact on your happiness as you decide how to spend your time. When the police conduct interviews with key witnesses, they attempt to reinstate the context of the crime by asking about mundane details such as the weather or what they ate for lunch on the day, which improves memory. To reinstate context in your mind, you could think about what the surrounding environment looked like there, such as rooms, the weather, any nearby people or objects. You might also consider changing perspectives by trying to place yourself in the shoes of someone else who was there.[19]

At other times, though, you might wish to take advantage of your natural inclination to remember the peak and end of an experience and to forget about how long it lasted. If you're scheduling meetings at work, plan the meeting with your favorite coworker at the end of the day. And if you want to remember sex in the most positive way, focus on making the last moments memorable without worrying too much about duration (within reason, of course). Just like everything else that you do in life, whether a longer sex session is a good use of time or not then depends not only on the happiness within the experience itself but also on the experiences of happiness after the event, which is the memory of it.

The critical issue is to monitor the feedback for your happiness of whatever it is you start doing. When the feedback is clear, you can then stop monitoring. Constantly monitoring the entire production process would be effortful and eventually hinder happiness. Once you know what brings you the best mix of pleasure and purpose, your production process of happiness will just need some adjustment from time to time. Let's say you've switched from the tube to the bus. Now you can check in once every so often to see if this is still making you happy. Perhaps the weather has changed, so you're no longer happy when waiting for the bus when it's raining. Feedback is the fuel for this fine-tuning.

PAY ATTENTION TO THE FEEDBACK OF OTHERS

Look at Others

We can get our own feedback, but we can also look to the experiences of others. Dan Gilbert, author of *Stumbling on Happiness,* says that one of the lessons happiness research teaches us is that the experiences of other people like you are a useful guide to the impact of an event on you, and often a much more useful guide than your own predictions about the impact of that event.[20] I agree with him.

Imagine you are about to go on a date. What would you rather know about your date ahead of time to help you project how you might feel — physical features, age, height, hometown, and favorite sport, or how a stranger felt when they met your date on a previous occasion? I'm guessing you would want the personal information, and most other people do, too. But women who were given personal information made worse forecasts about how they would feel when they met a man than when they were given reports of how another woman felt when she met him — even though they did not personally know the other woman who was providing the report.[21]

The key challenge is to know when your experiences will mirror those of other people and when yours will be different because you have a different set of preferences. You may have agreed with how many of the participants in the German DRM and the American Time Use Survey rated their happiness during different activities, but there were likely some differences, too. I know that you think you are special — and you are, of course — but, at least in how you react to events, just not as special as you think. Many of the experiences you have will be quite similar to the experiences of others, and probably more similar, more often, than you would imagine.

Ask Others

You could also solicit the advice of other people about your beliefs about your own happiness, particularly since the evidence suggests that your reports of your own happiness tend to correlate quite well with other people's reports of your happiness. In Estonia, a selection of visitors to GPs and hospitals nominated someone who knew them well (mostly spouses but also friends and other family members) to predict their overall happiness on a 0 to 10 scale. The correlation between the self-reported scores and the predictions made by others was a very high 0.75.[22] Similar results have been found in other studies using different measures of happiness.[23] If you believe you are happy but behave like you are not, then those close to you are well placed to point this out.

When your own mistaken desires for outcomes other than happiness conflict with your experiences of pleasure and purpose, other people can help you to refocus on what really matters. They might quite like the idea of you being the next Lady Gaga but also see, more clearly than you can, just how miserable the process of getting there is making you on a day-to-day basis.

Other people may also be well placed to help you overcome mistaken projections. Partly, this is because they will generally be less committed to your present self than you are; they will instead pay more attention to the consequences for you in the longer term. You will focus mostly on what *becoming* married, rich, or disabled will be like when you will be a newlywed, newly rich, or newly disabled for only a short time. Those close to you will be more inclined to consider what *being* married, rich, or disabled will be like, which lasts much longer and therefore more greatly affects your sentiments of pleasure and purpose.

When making a decision, you can use your friends to help you avoid focusing effects and the pitfalls of distinction bias, by asking them to imagine the consequences of your decision and not to pay attention to the decision itself. Say you have just been offered an attractive new job with the only anticipated downside being a longer commute. What will you think about as you decide whether or not to take the new job? Most likely you'll mistakenly consider the first couple of days or so when you are as excited as you ever will be about going into work, and when you are still making a direct comparison between your new job and the old one. So you could get those close to you to consider the next couple of months, when the pain of changing trains or being stuck in a traffic jam kicks in.

We have shown in our own research that longer commutes are associated with lower psychological health, especially among married women.[24] This is almost certainly because married women still pick up most of the household duties when they get home, while the commute does not eat into men's time in quite the same way. This is salient information but it's more likely to occur to your family or friends, who are not caught up in thinking about all the positive aspects of the opportunity. You may still take the job, but at least you are doing so armed with a better sense of the longer-term costs and benefits of *being* in that job.

It is vital that you ask the right questions in order to more accurately get at the likely effects of your decision on your happiness. So don't ask your friends, "What do you think about me taking the new job?" where the focus of attention will be on differences between the jobs that may not show up in the experiences of your decision. Instead ask, "How do you think my day-to-day life will be in a couple of months if I take the new job?"

Overall, it is entirely possible that other people might not be quite as susceptible to projection bias on your behalf as you are for yourself. In particular, your family and friends will be much more detached from your own current feelings about a decision. You might have fallen in love with a man, a car, or a house, and you would let this cloud your decision about whether to jump in, but your friends can adopt — or at least be explicitly asked to adopt — a "cooler" perspective on the likely consequences of your decision.

When others remember your happiness, they might not be as influenced by peak-end effects as you are. I am sure that Les remembers how good my nights out with her were in our prechildren partying days better than I do, and I am equally convinced that I remember how good her nights out with me were better than she does. As much as I hate to admit it, she probably has a better memory for them than I do. Studies have shown that under timed conditions, women remember both more positive and more negative autobiographical life events than do men.[25] In any case, the point is that other people might have a more accurate memory of what made you happy in the past than you do.

Recall also from our discussion of mistaken beliefs that you are likely to bring your attitudes in line with your behavior rather than vice versa. If you're thinking about getting married, you probably have a favorable attitude toward the person you are considering tying the knot with. You bring your attitude toward making a long-term commitment to that person in line with your behavior of already being in a committed relationship with that person. Ask your friend how being married might turn out and they could remind you how your prospective partner spends all their time at the office and that you will hardly see them (which might be a good thing, of course). To reiterate, the way you frame the question really matters. Don't ask "Should I get married?" but rather "What will being married be like?"

Far from being a weakness, it is a sign of strength to ask others for opinions about your behavior and your happiness. Just think how clearly you can see the mistakes others are making: they can see your mistakes just as clearly. Moreover, the conversations you have with other people about your and their happiness can be pleasurable and purposeful in themselves.

People in a boat similar to yours, or who know people that are, are ideally suited to helping you answer these questions. You probably wouldn't ask your dentist for advice about buying a car. So you won't want to ask someone who lives in Miami if you'd be happy in Alaska. Just as you need to ask someone who has recently purchased a car for advice before doing so yourself, you need to ask someone who has lived in Alaska, or knows someone who has, if you'd like it there. The more similar this person is to you in terms of values, beliefs, expectations, and experiences, the better the person will be able to advise you about your happiness. People like you affect what you do and they might also be a good guide to how you will feel.

Overall, other people are an excellent guide to how far you are away from allocating your attention in ways that bring you the most pleasure and purpose. They can help you pay closer attention to your experiences in life. In *Thinking, Fast and Slow,* Daniel Kahneman has claimed that the experiencing self does not have a voice (being drowned out by the evaluating self). When we had lunch recently, Danny and I agreed that other people are more likely to listen to our experiences.

By paying attention to your experiences of pleasure and purpose, other people are likely to arrive more quickly at the conclusion that perhaps you should stop doing something that is making you miserable, while you cling to the often mistaken belief that one day it will get better. Recall my friend who works at MediaLand and who evaluates her job positively — in spite of the fact that it makes her miserable on a daily basis. I can see an experiencing self that is suffering perhaps more clearly than she can.

Since reading a draft of this book, my friend has started looking for a new job.

Let Others Decide

Another more radical option is sometimes to let people you trust actually make decisions for you. Allow your desires, projections, and beliefs to be reflected in their choices. This will free up your attentional energy for use elsewhere. Psychologists have alerted us to the possibility that the psychological cost of a choice depends on how many options are available. You will often feel worse when you have more choices — this is known as the *paradox of choice.*[26] How long do you spend at the store selecting from twenty-five different shampoos? Letting someone else choose for you, or at least letting them help you choose, may be particularly effective if there is uncertainty about the outcome of a choice, because you'll have very little idea about what would have happened if you'd selected the other option; or if the stakes aren't particularly high, because the outcome won't have as big an impact on you as agonizing over the decision will.

As a small example of limiting choice to benefit myself in the end, I often let someone else choose my meal for me when I go out for dinner. Anyone who knows me knows that it's all about protein, so as long as the meal is loaded with it, I'm happy. Not only do I not have to agonize over the menu, but it's quite exciting not knowing what someone will order for me. And I also get to engage in general chitchat rather than being distracted by the menu. Now, this works for me, but it would be tricky for us all to do this and some people might not like the added pressure of choosing someone else's dinner as well as their own. But I reckon a happiness-improving strategy could emerge as we each choose different degrees of control and delegation over different decisions. You might want to consider a decision you could delegate, and who you would delegate it to.

DON'T TRY TOO HARD

It is important not to try too hard to be happy. I think this could go some way toward explaining why I (and I am speaking entirely for myself here) hate taking part in "organized happiness." I hate pub trivia and karaoke with a passion. I am not a big fan of weddings or birthday parties, either. All these events are supposed to be enjoyable but the pressure to have fun can sometimes ruin the experience. So don't think about it too hard.

Moreover, if you're thinking too hard about being happier and aren't feeling any happier, you're likely to become *less* happy as you get frustrated with yourself (as I surely would if I tried to enjoy members of the public murdering some rock and pop classics). Some of the most influential books on happiness focus a lot about how to think yourself happy, take a positive approach, and so on — and you might well be someone who wants to adopt a positive approach. But imagine that you dedicate effort to thinking positively, and it doesn't work immediately. Now there's an even greater incongruity between the person you are and the person you want to be and this makes you even more miserable.

You can also try too hard not to be miserable. It turns out that paying lots of attention to a recent traumatic event only serves to lock in the extreme and negative emotions that might have subsided had they not had such attention focused on them.[27] Intensive trauma therapy, which does exactly this, is a damaging solution searching for a problem that may not actually exist. In spite of good evidence that too much attention to a trauma within the first month or so after the event can make things worse, this therapy is still offered to — in fact, largely foisted upon — trauma victims, such as the first responders affected by the terrorist attacks in the United States on September 11, 2001. Moreover, as many researchers have noted, we need to accept some sadness in our lives from time to time. It is a natural human response and we should not always treat it as pathology.[28]

Indeed, given that we are prone to making various mistakes about our happiness, and given the important role of unconscious attention, you might consider not thinking too much at all.

In an interesting application of this idea, participants were shown photographs of men who had put pictures of themselves in personal ads. Half of the photographs were of men seeking women, and the other half were of men seeking men. It turned out that people were just as successful at discerning a man's sexual orientation from their photograph if they looked at it for fifty milliseconds as compared to ten seconds: participants in each of these time conditions were right about the guy's dating preferences about 60 percent of the time (statistically, this is much better than 50 percent, which chance would predict). Your gaydar in unconscious system 1 is just as good as it is in conscious system 2.[29]

In fact, it is possible that you will make even better decisions if you only briefly consider a choice, then stop consciously thinking about it for a while, and briefly return to thinking about it again later on. Imagine being shown a set of five posters from which you are allowed to select one to take home. Three of the posters are abstract art and the other two depict flowers and birds; so something for everyone. Now imagine you could either (1) choose a poster to take home immediately after looking at them simultaneously, (2) choose a poster after looking at them simultaneously and then solving anagrams for seven and a half minutes, or (3) choose a poster after thinking carefully about each one and viewing them one at a time. I suspect that you probably would like to be in the group that has the luxury of pondering their choice. But when students at the University of Amsterdam were called several weeks after making a choice in one of the three conditions, those who had taken a break and solved anagrams were the most satisfied with their choice than those in the other two groups.[30]

Choosing between cars is a little more complex than choosing between posters. Yet it would appear that giving our unconscious mind a chance to process information about fuel consumption, tire quality, and upholstery can improve our choices here, too. Participants were provided with descriptions of cars with a number of desirable and undesirable characteristics and then randomly divided into three groups along the lines of the poster study. Again, those who took a break had the best chance of picking the cars with the most positive attributes. When the researchers put these participants under MRI scanners to see their brains while they were making choices, they found that different parts of the brain were activated during conscious and unconscious thought, suggesting that the unconscious mind is processing decision information even when the conscious mind is otherwise occupied.[31]

All the participants in these studies were told how long they could consciously think about their choice. Yet when provided with information about a set of lottery outcomes to choose between, participants chose the one with the best odds when they got to think about it as long as they wanted to before making a choice, compared to being told they could think about their choice for exactly four minutes.[32] Context matters, as always, and the evidence base in this area is still growing and sparking much debate.

Nonetheless, it is interesting to consider whether you could make a better choice of a job or a house or a car if you allowed some time for unconscious contemplation rather than attending to the choice fully until a decision is made.[33] Or next time you are in the store deciding between a sassy peach and a saucy pink for your walls, you could think about it briefly, stop thinking about it, and then return to the decision. Or when you are next online looking at all those lovely clothes, go and read the paper or watch TV for a bit, and then come back and choose the best sweater.

Happier by Deciding

Mistaken desires, projections, and beliefs are pretty pervasive problems, and so you should be realistic and expect to succumb to them now and again. But there are ways of dealing with them. Handily, you get to experience the consequences of your decisions: what you attend to and do affects how you feel (and vice versa). So if you can more accurately monitor the feedback for your happiness from your decisions, you might be able to make more decisions that make you happier. Making your own feedback salient (noticeable and relevant) is the key challenge.

As we've seen, other people can also be a great source of information about your happiness. But a final word of caution here. You do need to weed out those who focus less on your happiness. You may very well receive feedback from others that the attainment of goals matters above all else: for example, from your boss to hit those weekly sales targets or from your partner to take that higher-paying job. Indeed, when you accept a new job that pays more than your old one, typically no one bats an eyelid. It is obvious to them why you changed jobs. But if your new job pays less than your last, your family and friends might well ask what you are playing at. Taking a lower-paying job somehow requires justification, making it less likely that you'll accept it even if you know it would make you happier. Judgments based on tangible factors that are easy to measure, like salary, are of course much easier to justify than decisions based on intangibles, such as getting on with colleagues or doing more fulfilling work.[34] So you need to learn to discard advice that doesn't include a consideration of how striving for these or other goals affects your happiness.

And remember not to overmonitor. Your attentional energy needs to take a break from time to time. Indeed, once you have achieved equilibrium, there is no incentive to reconfigure your production process until there is good reason to (e.g., if the stimuli or their effects change). Sometimes not consciously thinking about a decision at all could even result in better decision making if you allow your unconscious attention to process the choice while your conscious attention is allocated elsewhere.

6
DESIGNING HAPPINESS

The end of the previous chapter gave us a further look at the impact that unconscious attention has on what we do. Now we'll focus squarely on how you can organize your life in ways that give your unconscious attention the best shot of being allocated in ways that make you happier.

In all of this, context is king. The idea that behavior can be changed by "contextology" as much as by our own internal psychology lies at the heart of *Nudge* by Richard Thaler and Cass Sunstein.[1] *Nudge* recommends that policy makers seek to change behavior by going with the grain of human behavior; to change behavior with a contextual nudge rather than by a cognitive shove.

The really basic insight here is that if you want people to act in a particular way, make it easier for them. In one of many classic examples of this, students were more likely to get vaccinated for tetanus when they had a map of where to get vaccinated than if they were just simply given a pamphlet about the importance of the vaccination.[2] And, equally, if you don't want people to do something, make it harder for them. This is common sense, but it does not mean policy will be designed on the basis of it.

Around the time that I began working closely with the UK government to bring about population behavior change in areas such as health, energy, and tax payments, I worked with colleagues on a paper called "Mindspace," developed in the spirit of changing behavior by changing contexts. *Mindspace* is a nine-letter mnemonic for the most robust influences on behaviors that are driven largely, but not exclusively, by automatic and unconscious processes.[3] Based on earlier attempts to develop a checklist by Rob Metcalfe, Ivo Vlaev, and me, *Mindspace* is deliberately in the form of a checklist so that policy makers can work through the elements, ensuring that they properly account for situational factors that they might otherwise be blind to. We have already seen the power of checklists in chapter 3. Here are the nine elements.

Messenger	We are heavily influenced by who communicates information.
Incentives	Our responses to incentives are shaped by mental shortcuts.
Norms	We are strongly influenced by what others do.
Defaults	We "go with the flow" of preset options.
Salience	Our attention is drawn to what is novel and seems relevant to us.
Priming	Our acts are often influenced by unconscious cues.
Affect	Our emotional associations can powerfully shape our actions.
Commitments	We seek to be consistent with our public promises.
Ego	We act in ways that make us feel better about ourselves.

You can apply a checklist approach in your own life. From *Mindspace,* messenger and incentives are largely suited to policy; we have already touched on affect and ego in chapter 4 under mistaken projections and mistaken beliefs, respectively; and chapter 5 showed us that salience is a critical factor in getting useful feedback about our happiness. This leaves four overarching and related elements for you to consider: how to *prime* yourself to act differently, the *defaults* you set up, the *commitments* you make, and the *norms* of those you surround yourself with, as well as using these elements to alter your habits.

Companies are constantly nudging and priming you into buying their goods and services. You only have to catch a whiff of some freshly baked bread in your local supermarket to be enticed toward the pastry section, whether you were planning on buying baked goods or not. Defaults are used in pensions, where moving to an opt-out pension plan increases contributions, and for organ donations, where moving to an opt-out donor registry increases the number of donor organs.[4] Commitments have been used in health policy by offering quitting contracts to smokers and in taxation to reduce fraud, where placing signatures at the beginning rather than the end of tax forms reduces cheating.[5] And in terms of social norms, building upon some innovative work undertaken by Opower in the United States, Rob Metcalfe and I have been working with UK energy suppliers to give feedback to consumers about their own energy consumption relative to the consumption of their neighbors. The latest results show that social norms reduce consumption by around 6 percent.[6]

By using priming, defaults, commitments, and norms in your own life, you can become a whole lot happier without actually having to think very hard at all about becoming happier. You will be happier by design. You can then save your attentional energy for those occasions where you really do want to pay attention to a decision or to what you are doing.

PRIMING

Would you be happier if your house were clean or your children tidied up after themselves? Something as simple as using an air freshener makes it far more likely that you and they will clean up. People who ate a biscuit after sitting in a cubicle with citrus air freshener pumped in made three times as many hand movements to clean crumbs off the table compared to those who were not exposed to this cleanest-smelling of all scents.[7] And medical students who went to examine a patient complaining of heart palpitations were much more likely to comply with hand hygiene regulations when the smell of citrus was in the air.[8]

You might also think about how you use light to design your happiness landscape.

Light is responsible for setting our circadian rhythm, the twenty-four-hour sleep-wake cycle marked by changes in body temperature and levels of hormones like cortisol (related to stress) and melatonin (related to sleepiness).[9] Blue light, the sort emitted by electronics and energy-efficient lightbulbs, has a particularly powerful effect on our circadian rhythms and enhances alertness by suppressing the release of melatonin.[10] I know it might sound obvious, but by increasing your exposure to light in the morning and throughout the day, especially blue light, you'll optimize your alertness. By reducing your exposure at night, you prepare yourself for sleep. So charge your electronics outside of the bedroom and set up plenty of lights where you work. Laura Kudrna has a portable sunlamp that she carries with her when she needs to spend time analyzing data in dark university computer labs during the day.

One further environmental trigger you might consider is the natural environment. Nature (even through a window) grabs and retains your attention in positive ways because it's constantly changing, even in subtle ways, which prevents adaptation. It's been shown that prison inmates who had a view from their cell made fewer visits to the prison's health care facilities than those who did not have a view, and surgical patients randomly selected to have a view of nature from their hospital room recovered more quickly than those who had a view of a brick wall.[11] The resulting advice here seems simple: get out more. If you can't get out (and in fact even if you can), buy some plants or install a fish tank, both of which help to reduce stress.[12]

When it comes to priming yourself to lose weight, there is much out there that we can learn from. We're primed to fill our plates, irrespective of the plate's actual size.[13] The bigger the plate, the more you will have ate. So if you do want to lose weight, you could buy smaller plates. This conscious decision to choose smaller plates then drives the unconscious behavior of filling the plate. In an experiment where people were given a variety of larger containers to eat out of, they ate about a third more than those who ate out of smaller containers.[14] As further evidence that size matters, imagine being invited to a Super Bowl party and being offered some snacks before the game. If you were offered a four-liter bowl you would eat more than if you were offered a two-liter bowl — about 140 calories more on average.[15]

In all of this, be alert to possible spillover effects (discussed in chapter 3). With the hopes of encouraging patrons to eat more healthily, a group of six hundred US restaurant patrons were given a menu with healthy sandwiches on the front and unhealthy ones on the back (by the way, this is the same group from earlier that underestimated their calorie consumption). The patrons were 35 percent more likely to choose a healthy sandwich than those without the new menu. So far, so good. But because many of them picked potato chips instead of fruit as a side dish to accompany their healthy sandwiches, they completely offset the calorie-saving effects of the healthier choice. Overall, the new menu had no effect at all on total calorie consumption. Choosing healthy meals when there is no opportunity for discretionary side orders would be one way to overcome this permitting spillover effect.

Recall also that thinking you've just had a great workout can give you the moral license to eat more than if you hadn't exercised in the first place. Other healthy behaviors can have some of the same spillover effects as exercising. A lovely study shows how one group of students, who thought they had just taken a multivitamin pill, exhibited multiple forms of personal licensing in comparison to another group who were told that the pill was, in fact, a placebo. In particular, those who thought they had taken the vitamin pill expressed a greater preference for a buffet over an organic meal.[16] There is nothing wrong with a little moral licensing here and there, but, if it really will get in the way of being happier, design your environment to limit its extent. Join a gym without a fast-food restaurant on your route home from it.

You might now be wondering if designing your environment to change your unconscious behavior will work when you are consciously aware of how you are designing it. If you deliberately use a smaller bowl in order to eat less, won't you just serve yourself a second helping and ultimately eat the same amount anyway, because you know why you bought the smaller bowl? Thankfully, research suggests otherwise, supporting the efficacy of priming effects. There is even evidence for a "meta-placebo" or "open-label placebo" effect in medicine, where placebos (usually pills with no active ingredient) work *even when* people know they are taking a placebo.

In one study, eighty participants with irritable bowel syndrome (IBS) were randomly divided into two groups. The first group received a container presented as "placebo pills made of an inert substance, like sugar pills, that have been shown in clinical studies to produce significant improvement in IBS symptoms through mind-body self-healing processes." The second received no pill or medical treatment at all and simply interacted with the medical practitioners, who behaved in the same way as did the providers who interacted with the group receiving the placebo pills. Three weeks later, the researchers found that the first group had fewer symptoms of IBS than the second group.[17]

So, all in all, the current evidence suggests that being happier by design does not require design by deception.

DEFAULTS

If your home page is Facebook, it's inevitable that you will spend more time networking and less time working. Most of us "go with the flow." In general, humans are pretty lazy and are usually content to do whatever is the preset option. *Defaults* are passive commitments and you rarely notice them. So to become happier you need to make small adjustments to your life so that going with the flow is consistent with being happier. It is very efficient to use a little of

248

your attentional resources now to set defaults for scenarios that might otherwise require a lot of your attentional resources in the future.

So if you're used to checking your Facebook first thing in the morning, try changing your default for a few days to another home page, such as the news, and see what effect it has on how you feel. Shifting a few minutes of your time from one activity to another could spill over to your happiness in an extended way throughout the day.

If you decide you want to spend less or start saving more, there are online budgeting applications that will send alerts through your phone when you go over budget or have a low bank balance. You can also select a default banking password that reminds you of what you have decided will make you happier about your finances and how you manage them. People primed with negative feelings, like "sorrow," "grief," and "heartbreak," are willing to pay less for a box of chocolates than those who aren't primed with anything, so shopaholics could consider these as logins to their most tempting sites.[18] Or perhaps you'd like to e-mail less. Try a password that says something like "dontcheckmeagain."

Setting a default to be with people whose

company you enjoy is likely to increase the pleasure and purpose you experience, as well as improve some of the decisions you make. You may have withdrawn attention from your house but having an old friend around provides a fresh perspective on your dining room. If a friend lives far away, you could set up a default for an agreed time to talk each week or so. You then have to opt out of talking at that time if you cannot make it. This is the strategy that Mig and I have adopted — we talk on Skype at 9:00 a.m. UK time (10:00 a.m. in Ibiza) on Thursdays. The engagement has served to cement our friendship still further, and it makes us both happy (especially him, of course). Another way to default to being with others is to set up meetings on a particular work project or exercise program. Not only are you more likely to spend time on the activity if you have to actively "opt out" of your commitment, you will also work harder once you are there if you have someone encouraging you. The next section builds on this idea.

Making Them

Tell a friend you will stop smoking, and you are more likely to do so. We like to be consistent with our public promises. We are more likely to enroll in a curbside recycling program if we have to make a written commitment to do so than if we learn about the program in another way, such as on a flyer or by telephone.[19] And those who tweet about their attempts to lose weight are more likely to do so than those who just listen to a podcast about weight loss. At the end of six months of tweeting, every ten posts to Twitter were associated with 0.5 percent loss in weight, which is about one pound for an average-weight male in the United States.[20]

What would you like to make a commitment to do or to stop? A key challenge here is to commit to things that are actually going to make you happier if you do them — but that also won't make you overly miserable if you fail to do as you promised. If you set goals where you have some degree of control over the outcome, such as your physical health and feeling connected to others, you will experience more positive emotions than if you set a goal where you have less control over the outcome, such as being rich and famous.[21] This does not mean that goals that aren't entirely in your control are mistaken desires: if you can accept failure, you are better able to bounce back if you fall short of your ambitions.

Whatever form the commitment takes, start with small changes and don't put yourself under too much pressure. Bite-size commitments are more effective than mouthfuls. Recall also that you want future behaviors to be consistent with past ones so each next step can build on the last. You are more likely to complete a degree if you commit to going to class tomorrow, as opposed to saying "I am going to complete my college education." Commit to reading *Macbeth* to see if you like Shakespeare; don't commit to reading Shakespeare's entire collected works before deciding whether you have a taste for his style. You are more likely to run a marathon if you first commit to going out for a run a couple of times a week and building up from there, as opposed to saying "I'm going to run a marathon." I have put on a considerable amount of muscle by committing to put on a pound a week for six weeks at various times over the past decade.

Making bite-size goals becomes easier

with practice. It can be helpful to state what the overall goal is, break it down into more manageable chunks, and then ask yourself what you can do right now to work toward it. The basic insight, as noted earlier but which cannot be said often enough, is that you are more likely to do something if it is easy to do. So make each step on the path to the overall goal a simple one. Try it out for yourself in the box on next page, where I have used making new friends as an example.

Wherever you are "on a journey" — or working through a goal that has some discernible start and finish points — the evidence suggests that you can make reaching the destination more likely by the "law of small numbers": in plain English, "20 percent gone" is a good motivator, as is "20 percent to go" when you get there (rather than their inverses, "80 percent to go" and "80 percent gone"). Korean students who had to complete words based on the first few consonants in each word (this is evidently much harder to do in Korean than English) returned to the task more quickly after taking a break when their progress was presented this way.[22] The law of small numbers makes your commitment to progress more salient. You now have about

Overall goal	"Bite-size" goal	"Right now" goal
Make new friends	Attend social events at which I can meet new people	Call a connected friend

30 percent of this book to go — sounds good, eh?

Economists are fond of saying that people respond to incentives, and you will recall that it is one of the nine elements of mindspace. How many times have you bought something just because it was half price? Most, but certainly not all, of the time you are more likely to do something if paid, and less likely if fined or taxed. We know from psychology that losses loom larger than gains in our minds — losing anything, but especially money, really grinds on us. Taking this into account, we can think about how to frame our commitments. In one aptly named study, "Put Your Money Where Your Butt Is," researchers offered smokers who wanted to quit a savings account where they had to deposit money for a six-month period. Once the period was up, participants took a urine test to see whether they had managed to stay off the cigarettes. If they came up clear they got their money back; if not, it went to charity. Participants offered the savings account were more likely to quit smoking than those who weren't approached at all. Even more impressive is the fact that when they went back to test the smokers twelve months later, the majority of those who quit were still not smoking.[23]

We can also be quite selfish and, whatever our proclivity to behave that way, we're likely to feel guilty about it from time to time. One way to overcome this guilt is to precommit to spending some money on yourself. This is consistent with the happiness-enhancing principle "pay now, spend later," rather than the other way around, as with credit cards.[24] Precommitting to indulgence is seen as one of the reasons why many of us prefer all-inclusive holidays.[25] So you could allocate some fraction of your income to the "me money" account and spend it each month on yourself, guiltlessly. Life is all about balance, and occasionally it's good for us to think about only ourselves.

Breaking Them

You should also consider when to *give up* on a commitment — when you might be better off breaking a commitment or cutting your losses. Consider a relatively trivial example. You are in the cinema watching a boring film that you can't imagine will improve. Would you get up and walk out before the end? You ought to if you expect to be made happier by the alternative use of your time. The time and money you have already spent in the cinema is a *sunk cost* — it's gone and you can't get it back. So it should not be relevant to what you decide to do next. But it feels like it is relevant, doesn't it? You made the effort to go to the cinema, you bought the ticket, and you've sat through some of the film already. All of this feels more like an *investment* than a sunk cost. And so you want to see your investment pay off — or at least stick around in the hope that it might. This explains why people stay in failing relationships and dull jobs for longer than they ought to.

Your reluctance to see the past as sunk can make you less happy in the long run. You are much more likely to say "I wish I had got out earlier" than "I wish I had stuck around longer." On a night out, I have learned to go home as soon as the thought of going home enters my head but I admit that it took me many more years than it should have done to realize this. Hopefully being more aware of it now might help you to wise up sooner than I did.

Commitments matter, then, but so, too, does the ability to recognize when to give up on them. Time is a scarce resource and you should not waste it on remaining miserable. This is yet another difficult challenge as there is no cast-iron way of ever knowing whether you were right to hold or fold. But

I suggest that once you start seriously considering folding, you should probably move quite quickly from considering to doing. I say this as someone who has walked out of the cinema and not regretted doing so. But it is also based on our ability to adapt; to make sense of things that happen; and to regret those that have not.

If you are spending more and more time seriously thinking about quitting something, don't spend too much longer committing to it. Much as you might not like to accept it, sometimes it is better to hold your hands up and admit that you made a mistake. Most of the time in relationships, it seems, we translate negative feelings about a partner into active attempts to repair our beliefs about him or her that may otherwise be challenged by those feelings.[26] Put simply, we work to maintain and stabilize our mistaken beliefs about our partner. This is often conducive to happiness but sometimes it is not. Sometimes it is better to move on. And if you decide to leave a relationship, expect to feel low for a while. This is a natural and entirely healthy process. Keep this in mind, and you may be slightly less inclined to jump into an even worse "rebound" relationship. But you should certainly get out and socialize. Those who do socialize adapt better to the change and are less likely to go back to the previous partner simply because they feel lonely.

If you do decide to stay put, try to see your decision as a new commitment rather than as simply staying put at the same thing. See your attempt to accept your partner for who he or she is as a positive commitment. Turning down new job offers in the past has made me feel more committed to my existing job, for a while at least.

Difficult decisions of these kinds are not made easier by the sometimes complex relationship between pleasure and purpose. The pursuit of pleasure might push you into a new relationship but the continuation of purpose might pull you back to the old one. The balance between pleasure and purpose ebbs and flows in life as it does in relationships. So a key challenge will be to try, so far as it is possible, to separate out the experience of the current context from the general experience. Framing your commitments in terms of pleasure and purpose does, however, allow you to commit to more purpose if you are a pleasure machine (publicly promise to mow your elderly neighbor's lawn) and to more pleasure if you are a purpose engine (publicly commit to a night out with friends).

SOCIAL NORMS

Our modern age of information, technology, and social media means that we learn from the experiences of many other people. You might take into account the ratings of others when booking a holiday, hotel, or restaurant. We trust the judgments of others, to some extent at least, because they have information about an experience that we do not. If lots of people have had a specific experience, you can look at the average response, as well as the range of responses if you consider yourself to be more of an outlier. It has been shown that the *wisdom of crowds* can actually provide a great deal of insight.[27] Social norms affect your behavior through your unconscious attention and your automatic inclination to put people into groups.[28]

Surround Yourself

People around you influence you much more than you think. We are all social animals. You want to be like people like you and you will do what others like you are doing. You unconsciously want to fit in (even if, consciously, you say that you want to stand out). We are wired, automatically and unconsciously, to mimic and absorb the emotions of others around us. If you were to see pictures of happy and angry faces flash across a screen, you would react by moving the muscles on your face that create smiles and frowns, even if the flash of the faces was so quick that you would not be consciously aware of having seen them.[29] And if you kept a diary about your moods and your perceptions of the moods of those around you, there would be a close correspondence between your moods and their moods.[30]

It is not surprising, then, that having a friend who lives within a mile of you become happier increases the probability that you feel happy, too, by 25 percent.[31] Now, this could also be due to shared experiences: friends may all experience the same loss of a friend, which makes them all feel sad, and it is not always possible to properly account for this. But studies show that cricket players are affected by their teammates' emotions completely independently of how well their team is doing, suggesting that at least some of this contagion effect may not be attributable to shared experiences.[32]

You are especially likely to be affected by how someone else feels if you like them.[33] Nowhere is the contagion effect of happiness stronger than in families. When a sample of fifty-five teenagers, their mothers, and their fathers were asked about their emotions at random times of day over a week, the moods of the family members were highly correlated. The results also suggested that the similarity in moods was partly attributable to the transmission of emotions, particularly from daughters to their parents. Why is this, you might ask? We can't be sure but we can speculate that girls may communicate with their parents more about personal issues than do boys.[34] Regardless, it is clear that happiness is contagious and a social phenomenon.

Since other people matter so much to your behavior and happiness, the proximity of your family and friends is something to take into account when thinking about a new job or a new place to live. A basic starting question for any locational decision should be, "Where do the people who contribute most to my happiness live?" The distance between our friends and ourselves has grown over time as more people leave their hometowns and as we commute farther to work, which leaves us less time to spend with the people we care about.[35] You can draw your own "map of mates," similar to the one shown on next page. The map will help you flush out who matters to you and how far away they are. You can reappraise your portfolio of friends by drawing attention to who you see most often and whether this accords with whose company you enjoy the most. You might well realize that you are surrounded by a whole load of miserable gits. There are now sophisticated apps that allow you to map your friends online, too.

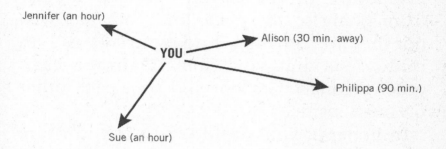

Thanks to social media, the term "friend" has taken on a whole new meaning. Your friends on Facebook can influence what you do and how you feel just like friends in the real world can. So it is worth taking stock of these "friends," too. Doing a bit of "Facebook culling" once in a while to reorient and reboot your social network can have huge payoffs as you prioritize those people you genuinely care about. You probably look at your financial portfolio from time to time, and you should do similarly with your friends.

There can be little doubt that my weight

training has been made considerably more pleasurable and purposeful by training with a seasoned bodybuilder, who has also become a close friend. Dixie is fifty-four and has been bodybuilding for thirty years. During this time, he has been in the top three in many national and international bodybuilding competitions. He is a training inspiration. Insofar as you would be happier from going to the gym (and you may well not be, of course), find yourself a gym buddy, so that you can encourage each other through the door and spur each other on once inside.

In general, you could try to spend more time with pleasure machines if your life is light on pleasure and more time with purpose engines if your life is light on purpose. You might want to think about the most important people in your life. Using the pendulum from chapter 1, do you live nearer to, or spend more time with, pleasure machines, purpose engines, or "balanced folk"? I do a lot of purposeful things these days, even going to the gym, so I make the most of the few times each year I get to see the pleasure machine that is Mig. I appreciate that I have a much greater choice of who I work with than most people, but where there is a choice, many people, perhaps motivated out of a mistaken desire for achievement, will work with those who are most likely to further their career. I try to work with people whose company I enjoy.

Finding the Sweet Spot

We want to be like people we consider to be similar to us — but we can also be adversely affected by their successes. Studies have found that life satisfaction and reports of pleasure fall when the income of those living in your local area rises.[36] The income of those around you doesn't have to increase for it to adversely affect you — you just need to find out that others are earning more than you. Researchers recently made employees at the University of California feel worse off by providing them with a Web link to the salaries of their colleagues (made possible by the state's "right-to-know law"). Those who were earning less than the median wage were less satisfied with their jobs after they viewed that link.[37] Perhaps there is something to be said for the coyness we have, especially in the UK, about talking about money.

This "relative income effect" does not appear everywhere, however: in transition economies, the higher income of similar others actually increases life satisfaction because financial success acts as a signal of opportunity for others to achieve the same.[38] In a very different study but with similar conclusions, African American participants took a bogus IQ test in which they were told that they either did better or worse than the person sitting near to them. They reported lower self-esteem when they were told they did worse than a white person but higher self-esteem when the person who did better than them was black.[39]

There might be a sweet spot with social comparisons, then, where we can benefit from looking down on some and upward at those we aspire to be. When people ask me how they can get happier, have more sex, lose weight, and so on, I reply that they should get happy friends and ditch the miserable ones, get friends who have lots of sex and ditch those who don't, get thin friends and ditch the overweight ones, and so on.

Although I say that half-jokingly, you do need to think carefully about this. Imagine a friend who insists on bragging about her zesty sex life while you are going through a dry spell. Having more sex might make you happier but you will be made less happy if your friends are having more than you (or at least say that they are).[40] The same logic applies if your friend brags about how easy it is to stick to her diet after you've just ordered more takeout. You might "win" by becoming more like your friend or you might "lose" by the negative impact of her doing well relative to you. If you want to be dragged up by others, then make sure you are not dragged down by envying their success. Select social norms that allocate your unconscious attention to sensible expectations for yourself. This will keep your attention away from unattainable upward comparisons that only serve to make you feel worse.

Expectations matter, and so you could focus more time on those people you want to be — and can be — more like. For a start, recall that happiness and misery are contagious and you should do all you can to catch the former and avoid the latter. Choosing the right reference groups will be central to this. Social media allow you more flexibility in your choice of peer group. Think about all those friends you have on Facebook and start prioritizing those whose behavior you want to copy. But be realistic — if they are all marathon runners or bodybuilding champions, you might make yourself a whole lot less happy from unattainable upward comparisons.

With a little effort, and a bit of trial and error, you should be able to tweak your reference groups so as to reallocate your attention in ways that will make you happier. Much of what you assume about the causes of happiness will be governed by the assumptions of those around you. Once you are aware of this, you can reconfigure your social norms.

DESIGNING HABITS

Recall that your brain is constantly looking to conserve attentional energy — seeking ways to *go with the grain.* Consequently, much of what you do will be habitual. As I'm sure you are only too well aware, habits are easy to create but they are a lot harder to break. A "habit loop" gets formed in three steps: (1) the cue — a trigger to send your brain into automatic mode; (2) the routine — the physical or mental act itself; and (3) the reward, which determines whether any loop is worth remembering.[41] Once a habit loop is established, it becomes difficult to inhibit even when it conflicts with changes in motivation and conscious intentions.[42]

The best way to change a habit is to change the routine, leaving the cue and reward alone. As a smoker who wants to quit, you may sometimes experience stress at work, which is the cue, and relieving it, which is the reward. Your routine might be to relieve the stress with a cigarette. It is much harder to remove the stress or the need to relieve it than it is to look for routines other than lighting up. Again, the simple principle of making good things easier to do and bad things harder applies here. Don't take cigarettes into work; and get a commitment from your work colleagues that they will not share theirs with you. Then reach for the kettle when the urge to smoke takes hold. I know that a cup of tea might not feel like much of a substitute for nicotine but it will become so within a few weeks.

Addictions of various kinds are some of the most difficult habits to break. Beyond any physical or psychological dependency, though, environment also matters greatly. There is also often a wider range of external cues for feeding the addiction, which explains why it's more likely that a smoker will become a regular user of nicotine than it is that a cocaine user will become a regular user of cocaine.[43] This does not mean that nicotine is more physically addictive than cocaine; simply that drug use is based on people and their contexts, not just on the physical properties of drugs. Recall that much of what we do is driven by the opportunity to do so. We have already seen that making a commitment to stop smoking can be quite effective but you need to additionally remove as much of the temptation as possible. Hanging out with non-smokers will help.[44]

Other habits are somewhat looser than nicotine addiction. Have you ever noticed how easy it is to let your gym attendance fall away? Unless you have a gym partner who calls you when you miss a session, it is up to you to set the cues that get you to a workout. The hardest part might be getting through the gym door in the first place but that's only half of the story: it's also quite easy to stop going again. This would seem to be one behavior where an apparent habit is quite easily broken. For "loose habits" like this, you need constant "top-up" nudges. Finding a gym on the way to or from work is a good start but you need to get into a routine of going at the same time each day. So long as the context of your gym visits does not change, once you have been going for a couple of months (around the time it takes for a habit to be set), you should be able to keep it up.[45]

A big change in your environment, such as a house move or a new job, is the perfect time to change some of your most ingrained habits because you have an entirely new environment to design.[46] Many of the usual cues for your habits are gone. This helps explain why soldiers who were heroin users returning to the United States after the Vietnam War in 1971 were much less likely to be using heroin a year later than civilian heroin users: the soldiers' usage patterns changed when their context changed.[47]

A study of the newspaper reading, TV watching, and exercising habits of students transferring from one university to the next found they were better able to act on their intentions for changing these habits when the environments in which these habits occurred also changed after the move. If reading the newspaper went from being a solitary to a social activity and they wanted to change the frequency with which they read newspapers, then they did so. Their habits changed when the contextual cues for the habits also changed.[48] So, before a big change, decide what behaviors will make you happiest and look to create contexts that will make it easy for you to do those things.

Imagine deciding where all your old stuff

should go in your new house. Want to watch less TV? Then set up the TV in a spare room and not in the kitchen where it was previously. Want to work from home without the distraction of the Internet? Then set up a workspace out of the range of your wireless router. Or say you're starting a new job. Want to walk a bit more? Then reserve a parking space farther from your desk. Want to eat at McDonald's less often? Then pick up a load of coupons for a local restaurant. Start doing something once in a new environment that you have designed during your transition and you are more likely to continue doing it because you have a fresh array of contextual cues to reinforce the behavior.

HAPPIER BY DESIGNING

The key to finding happiness is to find the ways in which going with the grain of your human nature makes it easier to be happier. The main elements that will help you to do this are summarized in the table on page 274. You can refer to it to address any behavior you might wish to change from now on. Try it out now if you feel like it, or save it for later. I've given the example of wanting to read more, which was one of the top New Year's resolutions of 2013. It seems that doing something that feels purposeful is quite high on people's desires. With a little initial effort like this, you can help yourself become happier by design.

We are all creatures of our environments and so we need to pay careful attention to what other people do in the contexts we are likely to, or would like to, experience. Just as naturalists watch animals in their native environments, you must spend more time watching yourself and other human animals in your natural environments — and spend much less time asking yourself questions about what you intend to do or about the reasons for what you just did. Be more like David Attenborough and less like David Letterman.

Design element	Behavior to change (e.g., read more)	Behavior to change (e.g.,)
Priming	Put books in every room of the house	
Defaults	Set Internet home page to a book review website	
Commitments	Make a date with a friend to attend a book fair	
Social norms	Join a Facebook group that reads and reviews books	

7
DOING HAPPINESS

Once you have gotten the feedback about what makes you happy and what doesn't and designed your landscape accordingly, you then need to pay attention to what makes you happy. You should generally pay attention to what you are doing and who you are doing it with, while doing your utmost not to get distracted from those experiences.

PAY ATTENTION TO
WHAT YOU ARE DOING

In general, you should focus on what you are doing rather than looking for a mental escape route to somewhere or something else. When you are in the *flow* of an experience, you will become completely absorbed, even losing track of time and pretty much everything else except, eventually, tiredness, thirst, and hunger.[1] Think about when you become engrossed in a good film: time passes really quickly. If you are purposely engaged, attention is directed only at what you are doing and not at how long the experience lasts. As someone who is quite easily distracted, I am sure that one of the reasons I enjoy going to the gym so much is because it is one of the very few activities that receives my undivided attention.

Experience Expenditure

If we are happier by attending to our experiences, then it makes sense that we should spend our money on good experiences. Indeed, most of us will say that spending money on an experience, such as a helicopter ride, makes us happier than spending it on a material possession, like a flat-screen TV.[2] In general, we adapt less quickly to happiness brought about by experiences, which means that their impact persists for longer. Not only does the impact of a new possession wane more quickly as an input into the production of happiness, but alternative choices can remain salient for longer as we think about what other material goods we could have bought.

We also don't make other people miserable when we buy our family dinner in the way we do when we buy a new car.[3] In a series of experiments that gave participants a choice between an experience (say, a vacation) and a possession (such as an electronic gadget), there was less social comparison for the experiences compared to the possessions, where keeping up with the Joneses matters more.[4] Spending more on doing stuff and less on buying stuff allows you to reframe your decisions and reference groups so that the Joneses are no longer your comparison group. And you'll find that this allows you to be happier as a result.

Even simply talking about experiential purchases as compared to material ones can make us happier. When a group of undergraduate strangers were placed in pairs and each pair was randomly assigned to talk about either an experiential purchase (spending money with the primary intention of having a life experience) or a material purchase (spending money with the primary intention of having a material possession), those who discussed experiential purchases reported enjoying the conversation more than those who discussed material purchases. So to enjoy your conversations more, talk about what you have done or plan to do rather than what you own or plan to buy. People will also like you more if you do this: pairs of participants who discussed experiential purchases reported having more favorable impressions of their conversation partners than those pairs who discussed material purchases.[5]

Having said that, when material and experiential purchases turn out badly, people report experiencing about the same low levels of happiness from them.[6] A lot depends on the expectations you have. If you expect to own a home and you don't, this will make you miserable, just as those students who expected to earn a lot when they were older but did not earn as much as anticipated turned out to be dissatisfied with their lives.

It's also worth saying that the distinction between experiential and material purchases is not always clear-cut. A decade or so ago, I owned a TVR Chimaera. It was a lovely car. I bought it as much for the sound of the engine as anything else. Every time I started it, I smiled to myself a little bit; and this feeling did not fade much over time. It was also an amazing car to drive (if a little beastly, which resulted in me crashing it, but that's another story). Cars are often seen as material purchases but my TVR was pure experience; and I have some fond memories of those experiences (even the crash, by now). Like most things in life, you need balance, though probably with a shift slightly toward more experiential goods over more material ones.

Shaking Up Attention

Because of the law of diminishing marginal returns (to beer, pizza, happiness), the last few units of pleasure are less valuable to your overall happiness than the first few units of purpose, and vice versa. This means that, as soon as your happiness in a relatively pleasurable activity starts to wane, you should do something else that is relatively purposeful. And when the happiness from that activity starts to wane, it's time to flit back to a relatively pleasurable activity. Your attentional resources won't become as depleted as they might otherwise because you are able to change tasks when you start to feel tired or distracted, and you avoid adapting to what might otherwise become mundane. But remember to stay focused on each activity while engaged in it. So this is not the same as multitasking, which, as we shall soon see, is not at all good for happiness.

For a given activity, you can also seek to pay attention to different aspects of it to keep diminishing marginal returns at bay. Take commuting. You could try walking or cycling a bit more, which has been shown to make the journey to and from work quite pleasurable.[7] Okay, so this might not be possible for those of you with long commutes, but you could still change the nature of your commute so that you attend to stimuli that will make you happier. Make efforts to pay attention to what you listen to, what you do, or who you talk to on the train or in the car. I'm lucky in that I can work on the hour-long train ride from my home in Brighton to work in London, so I turn what would otherwise be only a painful commute into one that's also purposeful. Or if you drive your kids to school, you could use that time to quiz them on multiplication tables (as Liz Plank, one of my researchers on this book, told me her dad did with her when she was a kid).

Notice that purpose has been made salient in these examples, where pain would otherwise dominate. When activities might be quite boring, such as standing in line or waiting at an airport, you can look to pay attention to pleasure by listening to some music or to purpose by reading a book. Or strike up a conversation with a stranger if you're in the mood to chat. You probably do these sorts of things already and so it will simply be a case of reminding yourself to do them more often. If you can't change what you do, then change what you pay attention to in the experience.

We know by now that taking a break when making a choice could help us. Similarly, sometimes taking a break from what you are doing and then returning to it again can increase your happiness when you return to the activity. Imagine being asked to watch TV programs with or without commercials. I bet you would prefer to watch TV without those annoying adverts. Me, too. But in a study that randomly selected people into one of these two conditions, those who watched with commercials enjoyed the programs more — and, just like us, they had failed to predict this effect.[8] This is distinct from distraction because most television programs are designed specifically for commercial "interruptions" whereas other tasks are not: TV programs leave you with a cliff-hanger for a few minutes, allowing you to return to the program eager to find out what happens and happier when you do.

The type of break you take can affect performance. As a great illustration of this, 145 participants from the University of California, Santa Barbara, each completed "unusual uses" tasks, where they had to generate as many creative uses as possible for a common object, such as a brick. They then took a break, during which time some of the participants completed a nondemanding task (where they saw colored digits on a screen and indicated whether they were even or odd). When they returned to the task, these people performed the best the second time around because their brains weren't under- or overoccupied; just like Goldilocks's porridge, their break was just right.[9] Rob Metcalfe and I have shown that creativity is associated with greater happiness, and so giving your attentional resources an undemanding task to contemplate could improve your happiness as well as the quality of your ideas.[10]

If you are feeling a little more adventurous, try having a few new experiences. Start small and see how it goes. Change radio stations in the morning to take in different music. Buy tickets to see a comedian you have never heard of but who has had rave reviews. These will direct your attention in happiness-enhancing ways — and if they don't, well, don't do them again, and try something else. Also try new experiences with new people. There is some suggestion that they will make you more creative, which, as we have seen, is good for happiness: entrepreneurs report more innovation and are more likely to apply for patents when they have diverse social networks beyond just their family and friends.[11]

If nothing else, these or other new experiences will help to slow down the perceived passage of time. Part of the reason time passes so slowly for children is because they are constantly having new experiences.[12] In fact, a ten-year-old will think that the passing of one minute is more than two minutes.[13] It appears as if our brains actually calculate time based on the number of events that occur; so the more events, the more time we feel has passed. If you saw six slides for thirty seconds each and thirty slides for six seconds each, you would think that you had spent more time looking at the thirty slides even though the time is obviously the same overall.[14] This could help explain why you recall that a day has passed quickly when you're in meeting after meeting but slowly if you're just at your desk.

Those who are high in the personality trait "openness to new experiences" report being more satisfied with their lives and experience more positive emotions.[15] Yeah, great, you might say, but what if I'm not an open type of person? Well, it will certainly require more of a nudge to push you into trying something new, but what's the worst that can happen? You don't like the new experience and so you don't do it again. I tried Marmite once, and bloody hated it. But at least now I know it tastes awful. As always, attention is critical. You can attend to the pleasure and purpose of a new experience that turns out well, and you can also attend to the lessons learned from a new experience that turns out badly.

Good Vibrations

There are a few obvious but sometimes forgotten stimuli that we can pay attention to in order to be happier. One of the most important is listening to music. This is a primal stimulus that has been a part of all cultures for thousands of years, bringing people together at weddings, funerals, music festivals, and flash mobs. As the philosopher Nietzsche pointed out, we listen to music with our entire bodies, moving muscles automatically in response to it by dancing, tapping our feet, or just bobbing along. It is a powerful way to open up the mind, and it most strongly affects the brain region associated with positive emotions and memory in a way that no other input to our happiness production process can.[16]

Music therapy has been used in the treatment of heart disease, stroke, post-traumatic stress disorder, and kids with mood disorders and behavioral problems.[17] People with Alzheimer's disease who cannot respond to language respond to music; it can also prevent tics in people with Tourette's syndrome.[18] The British Armed Forces are now using music as a successful intervention for treating trauma in war veterans. Listening to music even reduces cognitive dissonance: children forced to play with one toy instead of another devalued the other toy less when listening to music than when in silence. A bit of music therapy could help to make you a little happier, too, and it's certainly cheaper than retail therapy.

I have long been grateful to my own parents for creating an environment where music could be enjoyed, and I would love my own kids to grow up to be as emotionally aroused by music as I continue to be. Music really was my first love. I was basically into pop and disco as a primary school kid, soul as a secondary school kid, indie music at university and in my early twenties, dance music in my late twenties and early thirties, and all of the above for the last decade. I have spent a considerable amount of money on records, CDs, and going to gigs, and it has all been money well spent. The Jam will always be my favorite group, followed closely now by Faithless, but I keep up with the latest music trends and have every intention of doing so until my hearing goes. Naturally, I am doing my best to indoctrinate Poppy and Stanley with my impeccable music taste.

So when you put this book down, dig out a favorite song, play it and pay attention to it, and see how good it makes you feel, both when it's playing and afterward. If you have trouble remembering to play some music, just flip back a few pages to chapter 6, where we talked about designing your environment. Download a music app onto your phone or put a waterproof radio in the bathroom. What about defaults? Dig out an alarm clock radio or leave the stereo on in your car after you turn it off so it turns on the next time you hop in. And commitment? Put "music time" in your diary or set aside some "music money" for concerts or guitar lessons. Last, what about social norms? You can prioritize being with people in your life who love music or hook up with them on a music sharing app.

Don't underestimate the effects of humor, either. Twenty minutes of watching a comedy reduces stress levels by about the same amount as twenty minutes on a treadmill.[19] One hour of watching a funny video is enough to increase infection-fighting antibodies in the bloodstream for twelve hours, as well as activate "natural killer cells," which selectively target infected and tumorous cells.[20] Laughter also promotes muscle relaxation: people who are about to receive an electric shock report being less anxious beforehand if they listen to a funny tape first.[21] You might consider having a quick laugh before an injection or job interview.

Humor has also been used successfully to reduce perceptions of loneliness and pain in older people.[22] It's a way of dealing with life's trials and tribulations, evident in hospital workers and first responders, who joke as a way to help them handle highly stressful situations.[23] Humor also promotes social integration. Fathers are more likely to get involved in Sure Start (an early-intervention program for children) when Sure Start workers have a good sense of humor.[24]

We have already seen, quite obviously, that laughter can make you feel happier. But it is far from obvious to remember this simple fact. Again, apply design principles. I encourage my friends at work to set up amusing out-of-office replies so I am primed to laugh when I see them in my in-box. For defaults, prerecord your favorite comedies and stock up for dismal days. Commit to watching them with friends. Simply being around people who share your sense of humor is a recipe for laughter.

Although we each find different things funny, humor, like music, is pleasurable for almost everyone.[25] I cannot think of generically purposeful activities in the same way, but it goes without saying that you must be interested in what you are doing — and interested while you are doing it, not just in the achievement of the end point.

Being Mindful

Some of you might have expected me to have discussed *mindfulness* by now. Mindfulness training is about developing a constant sense of awareness and an ability to remain in the present moment. Mindfulness fits under the larger umbrella of therapies that build upon traditional cognitive behavioral therapy (CBT). CBT is a talking therapy that aims to solve dysfunctional emotions, cognitions, and behaviors by focusing attention on the "here and now" rather than ruminating about another place and time. Some of the most effective CBT-type interventions are quite "light touch," such as writing down a few thoughts here and there.[26]

Mindfulness adds novel psychological

methods, such as meditation, to CBT techniques. It involves a greater focus on one's breathing and body as well as a deeper awareness and acceptance of thoughts and feelings. It aims to change how we relate to our thoughts, instead of changing the thoughts themselves.[27] One of the most effective aspects of mindfulness training is the conscious reorientation of attention. The focused attention task involves concentrating on only one thing, such as breathing. Open monitoring involves attending to everything in your environment that you might not otherwise notice, such as the wind or a ticking clock. Focused attention and open monitoring strategies have been shown to help people regulate their emotions and prevent the relapse into depression.[28]

Mindfulness definitely has its place. But I think it only goes so far for two reasons: first, people have to self-select into it; and second, it is quite effortful. The context-focused, rather than cognition-driven, approach in this book only requires that you or someone close to you can influence your environment and, once that is done, it only then requires you to go with the grain of your human behavior. As with much that I have suggested, it is generally easier and more effective to nudge system 1 than it is to shove system 2, and so I'm optimistic that the behavioral insights in this book can be incorporated into light-touch forms of CBT and mindfulness.

PAY ATTENTION TO WHO YOU ARE DOING IT WITH

There is one almost surefire way to be happier: spend more time with people you like. As well as the benefits of asking others for advice about your happiness, the evidence quite clearly shows a strong positive association between happiness and doing things with the people you like and for those you care about. Having more social contact is one of the main reasons why religious people are more satisfied with their lives, though having a strong religious identity helps, too.[29] Being around other people can also help facilitate adaptation to difficult experiences; widows appear to withdraw attention from their loss more quickly when they have social support.[30] Your friends not only make you happier because they're there to hang out with you but also because they make you feel like you matter.[31]

Recall from the data in chapter 2 that certain types of people bring us different amounts of pleasure and purpose as we engage in different activities. The data suggest that, for a more purposeful commute, carpool with your colleagues. Bring your relatives out to eat or include them in the time you spend with your kids to make these occasions more pleasurable. Get the kids to do the housework with you and then watch TV together, which increases the pleasure of both of these activities for most people. Taking care of our own kids is an experience that Les and I have found to be best shared with each other, and ideally also shared with other parents and their kids.

If the data do not convince you of the merits of being with other people, try answering a simple question: if you spent twenty minutes more each day with people you like or, failing that, talking on the phone to people you like, would you be happier? If you'll allow me to answer for you: the answer is yes, irrespective of how happy you are at the moment. I am not so confident that a pay raise of $1,000 would make all of you happier, by the way. Sure, $1,000 will mean a lot to many of you but an extra $1,000 will not make all of you happier.

So why don't many of us find the time? I think it has a lot to do with how mistaken we are about how much discretionary time we think we have, as discussed earlier. So

291

when we say that we cannot find twenty minutes out of the one thousand or so minutes that we are awake each day, we really mean that we are not prioritizing doing so. Many happiness books will tell you to schedule time in for others but that planning requires time in itself, which you may put off because there are always other things that seem to be more important. Consistent with many of my observations in this book, it's worth thinking about how you could *find* more time without having to *plan* more time.

So, instead of using the toilet across the hall at work, start using the one at the other end of your floor. It will force you to walk across the office, making it more likely you'll casually socialize with others. The managers at Pixar in Emeryville, California, were experimenting with redesigning the immediate environment and decided to have only one bathroom in the entire building so their employees would all have to walk to the same place if they wanted to have a wee.[32] The managers anticipated that it would make people more likely to speak to each other and that the entire office would be more prone to socializing. They were right. It also boosted creativity.

It is worth saying that even the introverts

among you are likely to be happier when you are around people you like. Introversion and extroversion are broad personality categories that describe a range of predispositions and behaviors, such as the propensity to select into social situations, where extroverts have a higher propensity to do so. Many aspects of our world are designed for extroverts, such as group work in classrooms and workplaces. But introverts still benefit from social interaction; they just require a different balance from extroverts and have less tolerance for unpleasant social situations.[33]

DON'T GET DISTRACTED

Someone who maximizes their happiness is someone who allocates their attention optimally. Unfortunately, most of us are some way away from the optimum. A big part of the problem emanates from the fact that we get distracted from paying attention to our experiences. Distraction is very different from taking a break. Distraction comes from internal disruption, such as intrusive thoughts about whether you left the car lights on or where to go on holiday this summer, and also from external stimuli, such as people and e-mails. Taking a break, on the other hand, is deliberately chosen to happen at that time. And as we saw earlier in this chapter, taking the right kind of break can increase creativity. The same cannot be said for distraction. So if you hear someone say "distraction is a good thing," what they ought to mean is that a designated break is a good thing.

Distraction Costs

Distraction is damaging because it requires *switching costs*. A switching cost is how much attentional energy is required to change from one task to the next.[34] Every time you shift your attention, your brain has to reorient itself, further taxing your mental resources. When you interrupt yourself to text, tweet, or e-mail you are using attentional energy to switch tasks. If you do this frequently, your attention reserves quickly become diminished, making it even harder for you to focus on whatever it is you want to do. Assuming that what you want to do is a pleasurable and/or purposeful activity, it will make you less happy if you give it limited attention.

So multitasking makes you less happy and also results in less productivity. One nice recent study involved 218 Dutch students being asked to solve a Sudoku puzzle and complete a word search in a fixed time of twenty-four minutes. Participants in the experiment were randomly assigned to one of three treatments: one where they were forced to multitask; one where they could organize their work by freely switching between the Sudoku puzzle and the word search; and one where they performed the tasks sequentially. They were awarded points for each correctly filled Sudoku cell and each word found. The total points scored were lowest in the first group and highest in the third.[35] These results suggest that having a clear schedule of work is better for productivity. So multitasking might sound cool, but it actually makes you a fool.

Multitasking can, however, make us *feel* as if we are more productive, thus resulting in a mistaken belief about ourselves. This is a good reason why so many of us continue to do it.[36] But now you can remember that you'd feel even better if you concentrated on one thing at a time — and you would also get more done. Multitasking takes effort and it's not worth it. I never use lecture slides for this reason: students don't waste their attentional resources going between the slides and my voice. This is also a nice example of adaptation, by the way; the unease among my students at the start of term is palpable but the lack of slides is the one thing that they comment on most positively at the end of the course.

The costs of distraction are now more transparent in the modern age. Recent technological advances have brought a range of benefits, including national income growth, lower consumer prices, and possibly even higher life satisfaction.[37] And as an academic, my life is made so much easier by being able to download journal articles instead of lugging around piles of books and papers. But modern technology has brought a few costs, too, the biggest of which is distraction. A recent study estimated the combined cost of distractions for US businesses to be around $600 billion per year.[38] Thomas Jackson, known as "Dr. Email" for his nearly two decades of work on . . . wait for it . . . e-mail distractions, estimates that e-mail alone costs UK businesses about £10,000 ($16,500) per employee per year.[39]

Research also shows that reading something online that is embedded with links makes us more likely to be confused about what we are reading, even when we don't even click on the links, compared to reading printed text.[40] The mere fact that there is a link forces your brain to make a choice to click or not to click, which itself is distracting. All the time you spend online sharpens the neural circuits dedicated to "skimming" rather than those for "reading and thinking deeply." When you then go off-line, you have trained your brain to attend to things that it wouldn't attend to otherwise. This is a waste of time where you could instead be experiencing pleasure and purpose.

If you need further convincing about the costs of distraction, consider the correlation between the increase in parents being distracted by Internet, text, and e-mail, and the increase in accidents in young kids, reversing a long-term downward trend, and also in contrast to the continuing decrease in accidents in older kids.[41] Or, in a more controlled setting, consider the causal effects of (1) using the phone, (2) texting, or (3) listening to music on the likelihood of being hit while crossing the road in a simulated environment. Which do you think would be the most distracting? Well, you are more likely to get hit by a car while texting or listening to music but all three conditions are more dangerous than not being distracted.[42] And when people pretended to drive cars in a simulator, switching between braking in response to the brake lights of a car ahead and counting the number of times a sound occurred, the result was a delay that equated to sixteen feet of stopping distance.[43] This might be something to remember the next time you're behind the wheel.

Money on My Mind

Paying attention to what we are doing can feel increasingly difficult as there seem to be ever-increasing demands on our time. As you get richer, you attach more value to your time, and attaching more value to time, or anything else for that matter, means that it feels scarcer. And so you pay it ever more attention. If you could charge $1.50 per minute for working at a computer you would feel more time pressure than if you charged only $0.15 per minute for exactly the same task.[44] In fact, the same authors show that you only need to have your wealth brought to your attention to feel time pressed. If you were made to feel rich by being given a scale where "high savings" was anything over $500, you would report feeling "more pressed for time today" than if you were made to feel poor by being given a scale where you needed to have over $400,000 to be deemed to have high savings.

Thinking about time as money also affects experiences of pleasure during leisure activities. Imagine you are asked some questions about how much you earned over the past year and that your friend answered the same questions as well as being asked their hourly wage. Then you each listen to eighty-six seconds of "The Flower Duet" from the opera *Lakmé.* Who do you think would enjoy the music the most and be the most patient? You would — because your friend has just been reminded how much she earns in a unit (an hour), which draws attention to itself. Similar effects were also found when the researchers allowed participants to create their own leisure experience by playing around online.[45] The moral of these various studies is that you are less happy when you are paying attention to time (and especially to time as money) rather than to the activities you are engaged in. So again, try to be fully engaged in what you're doing, which includes not looking at the clock every few minutes. For example, I try hard not to be too set in how much time I spend playing with the kids in breaks from working.

Moreover, the more money you have, the more you may think of all the things you could do with that money if only you had the time, such as taking longer holidays. Surely richer people would actually take longer holidays whenever they could, right?

This was indeed the trend in the United States in the 1960s and 1970s, but from the 1980s on, something quite interesting has happened. People with less than a college degree have had relatively more leisure time, and those with a college degree or higher have had relatively less. The gap between the incomes of the rich and the poor has widened considerably since the 1980s but the gap between the amounts of leisure time they have has widened, too, favoring those with lower incomes.[46]

Little wonder, then, that daily moods do not improve beyond making around $75,000 per year in the United States — there is no time to be happy if you are rich. Focusing attention on the scarcity of time or money can lead to all of us making decisions that place a great deal of emphasis on getting more of that resource now at the expense of lots of it later. As a great illustration of this, one study randomly assigned participants into groups that varied in how much time they were allowed to think about answers to trivia questions, and into further groups that determined whether or not they would be allowed to take more time to answer now at the expense of less time later. Time-poor participants had three hundred seconds to answer, whereas time-rich participants had one thousand seconds. The former group borrowed on average 22 percent of their budget (so, sixty-six seconds), whereas time-rich participants borrowed on average 8 percent of their budget (so, eighty seconds). As you might expect, the time-rich groups did better than the time-poor groups, whether or not they could borrow, but the time-poor group performed the best when they could not borrow at all. In a nutshell, time-poor participants borrowed their way into poor performance. If a resource becomes scarce, we will all act in very similar ways to those who are currently poor in that resource.[47]

And so in general, it's better if you don't pay too much attention to money at all. Given my upbringing, I appreciate that money matters when circumstances dictate that every penny counts but it might generally be worth chilling out a bit about it if you are not in that position. Sure, money matters and you should respect it, but not so much that it overruns your life. It's certainly not worth making yourself miserable over. Rob Metcalfe and I have shown that, while poorer people have more intrusive thoughts about money than do wealthier people, the latter's happiness is more negatively influenced by those thoughts.[48]

A Wandering Mind

There is evidence that general mind wanderings, whether about money or anything else, are frequent, occurring up to a third of the time when people are asked what they are thinking about at random times during the day.[49] It seems that we are predisposed to let our minds wander: neurological evidence from brain imaging studies shows that mind wanderings are more common when a particular network of cortical regions in our brains is activated — which are the same regions that typically correspond to periods of rest.[50] It can be difficult to separate out what is evolutionarily adaptive and what is simply an evolutionary mistake; simply because you are neurologically wired to let your mind wander does not mean that you should, in much the same way that being genetically programmed to eat a lot because our ancestors didn't know when they would eat next doesn't mean that we should necessarily do so.[51] Knowing that you are hardwired does help explain why it happens, though, which will hopefully help you deal more effectively with the mind wanderings you do have, and not to ruminate further on them.

You are doubtless made less happy if your mental escape from your current experience is to somewhere worse than where you are now, such as if you start worrying about your blood test results in the middle of a meeting you cannot leave. But it seems that you might also be made less happy if your intrusive thoughts are positive; that is, even if you mentally escape to somewhere better, like your next holiday, in the middle of that meeting.[52] But context matters. I have an electric toothbrush that whirs automatically for two minutes. When I pay attention to cleaning my teeth, those two minutes can feel like an eternity and I can't wait for them to finish. When I am thinking about other stuff, in contrast, the two minutes fly by and I tend to enjoy my mind wanderings.

So, let's focus on negative intrusive thoughts, which are nearly always damaging to happiness. Most of the relevant research has been conducted on clinical populations or those who have experienced a difficult event, such as loss of a loved one: one study found that men who experienced a lot of intrusive thoughts in the first month of their bereavement adapted less quickly, as indicated by their lower morale one year later compared to those who had fewer intrusive thoughts.[53]

In an attempt to consider the importance of intrusive thoughts in the valuation of health states (a subject, you'll recall, that is close to my academic heart), I asked more than a thousand members of the general population in the United States first to describe their current health status. I then asked them how often and how intensely they thought about any current health problems. Finally, I asked them to say how many years of life they would be willing to give up in order to alleviate their health problems. I found that participants' willingness to give up life years was better explained by the frequency and intensity of their thoughts about health than by the description of the actual health issue. This study highlights once more that you are affected by what you attend to more than by the objective circumstances of your life.[54]

If you begin to worry or think about other things when you don't want to, it is possible to redirect your attention by finding ways that prevent your mind from wandering. For a very long time people have been making "worry tables" by writing down their worries and distinguishing between those they can and can't control, in order to help them stop worrying about what they can't.[55] If you were to try writing down what you were worrying about a month ago, let alone a year ago, you would most likely have trouble remembering; and even if you could remember, it is likely that the concern rarely had consequences anywhere close to your fears.

Most of our concerns more generally are about what has not yet happened, and sometimes about what has already taken place. In contrast, we nearly always have nothing to worry about *right now*. This is a pretty compelling reason to attend to the here and now. If you always did this, the "there and then" that you currently worry about would never affect you. The focus of your attention would be here and now, which is nearly always okay. This certainly applies to my stammer, which rarely makes me feel as bad as I imagine it will. When I feel an intrusive thought taking hold, I ask myself, "What have you got to worry about right *now*?" When the answer is nothing at all, as it nearly always is, I feel a little happier.

One intervention aimed at suppressing intrusive thoughts among people waiting for medical test results showed that simply making a plan for how they would manage the thoughts was helpful (e.g., by starting a conversation with someone to bring attention to the present).[56] Using this method, you could consciously write down a few things you might do to help yourself when situations arise where negative thoughts are most likely to pop up.

You could also remind yourself to "phone a friend" when your mind begins to wander. We have already seen that time with family and friends is a vital part of being happy, so how better to take advantage of them, in the nicest possible way, than when your mind starts going to places that would make you less happy?

New experiences can also mitigate intrusive thoughts. Those of us who do something new as opposed to something routine are much less likely to experience intrusive thoughts because new experiences require more attention in the moment than do routine ones.[57] So in addition to fostering creativity and slowing down time, which we have already discussed, new experiences have further benefits, which adds to our understanding of why people who are open to them are happier. "Try something new" is probably one of the more evidence-based suggestions in self-help books.

It is likely that your mind will wander from purpose toward pleasure, and your behavior might as well. Too often to be consistent with the maximization of my happiness, my attention while writing this book has been diverted from experiencing purpose toward searching out pleasure. Sometimes those mind wanderings have led to mouse wanderings, too, as I have searched the Internet. Even at the time of the distraction, I have been aware that I would rather be concentrating more fully on the book. I can more easily concentrate on pleasure without getting distracted, and I suspect you can, too. It will not come as any surprise to anyone who knows me that, in general, I am quite easily distracted. Ask any of the students who have sat through my mind wanderings in lectures. It's hard to be sure, and I get distracted thinking about it anyway, but I reckon I have always only ever concentrated in short bursts. In our own ways, we are each susceptible to being distracted, but we're also able to mitigate its effects.

I wonder what you are distracted by. Now's a good time to take a few moments to think about three things that interrupt you from attending to your experiences.

I get distracted by . . .

1. _____
2. _____
3. _____

Done it? I suspect that at least one item on that list has something to do with texts, tweets, e-mails, or the Internet.

A Wandering Mouse

We've all heard about attention deficit disorder but the modern world is making us all victims of "attention distraction disorder." It is important to note here that I am making a deliberate and important distinction between the two. The former is attributable to the person: some people are more likely to have it than others. Attention distraction disorder, on the other hand, is the result of contextual influences outside the person: some situations are more conducive to it than others, and they usually involve modern technology.

Although we've always needed to deal with the perils of distraction, the modern age is constantly removing obstacles to becoming addicted to checking e-mails or checking the Facebook updates of your virtual friends.[58] Medical doctors are now warning about "digital dementia," which is defined as irreversible deficits in brain development and memory loss among children who spend a lot of time on electronic devices like laptops and mobile phones.[59]

Internet addiction was recently suggested

to be a major contribution to mental disorders. Naturally, it's difficult to avoid being distracted when you are addicted to the source of the distraction. There is now evidence to show that the brains of heavy Internet users (people who report symptoms of addiction) literally shrink, just as they do in people who have addictions to heavy drugs such as cocaine and heroin.[60] Your brain becomes less efficient at filtering out irrelevant information when you allow yourself to become bombarded by information from the Internet.

In a recent study of people's desires and their ability to keep those desires under control, more than two hundred adults were given BlackBerries for a week. They were beeped seven times a day and asked if they were currently experiencing, or had experienced in the last half hour, a desire (described as an urge, craving, or longing) for a range of activities. The desire to engage in media activities was very difficult for the participants to control — they reported desiring them more frequently than sex, smoking, drinking coffee, drinking alcohol, and eating.[61] I have the feeling that this is a mistaken desire.

All in all, we have an "attentional commitment" to our communication devices.[62]

Even when you aren't stimulated by incoming updates, texts, or calls, you might imagine them. If you are anything like me, you will have experienced "phantom vibration syndrome": imagining the sensation of your phone vibrating, only to pick it up and realize that it wasn't doing anything at all.[63] Even when your devices aren't fighting for your attention, your brain is still wired to pay attention to them.

So you should look to find ways of breaking free from the addiction of virtual interaction; you have nothing to lose but your chains of e-mails.

Now, I do appreciate that you might be quite fond of the Internet and your phone. Indeed, I think there are many people out there who would be more affected by losing their phone than the friends whose information is recorded in it. So you'll probably have to take an initial hit to your happiness as you try to wean yourself off, even if only ever so slightly. But I reckon within a few days you will adjust and be happier than before as you free your attention up for more pleasurable and purposeful activities.

Distraction is an attentional thief and so you should look to keep the thief out by erecting barriers to being distracted. Some of the design features discussed in chapter 6 can be utilized here. Perhaps your wireless router does not require that extra add-on that extends its range to the backyard, too. It will be much easier to design your way out of distraction by preventing distractions from getting to you in the first place, than to use your willpower to counter them when they occur.

Use technology to counter its negative effects — set up new defaults by turning off notifications, leaving your phone on silent, turning off the chat function on your computer at work, and taking advantage of the new apps and programs that actually block you from using the Internet. This will allow you to pay attention to your activities and to pay attention for longer because you have designed a distraction-free zone.

You can also overcome your attentional commitment to your mobile devices with a public commitment to pay attention to your experiences. My friends and family know that I don't take my phone to the gym and, unless I am out for the night, I turn it off at 7:00 p.m. To avoid your own distractions on a night out with friends, put your phone on silent: you commit yourself to not being distracted by "pop-ups" in your head or on your phone. If your friends were to do likewise, you and they would be happier. It would seem that inventors of the "Phone Stacking Game" (also known as "Don't Be a Dick During Meals") agree with me. Before the meal, everyone stacks up their phone in a pile on the table. Whoever touches their phone first has to pay the bill.[64] Although purposeful activities are the most vulnerable to distraction, the invention of this game suggests that even more pleasurable ones, like socializing, are also now requiring design-based solutions to overcoming distraction.

Embed yourself in social networks made of the sorts of people who also prefer not being distracted. My friends and I try to avoid text conversations, which take so much longer than a single real conversation. It seems as though we are in the minority, as it looks like text is overtaking talk as the preferred means of communication. A whopping 129 billion text messages were sent during 2010, which is an increase of 24 percent compared to 2009.[65] In contrast, time spent talking on the phone actually dropped by 5 percent from 2010 to 2011.[66] If you are going to text chat, at least try to make some of it purposeful alongside the general small talk. This all reminds me of something a taxi driver said to me once. He asked me to imagine that voice calls were invented after text messaging. "Do you really think," he said, "that anyone would be sending texts? Of course they bloody wouldn't — they would be bloody marveling at their ability to actually have a conversation." I think he is bloody right.

Apologies, I got a little distracted there. There are so many stimuli vying for your attention — sounds, places, people, smells, and your own thoughts rattling around in your head. You only have so much attentional energy and it will make you happier, more efficient, and healthier if you are able to focus it properly.

HAPPIER BY DOING

It should come as no great surprise to anyone that we are happier when we pay attention to good experiences and to people we like being with. The problem is that we act in ways that make it appear as if this is not at all obvious. There are some simple yet effective things that you can do to reorient your attention to being happier. Buy a few more experiences and a bit less stuff, switch between pleasurable and purposeful activities, and listen to music. Make a commitment to spend a little more time each day talking to people you like. And look to spending a little less time each day glued to your computer or phone. Distractions drain you and leave you feeling tired and less happy, so stay focused on one thing at a time — and stop continually checking those darn e-mails and Facebook updates.

8
DECIDE, DESIGN, AND DO

You are now armed with the three pillars of the production process of happiness. Producing happiness involves deciding, designing, and doing, and the most effective ways to be happier involve joining up these various components.

To illustrate how to bring them together, let's consider two behaviors that I think will resonate with many readers: first, how to procrastinate less; and second, how to help yourself by helping others more. Procrastination involves avoiding paying attention to a task that you know you should complete. It is a good example for our purposes because most of us admit to procrastinating, which makes us less happy, strains our relationships with other people, and worsens performance at work and school.[1] Doing more for others is another good example, I think, because it makes us happy, but our behavior often does not reflect this fact.

Don't worry if you feel like these two behaviors don't strike a strong chord with you; I'm confident that knowing the reasons why we depart from being as happy as we can be in these contexts, and the related suggestions, will surely spark ideas in your mind about how you can tailor them to fit other behaviors that you are more concerned about.

DITHER LESS

Procrastination and distraction go hand in hand. If we could completely avoid the task, that would be fine and we wouldn't need to avoid paying attention to it, but procrastinators worry because the task simply can't be avoided (and we have seen how damaging intrusive thoughts can be for happiness).[2] Distraction also causes procrastination when stimuli other than the task at hand get in the way of getting it done. Let's first look at how we get into this misery of procrastination and then look for solutions to get out of it.

Departures from Happiness

The first step in tackling procrastination is to decide whether or not you want to perform the task. Perhaps the task is not worth bothering with at all. A mistaken

316

desire might be driving it, for example. It would appear that we procrastinate more over tasks we deem to be particularly important, like working toward lofty goals, because they require more effort and we seek to avoid expending this effort.[3] We also dither over tasks that will be evaluated, such as when students procrastinated over writing essays when they believed their university would randomly select some students' work and make them read it to students at a local high school as compared to students who just handed in their essays.[4] Moreover, tasks that don't match your skill set get in the way of becoming absorbed in the activity.

Mistaken projections make it easy to procrastinate. I'm sure we would like more time rather than less. But think about when you have to leave for work early as compared to having loads of time. If you are anything like me, you rush around more when you have more time and not less. This is probably because you will plan for the earlier departure and procrastinate more over being ready for the later one. Medical students evaluate more patients per hour and have more patient contact on nine-hour shifts as opposed to twelve-hour ones.[5] Further, as we have already seen, our memories do not accurately recall the duration of past events, and so we will project these errors into the future.[6] For example, we would seem to both remember and predict that short tasks of a couple minutes or so take longer than they actually do, but when it comes to longer tasks, we believe they will take less time than they actually do.[7] Most things take more than two minutes, so bear this in mind and plan extra time.

It's our mistaken beliefs that are perhaps at the root of our procrastination. Many of us mistakenly believe that we work best under the pressure of a last-minute deadline but this is generally not true. A review of twenty-four procrastination studies involving nearly four thousand students found that those who put off their work tended to have lower grades than those who didn't.[8] And even when we know that we tend to complete projects about a day before deadline, we'll still estimate overly optimistically that we'll be done about four days ahead of schedule.[9]

You might also think you're more creative under pressure. But when writers for the *Harvard Business Review* asked nearly two hundred highly educated employees from US businesses to describe, in separate sections of an online diary, how much time pressure they felt at the end of their workday and something that stood out in their minds from that day, they found that greater time pressure was associated with fewer instances of reported creativity.[10] You should also have realistic expectations about what you can achieve. Perfectionists are thought to be notorious procrastinators because they set goals that are too high, which they then fail to achieve, though this has been disputed.[11]

I would like to add that procrastination can adversely affect policy objectives, too. Together with Caroline Rudisill, I have shown that changing the maximum age that women in the UK can receive a state-funded cycle of in vitro fertilization (IVF) treatment from thirty-nine to forty-two will almost certainly result in fewer babies being born than before as women, whose fertility is declining, delay trying for a baby in the presence of the new deadline.[12] This is one of many examples where policy makers need to consult behavioral scientists (ideally me, of course) before intervening.

Decide

So how might you decide to procrastinate less? You can overcome the three attentional obstacles with salient feedback about how working toward your goals makes you feel.

Procrastination is about avoiding something you are torn about doing, so what is it that makes you want to avoid it? Consider reconstructing a similar task from the past. How did you feel the last time you did something similar to what you're procrastinating over? What was the environment like the last time you did it, and who was there?

You can also look to get more immediate feedback about how it feels to be working toward your goals and achieving them. Loan officers at the Colombian bank Bancamía put this principle into practice to tackle their serious procrastination problem. They had the bad habit of putting off finding new loan clients until just before their monthly bonuses were calculated, during the last two weeks of each month. Seventy percent of these officers reported being stressed or very stressed, and over half reported having trouble organizing their work or sticking to their plans. To shift their workload, they broke down their tasks into weekly elements and received small prizes, like movie tickets and restaurant coupons, for finishing each week. Compared to a group of loan officers who didn't enter this antiprocrastination program, they increased the attainment of their goals by 30 percent and their bonus payments by 25 percent. As discussed, feedback can help you decide what to input into your production process, as well as set behavior change in motion.[13]

Feedback from others can be an important means of overcoming procrastination. Other people might be better placed to help you get things done right now because they are less committed to your present self than you are. Other people can also help you rein in your overoptimism about the time it will take you to complete a task — indeed, perhaps erring on the side of assuming it will take longer than it actually will.[14] Ask someone to play devil's advocate with you and incorporate this into your decisions.

Being too hard on ourselves, and not accepting the fact that we procrastinate, just leads to more procrastination and makes it harder to change. Students who were self-critical and reported disliking themselves because of their procrastinating past were more likely to procrastinate the second time around than those who forgave themselves.[15] If you have never forgiven yourself for procrastinating before, start now; and if you have, remind yourself of how good it felt to do so the last time. The students in this study who forgave themselves also reported experiencing more positive emotions.

Design

How might you then design your way to less procrastination? Start by considering whether the primes in your immediate environment are conducive to getting things done. Perhaps a picture of a clean kitchen on your fridge will prime you to do the dishes just as the way clean and fresh smells (like citrus) get people to clean up and to wash their hands. And those of us who work or study in the same location appear less likely to procrastinate because the location nudges us to do what we did the last time we were in it.[16] So if you always work in the same place but never get anything done, change spaces, or just rearrange the space, and then see what happens.

Then what about using a default to preserve your attentional resources? You probably already opt out of many distracting scenarios that breed procrastination, like pop-up ads, and opt into many attention-saving ones, like automatic bill paying. Apply these principles elsewhere when you can. If you can set default deadlines, don't assume later is better. Most people think they'll use a gift certificate with an expiration date further into the future, but the opposite is true: they're more likely to redeem it before it expires if they are given just a few weeks to use it as opposed to if they are given a month or more.[17]

Also use the power of commitments and consider how best to spread them out. In a well-known study, researchers hired sixty proofreaders who responded to advertisements placed in the Massachusetts Institute of Technology's newspaper and on bulletin boards (little did the applicants know that they were about to read three very boring postmodern texts that often didn't make sense). Each participant was randomly assigned to do one of three things: (1) submit one of the three texts every seven days; (2) submit all three texts at the end of three weeks; or (3) set their own deadlines. Those with the weekly deadlines found the most errors and procrastinated the least — as did those who set weekly deadlines for themselves.[18]

So if you have a big project, consider breaking it down into smaller deadlines that are spaced evenly apart. Someone else could even do this for you (and might do a better job of it). If you get a friend to set your deadlines for you, your commitment will be to someone whom you do not want to let down, and so you might be more likely to meet the target by attending to them as well as it.

323

Breaking a project down has also been shown to reduce our tendency to be overly optimistic about how long a task will take. People who estimated the time it would take to prepare an hors d'oeuvre tray with miniature sandwiches, sliced fruit, stuffed vegetables, and skewered shrimp thought it would take about ten minutes less than it actually did, but when they reviewed all of the steps that would be needed to complete it (slicing fruit, boiling shrimp, etc.), there wasn't much of a difference between their predictions and the amount of time taken.[19]

Hanging out with highly motivated people will certainly help you create the social norm to procrastinate less by unconsciously guiding you to be more like those in your reference group. Take procrastination over retirement savings. If colleagues working in the same department as you are offered $20 for attending a fair about planning for retirement, you are three times more likely to attend — even though you will not get paid yourself — than if your colleagues are not incentivized to attend. Moreover, you will also be more likely to open and keep open a tax-deferred retirement account.[20] When you have a project to complete, spend some time with the purpose engines in your friendship group. Equally, when the pressure is off, hang out with the pleasure machines.

Do

And finally, how might you pay more attention to what you are doing? We generally procrastinate over purposeful activities, like work or study, and awkward situations, like delivering bad news to someone.[21] You therefore need to get right into engaging in these activities. If you have to deliver some bad news to different staff members, for example, set aside some time to do so in one hit rather than spreading it out over a day. I am not especially prone to procrastination but, in getting this book finished, I forced myself to get up before the rest of the family and get in a couple of hours of work while they were still sleeping. In so doing, I have turned myself from a night owl to a morning lark (though having kids had pretty much forced me to be a morning person already).

Also think about how you can better attend to others. Being with others when you're doing almost anything increases pleasure and purpose, so remember to pay attention to the people you may be with when you finally get around to whatever you have been procrastinating about. But don't let them distract you, of course, so perhaps consider giving each other feedback on the tasks you've been procrastinating about. Employees who report that they receive information about how well they are performing at work are more likely to say that they experience high meaningfulness while they are working, so this is a purpose-driven route out of procrastinating.[22] Also recall that conversations about experiences are pleasurable, so conversing about your experiences getting work done could be a way to promote pleasure, too.

Distraction will, of course, interrupt attending to experiences; one survey reported that over half of a sample of three hundred online survey participants reported using the Internet to procrastinate — and these are just the people who would have been consciously attending to doing so.[23] So this is yet further reason to work offline when you can. There are plenty of coffee shops without the Internet and apps that prevent you from accessing the Web.

DISTRIBUTE MORE

Many of us might be happier from doing more for other people. I am not suggesting that you immediately start giving more money to charity or rush out to volunteer but these are certainly the kinds of activities you could consider doing, even if you ultimately decide against it.

All of us care about our own happiness, but we also care about the distribution of happiness among other people. This is distinct from the effects that others have on what you do and how you feel, as discussed under social norms in chapter 6. Rather, it refers to the effects that other people's happiness *in itself* has on you.

There are many good reasons for wanting to spread happiness around. First of all, you could be made happier by reducing inequalities in society that you consider to be unjust, without any direct concern for any specific groups or individuals. This is caring *about* others. Second, you might feel happier from directly helping others, without any explicit concern for the impact this has on inequalities in society. This is caring *for* others. Let us first consider these motivations in turn, since the distinction affects what we might do in addressing them.

Concerns for Inequalities

In the figure on next page, the cake on the left is bigger than the one on the right, and the light gray slice on the left is bigger, too. So if only size matters, you would prefer the slice on the left. But the light gray slice on the left is smaller than one of the other slices and this might upset you. So you might well be happier with the smaller slice on the right because it is the same size as the other slices. If the cake on the right were any smaller, though, you might prefer the slice on the left. Herein lays the trade-off between size on the one hand and distribution on the other.

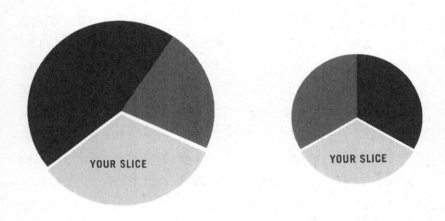

With many wonderful colleagues over many years, I have conducted numerous studies that show that we care greatly about the health of other people.[24] I got into this research because, along with other academics around that time, such as Alan Williams, I recognized that citizens and policy makers care about who gets which slices of health benefits, as well as how big the cake is overall. If I were doing these studies now, I would focus more directly on the distribution of happiness, but I was much more immersed in health issues a decade ago. Fortunately, though, health is an important input into the happiness production process, and what we know about people's preferences regarding the distribution of health in society can inform what we infer about their preferences for distributing other key inputs, as well as happiness itself.

At the time I started this research in the mid 1990s, there were no large-scale studies of the public's preferences about the distribution of health benefits. So I basically began asking as many people as I could get research funding for lots of questions about how to distribute health benefits. In various studies using a range of methods, including discussion groups and surveys, I have found that the general public do care about how much health can be generated by health and other policy interventions; they care about the size of the health cake. But they also prefer a more equal distribution of health: a more equal cut of the slices.[25] Similar findings have been found in studies that investigate preferences for the distribution of income in society.[26]

More recently, and in one of the largest

studies into what the public think about equity in health, Aki Tsuchiya and I, along with other colleagues at the University of Sheffield, conducted a study in which six hundred members of the UK general population were asked a series of binary choices. The basic setup was that one choice was preferred from a health-maximizing perspective and the other was preferred from another perspective, such as the reduction of inequalities. Encouragingly, the results suggest most members of the general public are sensitive to the trade-offs they are asked to make: they care about reducing inequalities in health when the sacrifice in overall health is not too great as they see it, but then they switch to maximizing health when they are asked to give up too much health.[27]

There have been far fewer studies that have focused on the general public's preferences about the distribution of happiness itself. In work supported by the Office for National Statistics, Rob Metcalfe and I asked nearly one thousand members of the UK general public in face-to-face interviews the following question:

Which do you think is better, a policy which achieves a reasonable level of well-being for everyone, or a policy which leads to higher total well-being overall, but results in high well-being for some people and low well-being for others?

Eighty-nine percent chose the first option, suggesting that people care about the distribution of happiness more than they do about the total amount of happiness overall. We then asked another one thousand people, this time in an online survey, two questions about efficiency-equality trade-offs in life satisfaction of the kinds that have been asked about health:

Imagine that, from policy 1, one person has a life satisfaction rating of 5 and another has a rating of 9. From policy 2, one person has a rating of 6 and another has a rating of 7. Which of the two policies brings about the best outcome?

Imagine that, from policy 1, one person has a life satisfaction rating of 2 and another has a rating of 6. From policy 2, one person has a rating of 3 and another has a rating of 4. Which of the two policies brings about the best outcome?

In both questions, there was a clear preference for narrowing the gap in happiness. Nearly two out of every three participants

331

chose the second option, with only about one in seven people strongly preferring the first (the remaining participants were undecided about which option to pick).

But — and it is a pretty big but — all of these studies are also subject to focusing effects because people are asked to think about how much the distribution of health and happiness in society matter in order to find out how much it matters, which (as you know by now) could make it seem like they matter more than they do. Along these lines, we have shown that people's preferences about the ideal distribution of health depend on what the current distribution looks like.[28] All of these issues are extremely important to consider when deciding whether and how to include public preferences in resource allocation decisions. The results of empirical studies need to be handled with a considerable degree of caution. As things stand, I am confident that we are affected by, and do care about, the distribution of happiness in society, even if I can't be quite so confident about the precise trade-offs between the size of the cake and the distribution of its slices.

Fortunately, there might be more "factual" information we can rely on to make decisions. While economic growth is associated with a reduction in the gap between the happiest and the least happy people within developed countries, rising income inequality acts as a barrier to achieving greater happiness equality.[29] Americans and Brits seem to be happier during periods when inequalities in income are lower.[30] Happiness is also higher in Japan, urban China, and Latin America when inequalities are lower.[31] In contrast, in rural China greater inequality has been associated with greater life satisfaction.[32] This suggests that income inequality may sometimes serve as a signal of opportunity, depending on how fair the opportunities to earn more are perceived to be.

Overall, though, it makes sense from a happiness-maximizing perspective to care about helping those who are in the worst-off sections of society, especially when those with the smaller slice of the cake have little opportunity to get a bigger slice. And given that more equal societies are generally happier, we might not need preference data at all to show the benefits of caring about others.

Helping Others

In addition to feeling better when unfair inequalities are reduced, we also feel better when we more directly care for others. We saw in chapter 2 that people who volunteer experience a fair dose of purpose from doing so. In other studies, people who volunteer, help others, and give to charity report greater life satisfaction and better moods than others.[33] But, as elsewhere, we need to exercise some caution in making inferences about causality from studies that show correlations between happiness and other outcomes: those who do more for others might also be happier to begin with. Having said that, there does appear to be good evidence for the causal effects on happiness from caring for others. Imagine being given the luxury to spend $20 of someone else's money today. If you were told to spend it on someone else, you would be happier than if you were told to spend it on yourself.[34]

There is also evidence that giving your time away to help others, as in volunteering, will help you to feel less time pressed.[35] So devoting some of your time to purposeful activities can in fact make you feel as if you have more time overall. Caring for others by being with them can also help to reduce loneliness, both on your part and on the part of the people you spend time with. Loneliness, like happiness, is contagious: it spreads even more strongly than feelings of connectedness with others.[36] Loneliness is also horrible for your health. Older adults who feel that they lack companionship, are left out, or are isolated from others are more likely to die in the next six years, largely because loneliness has a direct and detrimental impact upon their health.[37] Simply giving others the opportunity to be with you is good for your health and happiness as well as for theirs.

A major part of why we all care for others is because it makes us feel good about ourselves. When Les, Poppy, or Stanley is feeling down, I feel down, too. So I try to cheer them up, partly because I care about them and partly because it makes me happier. As I think Mark Twain said, "The best way to cheer yourself up is to try to cheer someone else up." There is a suggestion in the literature on charitable giving that the "purchase" of *warm glow* — the positive feelings obtained from helping others — is the principal reason for giving.[38] Warm glow strikes me as an excellent example of a good sentiment. And there is absolutely nothing wrong in saying that the reason you care for other people is because it makes you feel good. We feel good about helping others in much the same way that we feel good about having just finished a work project, with the added bonus that someone else benefits, too (which is not always the case with work projects).

Many of us do a great deal that feels purposeful and that is good not just for ourselves but also for our families and our friends. You may even feel from time to time that you are sacrificing your own happiness for those you care about, and that other people are doing likewise for you — and that none of you resent doing so. In my own family, Les and I feel we are making various sacrifices of our own happiness for each other's happiness and especially for the happiness of Poppy and Stanley. It could be argued that having children in the first place is a sacrifice of happiness for the sake of the evolution of our species but, as you now know, I think the addition of purpose to our experiences makes it less of a sacrifice. But beyond that, it feels as if I sometimes give up both pleasure and purpose for my kids' happiness, and Les definitely does. We are not especially self-sacrificing people, but we do care for our kids by attending to their happiness, and sometimes more than to our own.

I have no great desire to dig deeper into the underlying motivations for why people generally care for one another, since this has been done to death elsewhere. Suffice it to say here that it is generally to your evolutionary advantage to help other people on the assumption that, if roles were reversed, they would help you, too. Reciprocity — scratching someone else's back if they would scratch yours — is good for your survival; being completely selfish or completely selfless much less so.[39]

In 1984, Gerald Wilkinson set out to demonstrate this phenomenon among vampire bats. Vampire bats die quite quickly if they don't eat, reaching a dangerously low body weight in just twenty-four hours. Fortunately for them, they have the lovely habit of regurgitating blood into other vampire bats' mouths. Usually they do so into their relatives' mouths, but sometimes they share with non–family members. To find out whether reciprocal forces were operating among vampire bats, Wilkinson took nine mostly unrelated bats from California and put them in a small cage. Each evening, eight of the bats were allowed to feed and one bat had to go hungry. When the hungry bat was reintroduced into the group, some of the other bats would regurgitate into the starved bat's mouth, even though they weren't genetically related. Those who regurgitated were subsequently more likely to be fed by the bat they had previously fed when it was their turn to be left out of the evening feed.[40] Not all researchers agree that there is conclusive evidence to state that reciprocity operates among nonhuman animals, but you get the point. If vampire bats understand reciprocity, there is nothing stopping us.

It is certainly possible to care too much, though. Children who care for people in their household who are elderly, sick, or disabled are consequently less happy with their lives, more likely to be bullied, and do worse at school than their peers.[41] People who have dedicated their careers to caring for others in stressful situations, such as emergency care nurses and social workers, are at risk of overwhelming stress and burnout — an effect dubbed "compassion fatigue."[42] It is also possible that kindness could arouse suspicion in the recipients. For example, medical professionals are often suspicious that living organ donors who are not related to the organ recipient may be emotionally imbalanced. Even if they are related, there can still be lingering suspicions that their family is putting undue pressure on them to donate their organs.[43]

I will make the same point about your sacrifices of happiness for other people as I made about those sacrifices for yourself in the future. You need to be as confident as you can be that the sacrifice will be worth it: that those other people you care for so much really will be made happier from your own sacrifice. Fortunately, given that caring for others feels purposeful, you don't have to dwell too long on the "tough choices" of sacrifices and can focus instead on the "easier choices" of making yourself — and other people — happier.

Departures from Happiness

Since we generally get a little more pleasure and a whole lot more purpose out of our experiences when they are to the benefit of others as well as to ourselves, it's intriguing why we don't do more for others, especially those outside of our families and close friends. My strong suspicion is that we allow mistakes about the sources of happiness to get in the way of us doing more for others, such as the idea that personal spending will bring us more pleasure and purpose than prosocial spending. As evidence of this, people who heard about the experiment where participants were made happier by spending $20 on someone else rather than spending it on themselves thought it would have been the other way around.

We may also make mistaken projections when our attention is focused on a decision rather than its consequences. We focus on the financial difference between keeping $20 to spend on ourselves and giving it away by spending it on others rather than on the happiness we would experience from each of these actions. The label of the activity "helping others," does not lend itself to thinking about our own happiness, either; rather, it mistakenly focuses attention on how happy other people will be from our actions.

Perhaps you like to think of yourself as too busy to care more, when it really comes from not making the time rather than not having the time, as I argued earlier. Or perhaps you consider yourself to be a generous person when, in fact, you don't behave as generously as you think you do. And consistent with the fundamental attribution error I discussed in chapter 4, we might blame others' dispositions for how they are and therefore think that helping them will not make any difference.

For all these reasons, it is not surprising that research has shown that we have a "blind spot" for virtuousness.[44] We need to consider how to turn the blind spot into a "sight spot" that will help us spread some happiness around.

Decide

Given our proclivities to mistaken desires, projections, and beliefs, and recalling the discussion in chapter 5, you could look for feedback to ensure that your expectations more accurately match reality. Try reminding yourself about how happy you were the last time you were caring about or for others, and then use this information when thinking about what caring will be like in the future. You can see how a DRM might be helpful here. Even simply remembering instances of when we have been kind to others has been shown to increase how happy we say we are.[45]

You could also make salient the impact of your contribution to redistribution. A group of willing donors to UNICEF were randomly divided into two groups, one where they were told about the general priorities of the children's charity and the type of work it did, and one where they were specifically told about the impact of their donation, including the statement "every $10 collected purchases a bed net for a child in Africa." Larger donations were associated with greater life satisfaction among only those who received the specific information. Charitable giving seems to have the greatest impact on your happiness when it's clear to you where your money is going and who and how it will help.[46] So if you decide to give time or money, you'll reap more happiness if you know some of the specifics of how it'll help.

With deciding generally, if you make a note of the contexts within which you care about and for others, you can look to reinstate those contexts in the future. For example, if you find that your workaholic self is too busy to do more for others during a typical working week, you might decide to plan visits to your stressed-out sister on weekends or holidays, when you're more likely to experience happiness when giving her a hand. You might also consider not thinking too hard about it. In games where players can earn more money if everyone cooperates, the quicker people are asked to make decisions about their moves, the more likely they are to cooperate.[47]

Design

How can you design a better distributional landscape? Well, you could try to prime yourself with cues to encourage you to care more for others. Princeton students who were asked to write a list of the behavior, values, lifestyle, and appearance of their favorite superhero and were then introduced to a charitable campus organization volunteered twice as many hours to it than students who listed characteristics of their dorm rooms.[48] And a group of students from the University of Arizona donated more than twice as much change to an American educational charity after writing down thoughts and feelings about their own death as opposed to writing about dental pain, a result dubbed the "Scrooge effect."[49] So the next time you select a movie, new screen saver, or banking password, choose something that might nudge you to care for others more. One of my friends uses the name of a wandering monk, a character from a book that embodies altruism, as her banking password. It's up to you to experiment and choose what works for you.

Also bear in mind that your happiness will affect your charitable giving. Rob Metcalfe, Dani Navarro-Martinez, and I conducted an online experiment with people living in and around London. Participants earned money by completing a boring but demanding task involving moving as many sliders as possible to their midpoint in forty minutes. A randomly selected sample of participants were then told that they had done well on the task (irrespective of how well they had actually performed). At the end of the experiment, all participants were offered the chance to give some of their winnings to charity. You can guess what's coming, right? Those who were told they had done well gave considerably less to charity than those given no feedback (34 percent compared to 50 percent).[50] This suggests that donation behaviors depend on motivations to regulate the way we feel. When we feel good, we have less incentive to do good. Recall that this is an example of a permitting spillover. One way to create some benefit from this spillover is to give to charity when you are feeling less happy, which will give your happiness a boost.

You can set up defaults here, too. If you want to donate to charity to reduce inequalities you care about, select your favorites once and then set up a monthly direct debit that comes out on payday so you never miss the cash. Consider also the commitments you make. Deciding to end world hunger is a noble but lofty goal that may wind up making you more miserable than before because you can't attain it right now. Instead, make smaller and more manageable commitments, such as pledging to spend an afternoon at a soup kitchen. By caring for others like this you can work toward acting on the fact that you care about reducing inequalities. And remember that making your commitments public makes it more likely you will keep them.

Here as elsewhere, don't underestimate the power of social norms. A study on the Hadza hunter-gatherer society in Tanzania showed that people who were willing to donate sticks of honey to other adults in their camp were more likely to have friends who were willing to make donations, too. [51] Giving spreads. Another study in the UK showed that putting a smiley or frowny face on a postcard to reflect a street's recycling performance improved recycling rates overall by activating a social norm for recycling.[52]

Social norms for status have a particularly strong effect on caring about and for others. Overall, we should all seek to actively encourage what I will call *conspicuous caring* — or what Jan Abel Olsen and I have previously labeled "conspicuous altruism."[53] We were somewhat less embracing of it in our work, but I think that was a mistake. The evolution of my work has taught me that our motivations are less important than if we behave in ways that have good consequences. I care only about outcomes, and most specifically about the outcome of happiness. If we nudge people into caring about and for others and into being happier themselves by tapping into their concerns for how others perceive them, then all well and good. Conspicuous caring is similar to the well-established idea of conspicuous consumption, which is when people buy luxury items that display their wealth to other people.[54]

When the names of donors are displayed for donations with ranges of donation amounts, the majority of donors donate at exactly the lowest amount in a given range. Carnegie Mellon University publishes the names of donors who have given between $1,000 and $4,999 but does not specify what amount donors give. Almost 70 percent of these donations in 1988–89 were exactly $1,000. A similar policy operated for donations to the "Cameron Clan" at Carnegie Mellon, where the names of donors who had given between $500 and $999 were published. The average donation to this fund was $525. The Harvard Law School Fund had the same policy in 1993–94 and 93 percent of the donations were exactly $500.[55]

We are more likely to purchase environmentally friendly products when shopping in public as opposed to private, and we are more likely to give money to our community rather than keep it for ourselves when others know we're giving it away.[56] Princeton University students who can earn money for the Red Cross by clicking on a keyboard make many more clicks when they have to tell others how much they earned than if they do not.[57] We're also more generous when we are competing with other people about who can be the most generous — and more so than when we are competing for personal gain.[58]

All in all, I can get a sense of how rich you are from your job, where you live, the car you drive, and the clothes you wear. But I have no idea how generous you are unless you find some way of showing me. We should generally look to celebrate the ways in which we help other people a bit more, not in a "look at me, aren't I great" kind of way but in ways that make us all feel better off from the contributions that we each make. Charity might begin at home but it is encouraged by being shown.

Do
In terms of doing happiness, pay attention to those around you who have a small slice

of the cake and for whom you can do something, whether this is giving to charity, signing up to be a mentor for vulnerable teenagers, or simply listening to an unhappy friend. So that you pay attention to the happiness that comes from any charitable donations you make, look to get reminded of your donations through newsletters and e-mails from the charity.

You know that being with others helps you to feel good, so being charitable alone (e.g., by making online donations) will not be as conducive to your experiences of pleasure and purpose as doing so with other people. As we know from the American Time Use Survey, volunteering is associated with greater pleasure and purpose when done with someone else than when done alone. When caring about others by redistributing to reduce inequalities, consider making joint contributions with other people.

There is also some evidence that distraction can make it more likely for you to blame others for their misfortune. Imagine being asked to think about the level of compensation to award to a guy called Mike whose foot was broken when a light fixture fell on it at a baseball stadium — but when he was sitting in a seat that he had "stolen." If you were asked to read and recall a list of words while thinking about this judgment as compared to cracking straight on with determining the compensation, you would be more likely to give Mike less and blame him more if you had to recall the words after making the judgment.[59] Insofar as you think that being focused allows you to act the way you wish toward others, avoid being distracted when caring about and for them.

EFFICIENT PRODUCTION

Maybe you never procrastinate and perhaps you care about or for other people to just the right extent so far as your happiness is concerned. But whenever you think the allocation of your attention is out of kilter with being as happy as you can be, the three Ds can be used to help you find equilibrium. *Decide* will help you answer whatever question it is you have about your happiness, *design* will make it easier to implement the answer, and *do* will ensure your attentional resources are running smoothly. These are flexible principles that can be applied to all of your experiences in life.

CONCLUSION

It feels like we've taken quite a journey together. I hope it has been as pleasurable and purposeful for you as it has for me, and that you've learned something about how to attend to your happiness more effectively. I also hope that you have a little attentional energy left for some final reflections.

Happiness is all that matters in the end. When asked enough times why something matters, you will eventually end up by saying, "So that I can be happy."[1] Audrey Hepburn was spot-on when she said, "The most important thing is to enjoy your life — to be happy — it's all that matters." Moreover, we know that happiness causes a range of other good outcomes and that it's also contagious. The pursuit of happiness is therefore a noble and very serious objective for us all.

If you are going to pursue or improve something, it makes sense to be clear about what you are shooting at. Happiness has most often been measured by global evaluations of life satisfaction, but it should, in contrast, be measured according to your feelings over time. The evaluative self is largely constructed, and I agree with Daniel Kahneman that we give it too much of a voice in determining our behavior — more than we give to our experiencing self. If nothing else, I hope this book has convinced you to listen more to your real feelings of happiness than to your reflections on how happy you think you are or ought to be.

Recall that feelings are the sentiments of pleasure and purpose associated with an experience, rather than the more common but narrower definition of feelings as emotions only. We should all be seeking to maximize those sentiments from cradle to grave for ourselves and all those we care about. Policy makers should look to do likewise, properly accounting for the fact that we care about the suffering of the worst off in society. Love, life, and the universe are about the pleasure-purpose principle.

The PPP can also explain a lot of behavior that might otherwise seem a bit odd. Please allow me one last foray into the world of amateur bodybuilding. (I apologize but it's one of the three main aspects of my life, alongside my family and my work.) On the face of it, the competitions make no sense. These guys (and it is mostly guys) spend a long time training hard and eating lots of food to put as much size on as possible and then spend about three months dieting hard to keep as much muscle as possible while getting down to about 3 percent body fat. The final couple of weeks before competition are especially grueling: the endeavor to keep muscle and shed fat involves days of eating chicken and green beans over and over again. Then, in order to look pumped up onstage, the diet in the couple of days before competition consists of a jacket potato and an apple, alternated on the hour, every waking hour.

All of this for a few seconds onstage flexing your muscles, so tanned that you make the tango man look pasty and — best of all — wearing a very small thong. And all safe in the knowledge that you are unlikely to win; and even if you do, your prize will be a tacky trophy worth less than the cost of getting to the competition itself. But bodybuilding does make sense if you think in terms of the PPP over time. The dieting is only ever painful but it is simultaneously purposeful. There is purpose in pushing your body to its limits.

Sometimes, though, activities will be neither pleasurable nor purposeful. You may of course be willing to give up your own happiness now for happiness later or for the happiness of those whom you care about, but if you are not expecting to benefit from your current course of action, and don't expect others to, either, then the answer is actually quite straightforward — change course. As the old joke goes: "I went to the doctor the other day. I said, 'It hurts when I do that.' He said, 'Well, don't do it.' " Too often, I think, we treat happiness as if it is fungible — as if, like money, it can be moved around relatively easily. But while saving money for a rainy day that never comes is sad, giving up happiness now for later happiness that never comes is truly tragic.

The economist in me considers attention in terms of the allocation of a scarce resource. The psychologist in me recognizes that your attention will be unconsciously pulled around by specific contexts as well as being allocated consciously. There are many potential departures from being as happy as we can but the production process of happiness allows you to reallocate your attention to become happier by *deciding, designing,* and *doing.*

Take a look at this sentence and count the number of *f*'s in it: "Finished files are the result of years of scientific study combined with the experience of years." Did you count three, or perhaps six? There are six, but if you counted three, you are like most of the rest of us: our brains do not notice the *f* in *of*. Figuratively speaking, if paying attention to those three *f*'s (inputs into your happiness production process) were to make you miserable, then you would be wise to ignore them. But, equally, they might make you happier if only you noticed them. So you first need to pay careful attention to every word in the sentence (to every input into the production of happiness) and then to decide, design, and do your way to greater happiness by making it easier for you to pay attention to what makes you happier.

I have learned to deal with having a stammer in part by deciding to have realistic expectations about myself and my fluency, by designing my defaults and commitments in ways that force me to confront my speech problems, and by doing activities that stop my mind from wandering to exaggerated fears about my speech and other people's reactions to it. The impact of some of your own concerns in life might not be a million miles away from the impact of a stammer, and so the solutions to reorienting your attention in ways that make you happier might also be quite similar.

In general, you can see by now that it is a lot easier for you to nudge yourself happier in small but effective ways than it is to try to "shove" yourself into becoming a whole new person or into adopting a wildly different lifestyle. If you recognize that much of what you do is governed by contextology and not just your own internal psychology, you can approach situations that will make you happier and avoid those that will make you unhappy. We have some control over the situations we place ourselves in and much less control over our predisposition to act in particular ways once we are in those situations.

I've learned that the word "attention" comes from the Latin for "reach toward." I really hope you are now better placed to reach toward the ultimate prize of maximizing your happiness according to the PPP. You can reach toward it from this moment on. The more time you spend attending to the things that make you happy, the happier you will be. And stop doing things that make you miserable. Change what you do, not how you think. You are what you do, your happiness is what you attend to, and you should attend to what makes you and those whom you care about happy.

A GENTLE WARM-DOWN

Before you run off to get a coffee or something stronger, there is one more thing that I would like you to do. Remember the exercise at the beginning of the book? I'd like you to do it again. Well, sort of: now we can distinguish between pleasure and purpose.

So from the same list of twenty items you saw before, repeated on next page, what are the two that would bring you the most pleasure? What are the two that would bring you the most purpose? Whatever answers you gave and however they've changed from last time, I hope this book has helped you understand more clearly what will bring you pleasure on the one hand and purpose on the other.

Now, for each of the two items you chose for pleasure, please rate how difficult it would be to achieve it on a scale from 0 to 10, where 0 represents "not at all difficult" and 10 means "very difficult indeed." For each of the two items you chose for purpose, please rate how difficult it would be to achieve it, using the same scale. I'm really hoping that you now think that it is easier

		Bring me the most pleasure	Bring me the most purpose	Difficulty in achieving (0–10)
1	More money			
2	New experiences			
3	Children			
4	More time with the kids			
5	The kids leaving home			
6	A new partner			
7	More sleep			
8	More sex			
9	A shorter commute			
10	More time with friends			
11	A new house			
12	A new job			
13	A new boss			
14	New work colleagues			
15	More exercise			
16	To be healthier			
17	To be slimmer			
18	To stop smoking			
19	More holidays			
20	A pet			

to achieve those things that will bring you the most pleasure or purpose. Either that or you have been more ambitious in your choice of items.

We really are done now. Writing this book has made me, Professor Happy, very happy, and finishing it even more so. I hope that reading it has made a sentimental hedonist out of you and brought you a good dose of pleasure and purpose, and that you have many, many more happy experiences in your life. I have thought long and hard about how to finish this book, especially because, as we know, it might end up being your abiding memory of all that I have written. So let me just restate that future happiness cannot compensate for current misery; lost happiness is lost forever. Powered by your own supercharged attention production process, there is no better time than now to crack on with finding pleasure and purpose in everyday life.

ACKNOWLEDGMENTS

This is the bit where I say how I couldn't have done it on my own. That's actually not true because I could have written this book on my own — it just wouldn't have been very good. There are many people who have helped to make *Happiness by Design* a book that I am very proud of, and I hope they are proud to be associated with it. Here they are:

Main personal support: My wife, Les, who took the kids out many times so that I could get on with writing. Among her many qualities, she keeps my feet firmly on the ground and she makes me laugh.

Main intellectual inspiration: Danny Kahneman, who is simply the smartest and nicest man I have ever met.

Researcher extraordinaire: Laura Kudrna, who was always on the other end of the phone or e-mail to listen to my ramblings, to help make them more coherent, and then find research evidence that supported (and often disproved) them. She was also responsible for all the analysis of new data on pleasure and purpose reported in chapter 2. Her ability to work (almost) as intensely and thoroughly as me in the final stages was remarkable.

Invaluable research support: Liz Plank, who was with me from the beginning and who found so many interesting studies that acted as a catalyst for many of my ideas, and Kate Laffan, who turned around the analysis of the ONS data in record time.

Additional research support: Daniel Davis and Merata Snedden in the early days of this project.

Main academic collaborators, whose joint work with me informs much of what is in the book, and who also provided detailed comments: Rob Metcalfe, who has felt like my intellectual child since doing his PhD with me a few years ago, but who may well end up as more successful than his academic father (when I will no longer like him, of course); David Bradford, who is a brilliant economist and who reminds me that there is an economist still lurking in me somewhere; George Kavetsos and Matteo Galizzi, two very smart postdocs who are also two of the kindest people I have ever met;

Grace Lordan and Caroline Rudisill, two of LSE's finest and most helpful lecturers; and Ivo Vlaev, who is sometimes on a different planet but has some great ideas when he is on this one.

Main comment providers: Miguel Llabres Hargreaves, my best friend; Dixie Deane, my best training partner; Paula Skidmore, who came up with some great ideas about the exercises; Daniel Fujiwara, who is a great PhD student and a wizard with happiness data; Dom King and Henry Lee, two surgeons whose PhDs I have had the honor to supervise; Lisa Witter, whose comments on an earlier draft led to significant improvements; Oliver Harrison, who provided some really insightful comments; Chloe Foy, who inspired some last-minute improvements; Steve Martin, who helped with the initial pitch; and Helen Coyle, who pointed me in the right direction to begin with.

Special agent: That'll be Max Brockman, who helped me write the initial book proposal and get the deals, and who also remained calm every step of the way.

Editors with faith (in me): Christina Rodriguez and Alexis Kirschbaum, for supporting this project and for helping me present the material in a way that has a much better chance of resonating with you than if I had been left to my own devices.

Thank you all so very much. If you judge someone by the company they keep, then I am a truly wonderful person — or very lucky (lucky it is, then). You have all helped with happiness by design but, much more than that, you continue to bring me considerable pleasure and purpose in everyday life.

NOTES

Introduction

1. Gordon N. Stuttering: incidence and causes. *Developmental Medicine & Child Neurology* 2002; 44: 278–82.
2. Peters ML, Sorbi MJ, Kruise DA, Kerssens JJ, Verhaak PF, Bensing JM. Electronic diary assessment of pain, disability and psychological adaptation in patients differing in duration of pain. *Pain* 2000; 84: 181–92.
3. James W. Does consciousness exist? In: The William James reader: vol. 1. Wilder Publications, 1898.
4. Currie J, Vigna SD, Moretti E, Pathania V. The effect of fast food restaurants on obesity and weight gain. *American Economic Journal: Economic Policy* 2010; 2: 32–63.
5. Mazar N, Amir O, Ariely D. The dishonesty of honest people: a theory of self-

concept maintenance. *Journal of Marketing Research* 2008; 45: 633–44.

1. What Is Happiness?

1. Kahneman D, Riis J. Living, and thinking about it: two perspectives on life. *Science of Well-Being* 2005: 285–304.
2. Clark AE. What really matters in a job? Hedonic measurement using quit data. *Labour Economics* 2001; 8: 223–42; Hirschberger G, Srivastava S, Marsh P, Cowan CP, Cowan PA. Attachment, marital satisfaction, and divorce during the first fifteen years of parenthood. *Personal Relationships* 2009; 16: 401–20.
3. Feldman F. Pleasure and the good life: concerning the nature, varieties, and plausibility of hedonism. Oxford University Press, 2004; Haybron DM. The pursuit of unhappiness: the elusive psychology of well-being. Oxford University Press, 2008.
4. Vitterso J, Oelmann HI, Wang AL. Life satisfaction is not a balanced estimator of the good life: evidence from reaction time measures and self-reported emotions. *Journal of Happiness Studies* 2009; 10: 1–17.
5. Deaton A. The financial crisis and the

well-being of Americans: 2011 OEP Hicks Lecture. *Oxford Economic Papers* 2011; 64: 1–26.

6. Schwarz N, Strack F, Mai H-P. Assimilation and contrast effects in part-whole question sequences: a conversational logic analysis. *Public Opinion Quarterly* 1991; 55: 3–23.

7. Watson D, Tellegen A. Toward a consensual structure of mood. *Psychological Bulletin* 1985; 98: 219–35.

8. Kahneman D, Deaton A. High income improves evaluation of life but not emotional well-being. *Proceedings of the National Academy of Sciences* 2010; 107: 16489–93.

9. Bentham J. An introduction to the principles of morals and legislation. Oxford University Press, 1907.

10. Watson D, Tellegen A. Toward a consensual structure of mood. *Psychological Bulletin* 1985; 98: 219–35.

11. Mauss I, Wilhelm F, Gross J. Is there less to social anxiety than meets the eye? Emotion experience, expression, and bodily responding. *Cognition & Emotion* 2004; 18: 631–42.

12. Oliver MB, Hartmann T. Exploring the role of meaningful experiences in users' appreciation of good movies. *Projections*

2010; 4: 128–50.

13. Ryff CD. Psychological well-being in adult life. *Current Directions in Psychological Science* 1995; 4: 99–104.

14. Nelson SK, Kushlev K, English T, Dunn EW, Lyubomirsky S. In defense of parenthood: children are associated with more joy than misery. *Psychological Science* 2013; 24: 3–10.

15. Dolan P, Metcalfe R. Comparing measures of subjective well-being and views about the role they should play in policy. Office for National Statistics, 2011.

16. Vitaglione GD, Barnett MA. Assessing a new dimension of empathy: empathic anger as a predictor of helping and punishing desires. *Motivation and Emotion* 2003; 27: 301–25; Harmon-Jones E, Harmon-Jones C, Price TF. What is approach motivation? *Emotion Review* 2013; 5: 291–95.

17. Hopfensitz A, Reuben E. The importance of emotions for the effectiveness of social punishment. *Economic Journal* 2009; 119: 1534–59.

18. Hansen T. Parenthood and happiness: a review of folk theories versus empirical evidence. *Social Indicators Research* 2012; 108: 29–64.

19. Kirchgessner M, Vlaev I, Rutledge R,

Dolan P, Sharot T. Happiness in action: using measures of pleasure and purpose to predict choice. Under review, 2013.

20. Einstein A. Relativity: the special and general theory. Henry Holt, 1920.

21. O'Brien EH, Anastasio PA, Bushman BJ. Time crawls when you're not having fun: feeling entitled makes dull tasks drag on. *Personality and Social Psychology Bulletin* 2011; 37: 1287–96; Eastwood JD, Frischen A, Fenske MJ, Smilek D. The unengaged mind: defining boredom in terms of attention. *Perspectives on Psychological Science* 2012; 7: 482–95.

22. Harris C, Laibson D. Instantaneous gratification. *Quarterly Journal of Economics* 2013; 128: 205–48.

23. Dehaene S. The neural basis of the Weber–Fechner law: a logarithmic mental number line. *Trends in Cognitive Sciences* 2003; 7: 145–47.

24. Guven C, Senik C, Stichnoth H. You can't be happier than your wife. Happiness gaps and divorce. *Journal of Economic Behavior & Organization* 2012; 82: 110–30.

25. Proto E, Sgroi D, Oswald AJ. Are happiness and productivity lower among young people with newly-divorced par-

ents? An experimental and econometric approach. *Experimental Economics* 2012; 15: 1–23.

26. Hinks T, Katsoris A. Smoking ban and life satisfaction: evidence from the UK. *Economic Issues* 2012; 17: 23–48.

27. Roese NJ, Summerville A. What we regret most . . . and why. *Personality and Social Psychology Bulletin* 2005; 31: 1273–85; Zeelenberg M, Van den Bos K, Van Dijk E, Pieters RGM. The inaction effect in the psychology of regret. *Journal of Personality and Social Psychology* 2002; 82: 314–27.

28. Kivetz R, Keinan A. Repenting hyperopia: an analysis of self-control regrets. *Journal of Consumer Research* 2006; 33: 273–82.

29. Wittgenstein L. Philosophical investigations, 4th edition. Wiley-Blackwell, 2009.

30. Russell B. Autobiography. Routledge, 1998.

2. What Do We Know about Happiness?

1. Scollon CN, Kim-Prieto C, Diener E. Experience sampling: promises and pitfalls, strengths and weaknesses. *Journal of Happiness Studies* 2003; 4: 5–34.

2. Kahneman D, Krueger AB, Schkade DA, Schwarz N, Stone AA. A survey method for characterizing daily life experience: the day reconstruction method. *Science* 2004; 306: 1776–80.

3. White MP, Dolan P. Accounting for the richness of daily activities. *Psychological Science* 2009; 20: 1000–1008.

4. Csikszentmihalyi M, Hunter J. Happiness in everyday life: the uses of experience sampling. *Journal of Happiness Studies* 2003; 4: 185–99; Dimotakis N, Scott BA, Koopman J. An experience sampling investigation of workplace interactions, affective states, and employee well-being. *Journal of Organizational Behavior* 2011; 32: 572–88.

5. Anxo D, Mencarini L, Pailhé A, Solaz A, Tanturri ML, Flood L. Gender differences in time use over the life course in France, Italy, Sweden, and the US. *Feminist Economics* 2011; 17: 159–95.

6. Verbrugge LM, Gruber-Baldini AL, Fozard JL. Age differences and age changes in activities: Baltimore longitudinal study of aging. *Journal of Gerontology B: Psychological and Social Sciences* 1996; 51B: S30–S41.

7. Hamermesh DS, Lee J. Stressed out on four continents: time crunch or yuppie

kvetch? *Review of Economics and Statistics* 2007; 89: 374–83.

8. Dolan P, Peasgood T, White M. Do we really know what makes us happy? A review of the economic literature on the factors associated with subjective well-being. *Journal of Economic Psychology* 2008; 29: 94–122.

9. Layard R, Mayraz G, Nickell S. The marginal utility of income. *Journal of Public Economics* 2008; 92: 1846–57.

10. Fujiwara D. Valuing the impact of adult learning. NIACE Research Paper, 2012.

11. Schwandt H. Unmet aspirations as an explanation for the age U-shape in human wellbeing. Centre for Economic Performance, CEP Discussion Paper No. 1229, 2013.

12. Deaton A, Stone AA. Grandpa and the snapper: the wellbeing of the elderly who live with children. National Bureau of Economic Research, 2013.

13. Frijters P, Beatton T. The mystery of the U-shaped relationship between happiness and age. *Journal of Economic Behavior & Organization* 2012; 82: 525–42.

14. Peasgood T. Measuring wellbeing for public policy. Imperial College London, 2008; Oishi S, Diener E, Lucas R. The optimum level of well-being: can people

be too happy? *Perspectives on Psychological Science* 2007; 2: 346–60.

15. Eichhorn J. Happiness for believers? Contextualizing the effects of religiosity on life-satisfaction. *European Sociological Review* 2012; 28: 583–93.

16. Schimmack U, Oishi S, Furr RM, Funder DC. Personality and life satisfaction: a facet-level analysis. *Personality and Social Psychology Bulletin* 2004; 30: 1062–75.

17. Sutin A, Costa Jr P, Wethington E, Eaton W. Turning points and lessons learned: stressful life events and personality trait development across middle adulthood. *Psychology and Aging* 2010; 25: 524–33.

18. Oswald AJ, Powdthavee N. Does happiness adapt? A longitudinal study of disability with implications for economists and judges. *Journal of Public Economics* 2008; 92: 1061–77; Lucas RE. Adaptation and the set-point model of subjective well-being: does happiness change after major life events? *Current Directions in Psychological Science* 2007; 16: 75–79.

19. Lucas RE, Clark AE, Georgellis Y, Diener E. Reexamining adaptation and the set point model of happiness: reactions to

changes in marital status. *Journal of Personality and Social Psychology* 2003; 84: 527.

20. Dolan P, Layard R, Metcalfe R. Measuring subjective well-being for public policy. Office for National Statistics, 2011.

21. First ONS annual experimental subjective well-being results. Office for National Statistics, 2012.

22. Stevenson BA, Wolfers J. Paradox of declining female happiness. *American Law & Economics Association Annual Meetings,* Paper 107, 2008.

23. How's life? measuring well-being, OECD Publishing, 2011: http://dx.doi.org/10.1787/9789264121164-en.

24. Dolan P, Kavetsos G. Happy talk: mode of administration effects on subjective well-being. Centre for Economic Performance, CEP Discussion Paper No. 1159, 2012.

25. Deaton A, Arora R. Life at the top: the benefits of height. *Economics & Human Biology* 2009; 7: 133–36.

26. Hosoda M, Stone-Romero EF, Coats G. The effects of physical attractiveness on job-related outcomes: a meta-analysis of experimental studies. *Personnel Psychology* 2003; 56: 431–62.

27. Krueger AB, Mueller AI. Time use, emotional well-being, and unemployment: evidence from longitudinal data. *American Economic Review* 2012; 102: 594–99; Knabe A, Rätzel S, Schöb R, Weimann J. Dissatisfied with life but having a good day: time-use and well-being of the unemployed. *Economic Journal* 2010; 120: 867–89.

28. Weiss A, King JE, Inoue-Murayama M, Matsuzawa T, Oswald AJ. Evidence for a midlife crisis in great apes consistent with the U-shape in human well-being. *Proceedings of the National Academy of Sciences* 2012; 109: 19949–52.

29. O'Brien E, Konrath SH, Grühn D, Hagen AL. Empathic concern and perspective taking: linear and quadratic effects of age across the adult life span. *Journal of Gerontology B: Psychological and Social Sciences* 2013; 68: 168–75.

30. Stone AA, Schwartz JE, Broderick JE, Deaton A. A snapshot of the age distribution of psychological well-being in the United States. *Proceedings of the National Academy of Sciences* 2010; 107: 9985–90.

31. Carstensen LL, Turan B, Scheibe S, et al. Emotional experience improves with age: evidence based on over 10 years of

experience sampling. *Psychology and Aging* 2011; 26: 21–33.
32. Dolan P, Kudrna L. More years, less yawns: fresh evidence on tiredness by age and other factors. *Journal of Gerontology B: Psychological and Social Sciences* 2013.

3. What Causes Happiness?

1. Ockham W. Philosophical writings: a selection. Hackett, 1990.
2. DellaVigna S. Psychology and economics: evidence from the field. *Journal of Economic Literature* 2009; 47: 315–72.
3. Hossain T, Morgan J. . . . Plus shipping and handling: revenue (non) equivalence in field experiments on eBay. *Advances in Economic Analysis & Policy* 2006; 5.
4. Davenport TH, Beck JC. The attention economy: understanding the new currency of business. Harvard Business Press, 2002.
5. Kaplan S, Berman MG. Directed attention as a common resource for executive functioning and self-regulation. *Perspectives on Psychological Science* 2010; 5: 43–57.
6. Maguire EA, Gadian DG, Johnsrude IS, et al. Navigation-related structural change in the hippocampi of taxi drivers. *Proceed-*

ings of the National Academy of Sciences 2000; 97: 4398–4403.

7. Chabris C, Simons D. The invisible gorilla: and other ways our intuition deceives us. HarperCollins, 2011.

8. Drew T, Võ ML-H, Wolfe JM. The invisible gorilla strikes again: sustained inattentional blindness in expert observers. *Psychological Science* 2013.

9. Haynes A, Weiser T, Berry W, Lipsitz S, Breizat A, Dellinger E, Herbosa T, et al. A surgical safety checklist to reduce morbidity and mortality in a global population. *New England Journal of Medicine* 2009; 360: 491–99.

10. Harmer M. The case of Elaine Bromiley: independent review on the care given to Mrs Elaine Bromiley on 29 March 2005. Clinical Human Factors Group, 2005.

11. Stanton NA, Young MS. Driver behaviour with adaptive cruise control. *Ergonomics* 2005; 48: 1294–1313; Vahidi A, Eskandarian A. Research advances in intelligent collision avoidance and adaptive cruise control. *IEEE Transactions on Intelligent Transportation Systems* 2003; 4: 143–53.

12. Laycock T. Mind and brain. Sutherland & Knox, 1860.

13. Dijksterhuis A, Nordgren LF. A theory of unconscious thought. *Perspectives on Psychological Science* 2006; 1: 95–109.
14. Kahneman D. Thinking, fast and slow. Penguin, 2011.
15. Ritzer G. The McDonaldization of society. Pine Forge Press, 2010.
16. Zhong CB, DeVoe SE. You are how you eat: fast food and impatience. *Psychological Science* 2010; 21: 619–22.
17. Hill RA, Barton RA. Psychology: red enhances human performance in contests. *Nature* 2005; 435: 293.
18 North AC, Hargreaves DJ, McKendrick J. The influence of in-store music on wine selections. *Journal of Applied Psychology* 1999; 84: 271.
19. Alter A. Drunk tank pink: and other unexpected forces that shape how we think, feel, and behave. Penguin, 2013.
20. Bojinov H, Sanchez D, Reber P, Boneh D, Lincoln P. Neuroscience meets cryptography: designing crypto primitives secure against rubber hose attacks. *Proceedings of the 21st USENIX Security Symposium* 2012: 129–41.
21. Bargh JA. The automaticity of everyday life. Lawrence Erlbaum, 1997.
22. Wilson T. Strangers to ourselves: discov-

ering the adaptive unconscious. Harvard University Press, 2002.

23. Lally P, Gardner B. Promoting habit formation. *Health Psychology Review* 2013; 7: S137–S158.

24. Margolis SV. Authenticating ancient marble sculpture. *Scientific American* 1989; 260: 104–10; Gladwell M. Blink: the power of thinking without thinking. Penguin, 2006.

25. Genakos C, Pagliero M. Risk taking and performance in multistage tournaments: evidence from weightlifting competitions. Centre for Economic Performance, CEP Discussion Paper No. 928, 2009.

26. Stroop JR. Studies of interference in serial verbal reactions. *Journal of Experimental Psychology* 1935; 18: 643.

27. MacLeod CM. Half a century of research on the Stroop effect: an integrative review. *Psychological Bulletin* 1991; 109: 163.

28. Tuk MA, Trampe D, Warlop L. Inhibitory spillover increased urination urgency facilitates impulse control in unrelated domains. *Psychological Science* 2011; 22: 627–33.

29. Dolan P, Galizzi M. Because I'm worth it: experimental evidence on the spill-over effects of incentives. Centre for the Study

of Incentives in Health. In press.

30. Mallam KM. Contribution of time-tabled physical education to total physical activity in primary school children: cross sectional study. *British Medical Journal* 2003; 327: 592–93.

31. Metcalf B. Physical activity cost of the school run: impact on schoolchildren of being driven to school (EarlyBird 22). *British Medical Journal* 2004; 329: 832–33.

32. Monin B, Miller DT. Moral credentials and the expression of prejudice. *Journal of Personality and Social Psychology* 2001; 81: 33–43.

33. Effron DA, Cameron JS, Monin B. Endorsing Obama licenses favoring whites. *Journal of Experimental Social Psychology* 2009; 45: 590–93.

34. Zhong CB, Liljenquist K. Washing away your sins: threatened morality and physical cleansing. *Science* 2006; 313: 1451–52.

35. Kahneman D, Thaler RH. Anomalies: utility maximization and experienced utility. *Journal of Economic Perspectives* 2006; 20: 221–34.

36. Metcalfe R, Powdthavee N, Dolan P. Destruction and distress: using a quasi-experiment to show the effects of the September 11 attacks on mental well-

being in the United Kingdom. *Economic Journal* 2011; 121: F81–F103.

37. Schkade DA, Kahneman D. Does living in California make people happy? A focusing illusion in judgments of life satisfaction. *Psychological Science* 1998; 9: 340–46.

38. Bradford WD, Dolan P. Getting used to it: the adaptive global utility model. *Journal of Health Economics* 2010; 29: 811–20.

39. Oswald AJ, Powdthavee N. Obesity, unhappiness, and the challenge of affluence: theory and evidence. *Economic Journal* 2007; 117: 441–14.

40. Samaan Z, Anand S, Zhang X, et al. The protective effect of the obesity-associated rs9939609: a variant in fat mass- and obesity-associated gene on depression. *Molecular Psychiatry,* 2012.

41. Katsaiti MS. Obesity and happiness. *Applied Economics* 2012; 44: 4101–14.

42. Graham C, Felton A. Variance in obesity across countries and cohorts. Unpublished working paper, 2007.

43. Gilbert DT, Pinel EC, Wilson TD, Blumberg SJ, Wheatley TP. Immune neglect: a source of durability bias in affective forecasting. *Journal of Personality and*

Social Psychology 1998; 75: 617; Wilson TD, Gilbert DT. Affective forecasting. *Advances in Experimental Social Psychology* 2003; 35: 345–411.

44. Schaller M, Miller GE, Gervais WM, Yager S, Chen E. Mere visual perception of other people's disease symptoms facilitates a more aggressive immune response. *Psychological Science* 2010; 21: 649–52.

45. Di Tella R, Haisken-De New J, Mac-Culloch R. Happiness adaptation to income and to status in an individual panel. *Journal of Economic Behavior & Organization* 2010; 76: 834–52.

46. Dolan P, Powdthavee N. Thinking about it: a note on attention and well-being losses from unemployment. *Applied Economics Letters* 2012; 19: 325–28.

47. Weinstein ND. Community noise problems: evidence against adaptation. *Journal of Environmental Psychology* 1982; 2: 87–97.

48. Cohen S, Glass DC, Singer JE. Apartment noise, auditory discrimination, and reading ability in children. *Journal of experimental social psychology* 1973; 9: 407–22.

49. Passàli GC, Ralli M, Galli J, Calò L, Paludetti G. How relevant is the impair-

ment of smell for the quality of life in allergic rhinitis? *Current Opinion in Allergy and Clinical Immunology* 2008; 8: 238–42.

50. Wilson TD, Gilbert DT. Explaining away: a model of affective adaptation. *Perspectives on Psychological Science* 2008; 3: 370–86.

51. Dolan P, Selya-Hammer C, Bridge JA, Kudrna L. The impact of cancer on the preferences and subjective wellbeing of patients and their carer. Under review, 2013.

52. Wiggins S, Whyte P, Huggins M, et al. The psychological consequences of predictive testing for Huntington's disease. *New England Journal of Medicine* 1992; 327: 1401–5.

53. Gardner, J, Oswald A. Do divorcing couples become happier by breaking up? *Journal of the Royal Statistical Society: Series A (Statistics in Society)* 2006; 169: 319–36.

54. Loewenstein G, Thaler RH. Anomalies: intertemporal choice. *Journal of Economic Perspectives* 1989; 3: 181–93.

55. Loewenstein G. Anticipation and the valuation of delayed consumption. *Economic Journal* 1987; 97: 666–84.

56. Forrest D, Simmons R. Outcome uncer-

tainty and attendance demand in sport: the case of English soccer. *Journal of the Royal Statistical Society: Series D (The Statistician)* 2002; 51: 229–41.

4. Why Aren't We Happier?

1. Benjamin DJ, Heffetz O, Kimball MS, Rees-Jones A. What do you think would make you happier? What do you think you would choose? *American Economic Review* 2012; 102: 2083–2110.
2. Benjamin DJ, Heffetz O, Kimball MS, Rees-Jones A. Do people seek to maximize happiness? Evidence from new surveys. National Bureau of Economic Research, 2010.
3. Koepp MJ, Gunn RN, Lawrence AD, et al. Evidence for striatal dopamine release during a video game. *Nature* 1998; 393: 266–68.
4. Nickerson C, Schwarz N, Diener E, Kahneman D. Zeroing in on the dark side of the American dream: a closer look at the negative consequences of the goal for financial success. *Psychological Science* 2003; 14: 531–36.
5. Translated and as it appears in Coelho, Paulo. (2010) The fisherman and the businessman. Paulo Coelho's Blog.

[online] http://paulocoelhoblog.com/2010/09/08/the-fisherman-and-the-business man.

6. Akerlof GA, Kranton RE. Economics and identity. *Quarterly Journal of Economics* 2000; 115: 715–53.

7. Loewenstein G. Because it is there: the challenge of mountaineering . . . for utility theory. *Kyklos* 1999; 52: 315–43.

8. Medvec VH, Madey SF, Gilovich T. When less is more: counterfactual thinking and satisfaction among Olympic medalists. *Journal of Personality and Social Psychology* 1995; 69: 603.

9. Dockery AM. The happiness of young Australians: empirical evidence on the role of labour market experience. *Economic Record* 2005; 81: 322–35.

10. Career Happiness Index 2012:| City & Guilds. http://www.cityandguilds.com/About-Us/Broadsheet-News/November-2012/Careers-Happiness-Index-2012.

11. Nozick R. Anarchy, state, and utopia. Basic Books, 1977.

12. Dolan P. Happiness questions and government responses: a pilot study of what the general public makes of it all. *Revue d'économie politique* 2011; 121: 3–15.

13. Dolan P, White MP. How can measures

of subjective well-being be used to inform public policy? *Perspectives on Psychological Science* 2007; 2: 71–85.

14. Dolan P, Peasgood T. Measuring well-being for public policy: preferences or experiences? *Journal of Legal Studies* 2008; 37: S5–S31.

15. Crisp R. Hedonism reconsidered. *Philosophy and Phenomenological Research* 2006; 73: 619–45.

16. Dolan P, Peasgood T. Measuring well-being for public policy: preferences or experiences? *Journal of Legal Studies* 2008; 37: S5–S31.

17. Cohen S, Doyle WJ, Turner RB, Alper CM, Skoner DP. Emotional style and susceptibility to the common cold. *Psychosomatic Medicine* 2003; 65: 652–57.

18. Neve J-ED, Oswald AJ. Estimating the influence of life satisfaction and positive affect on later income using sibling fixed effects. *Proceedings of the National Academy of Sciences* 2012; 109: 19953–58.

19. Lyubomirsky S, King L, Diener E. The benefits of frequent positive affect: does happiness lead to success? *Psychological Bulletin* 2005; 131: 803–55.

20. Golle J, Mast FW, Lobmaier JS. Something to smile about: the interrelationship

between attractiveness and emotional expression. *Cognition & Emotion* 2013: 1–13; Ritts V, Patterson ML, Tubbs ME. Expectations, impressions, and judgments of physically attractive students: a review. *Review of Educational Research* 1992; 62: 413–26; Hamermesh D, Biddle J. Beauty and the labor market. *American Economic Review* 1994; 84: 1174–94.

21. Pinquart M. Creating and maintaining purpose in life in old age: a meta-analysis. *Ageing International* 2002; 27: 90–114.

22. Siegenthaler KL, O'Dell I. Older golfers: serious leisure and successful aging. *World Leisure Journal* 2003; 45: 45–52; Whaley DE, Ebbeck V. Self-schemata and exercise identity in older adults. *Journal of Aging and Physical Activity* 2002; 10: 245–59.

23. Hackman JR, Oldham G, Janson R, Purdy K. A new strategy for job enrichment. *California Management Review* 1975; 17: 57–71; Steger MF, Dik BJ, Duffy RD. Measuring meaningful work: the work and meaning inventory (WAMI). *Journal of Career Assessment* 2012; 20: 322–37.

24. Wegner L, Flisher AJ, Chikobvu P, Lombard C, King G. Leisure boredom and high school dropout in Cape Town,

South Africa. *Journal of Adolescence* 2008; 31: 421–31.

25. Tsapelas I, Aron A, Orbuch T. Marital boredom now predicts less satisfaction nine years later. *Psychological Science* 2009; 20: 543–45.

26. Schkade DA, Kahneman D. Does living in California make people happy? A focusing illusion in judgments of life satisfaction. *Psychological Science* 1998; 9: 340–46.

27. Kahneman D. Thinking, fast and slow. Penguin, 2011.

28. Xu J, Schwarz N. How do you feel while driving your car? Depends on how you think about it. Unpublished working paper, 2006.

29. Dolan P, Gudex C, Kind P, Williams A. The time trade-off method: results from a general population study. *Health Economics* 1996; 5: 141–54.

30. Dolan P. Modelling valuations for Euro-Qol health states. *Medical Care* 1997; 35: 1095–1108.

31. Dolan P. Using happiness to value health. Office of Health Economics, 2011.

32. Dolan P, Loomes G, Peasgood T, Tsuchiya A. Estimating the intangible victim costs of violent crime. *British Journal of Criminology* 2005; 45: 958–76.

33. Dolan P, Kahneman D. Interpretations of utility and their implications for the valuation of health. *Economic Journal* 2008; 118: 215–34.
34. Shaw JW, Johnson JA, Coons SJ. US valuation of the EQ-5D health states: development and testing of the D1 valuation model. *Medical Care* 2005; 43: 203–20.
35. Dolan P, Metcalfe R. Valuing health: a brief report on subjective well-being versus preferences. *Medical Decision Making* 2012; 32: 578–82.
36. Menzel P, Dolan P, Richardson J, Olsen JA. The role of adaptation to disability and disease in health state valuation: a preliminary normative analysis. *Social Science & Medicine* 2002; 55: 2149–58.
37. Dolan P, Kavetsos G, Tsuchiya A. Sick but satisfied: the impact of life and health satisfaction on choice between health scenarios. *Journal of Health Economics* 2013; 32: 708–14.
38. Smith A. The theory of moral sentiments. Strahan, 1759.
39. Dolan P, Metcalfe R. "Oops . . . I did it again": repeated focusing effects in reports of happiness. *Journal of Economic Psychology* 2010; 31: 732–37.
40. Distinction bias: misprediction and mis-

choice due to joint evaluation. *Journal of Personality and Social Psychology* 2004; 86: 680.

41. Loewenstein G, O'Donoghue T, Rabin M. Projection bias in predicting future utility. *Quarterly Journal of Economics* 2003; 118: 1209–48.

42. Dutton DG, Aron AP. Some evidence for heightened sexual attraction under conditions of high anxiety. *Journal of Personality and Social Psychology* 1974; 30: 510–17.

43. Simonsohn U. Weather to go to college. *Economic Journal* 2010; 120: 270–80.

44. Conlin M, O'Donoghue T, Vogelsang TJ. Projection bias in catalog orders. *American Economic Review* 2007; 97: 1217–49.

45. Read D, van Leeuwen B. Predicting hunger: the effects of appetite and delay on choice. *Organizational Behavior and Human Decision Processes* 1998; 76: 189–205.

46. Chochinov HM, Tataryn D, Clinch JJ, Dudgeon D. Will to live in the terminally ill. *Lancet* 1999; 354: 816–19.

47. Baumeister RF, Vohs KD, DeWall CN, Zhang L. How emotion shapes behavior: feedback, anticipation, and reflection,

rather than direct causation. *Personality and Social Psychology Review* 2007; 11: 167–203.

48. Bar-Hillel M, Neter E. Why are people reluctant to exchange lottery tickets? *Journal of Personality and Social Psychology* 1996; 70: 17.

49. Gilbert DT, Morewedge CK, Risen JL, Wilson TD. Looking forward to looking back: the misprediction of regret. *Psychological Science* 2004; 15: 346–50.

50. Kahneman D, Wakker PP, Sarin R. Back to Bentham? Explorations of experienced utility. *Quarterly Journal of Economics* 1997; 112: 375–406.

51. Fredrickson BL, Kahneman D. Duration neglect in retrospective evaluations of affective episodes. *Journal of Personality and Social Psychology* 1993; 65: 45.

52. Wakin D. Ringing finally ended, but there's no button to stop shame. *New York Times,* Jan. 12, 2012.

53. Clark AE, Georgellis Y. Kahneman meets the quitters: peak-end behaviour in the labour market. Unpublished working paper, 2004.

54. Nickerson RS. Confirmation bias: a ubiquitous phenomenon in many guises.

Review of General Psychology 1998; 2: 175.

55. Mahoney MJ. Publication prejudices: an experimental study of confirmatory bias in the peer review system. *Cognitive Therapy and Research* 1977; 1: 161–75.

56. Ross L. The intuitive psychologist and his shortcomings: distortions in the attribution process. *Advances in Experimental Social Psychology* 1977; 10: 173–220.

57. Gilbert DT, Malone PS. The correspondence bias. *Psychological Bulletin* 1995; 117: 21.

58. Ouellette JA, Wood W. Habit and intention in everyday life: the multiple processes by which past behavior predicts future behavior. *Psychological Bulletin* 1998; 124: 54.

59. Webb TL, Sheeran P. Does changing behavioral intentions engender behavior change? A meta-analysis of the experimental evidence. *Psychological Bulletin* 2006; 132: 249–68; Astell-Burt T, Feng X, Kolt GS. Greener neighborhoods, slimmer people? Evidence from 246,920 Australians. *International Journal of Obesity* 2013.

60. Frijters P. Do individuals try to maximize general satisfaction? *Journal of Economic Psychology* 2000; 21: 281–304.

61. Festinger L. A theory of cognitive dis-

sonance. Stanford University Press, 1957.

62. Festinger L, Carlsmith JM. Cognitive consequences of forced compliance. *Journal of Abnormal and Social Psychology* 1959; 58: 203–10.

63. Masataka N, Perlovsky L. Music can reduce cognitive dissonance. *Nature Precedings* 2012; Knox R, Inkster J. Postdecision dissonance at post time. *Journal of Personality and Social Psychology* 1968; 8: 319–23; Foster JD, Misra TA. It did not mean anything (about me): cognitive dissonance theory and the cognitive and affective consequences of romantic infidelity. *Journal of Social and Personal Relationships* 2013.

64. Mullainathan S, Washington E. Sticking with your vote: cognitive dissonance and political attitudes. *American Economic Journal: Applied Economics* 2009; 1: 86–111.

65. Aizer A, Dal Bo P. Love, hate and murder: commitment devices in violent relationships. *Journal of Public Economics* 2009; 93: 412–28.

66. Dolan P, Lordan G. Moving up and sliding down: an empirical assessment of the effect of social mobility on subjective wellbeing. Centre for Economic Perfor-

mance, CEP Discussion Paper No. 1190, 2013.

67. Graham C, Pettinato S. Frustrated achievers: winners, losers and subjective well-being in new market economies. *Journal of Development Studies* 2002; 38: 100–140.

68. May DR, Gilson RL, Harter LM. The psychological conditions of meaningfulness, safety and availability and the engagement of the human spirit at work. *Journal of Occupational and Organizational Psychology* 2004; 77: 11–37.

69. Schooler J, Ariely D, Loewenstein G. The pursuit and assessment of happiness. In: Brocas I, Carrillo JD, eds. The psychology of economic decisions: vol. 1: rationality and wellbeing. Oxford University Press, 2003.

70. Polivy J, Herman CP. The false-hope syndrome: unfulfilled expectations of self-change. *Current Directions in Psychological Science* 2000; 9: 128–31.

71. Sharot T. The optimism bias: why we're wired to look on the bright side. Constable & Robinson, 2012.

72. Joule R-V, Girandola F, Bernard F. How can people be induced to willingly change their behavior? The path from persuasive communication to binding communica-

tion. *Social and Personality Psychology Compass* 2007; 1: 493–505.

73. Wegner DM, Schneider DJ, Carter SR, White TL. Paradoxical effects of thought suppression. *Journal of Personality and Social Psychology* 1987; 53: 5–13.

74. Hosser D, Windzio M, Greve W. Guilt and shame as predictors of recidivism: a longitudinal study with young prisoners. *Criminal Justice and Behavior* 2008; 35: 138–52.

75. Sifton E. The serenity prayer: faith and politics in times of peace and war. W. W. Norton, 2005.

76. Dennett DC. Intuition pumps and other tools for thinking. Penguin, 2013.

77. Shakespeare W. Macbeth, annotated edition. Wordsworth Editions, 1992.

5. Deciding Happiness

1. Hughes JR, Higgins ST. Nicotine withdrawal versus other drug withdrawal syndromes: similarities and dissimilarities. *Addiction* 1994; 89: 1461–70.

2. Richardson CR, Newton TL, Abraham JJ, Sen A, Jimbo M, Swartz AM. A meta-analysis of pedometer based walking interventions and weight loss. *Annals of Family Medicine* 2008; 6: 69–77.

3. Glynn LG, Murphy AW, Smith SM, Schroeder K, Fahey T. Interventions used to improve control of blood pressure in patients with hypertension. In: The Cochrane Collaboration, Glynn LG, eds. Cochrane Database of Systematic Reviews. John Wiley & Sons, 2010.

4. Wisdom J, Downs JS, Loewenstein G. Promoting healthy choices: information versus convenience. *American Economic Journal: Applied Economics* 2010; 2: 164–78.

5. Wing RR, Tate DF, Gorin AA, Raynor HA, Fava JL. A self-regulation program for maintenance of weight loss. *New England Journal of Medicine* 2006; 355: 1563–71.

6. Stice E, Yokum S, Blum K, Bohon C. Weight gain is associated with reduced striatal response to palatable food. *Journal of Neuroscience* 2010; 30: 13105–9.

7. Rozin P, Kabnick K, Pete E, Fischler C, Shields C. The ecology of eating: smaller portion sizes in France than in the United States help explain the French paradox. *Psychological Science* 2003; 14: 450–54.

8. Hetherington MM, Anderson AS, Norton GNM, Newson L. Situational effects on meal intake: a comparison of eating alone and eating with others. *Physiology &*

Behavior 2006; 88: 498–505.

9. Ogden J, Coop N, Cousins C, et al. Distraction, the desire to eat and food intake: towards an expanded model of mindless eating. *Appetite* 2012.

10. Wansink B, Just DR, Payne CR. Mindless eating and healthy heuristics for the irrational. *American Economic Review* 2009; 99: 165–69.

11. Zajonc RB, Murphy ST, Inglehart M. Feeling and facial efference: implications of the vascular theory of emotion. *Psychological Review* 1989; 96: 395.

12. Niedenthal PM. Embodying emotion. *Science* 2007; 316: 1002–5.

13. Grandey AA, Fisk GM, Mattila AS, Jansen KJ, Sideman LA. Is "service with a smile" enough? Authenticity of positive displays during service encounters. *Organizational Behavior and Human Decision Processes* 2005; 96: 38–55.

14. Umbreit J, Lane KL, Dejud C. Improving classroom behavior by modifying task difficulty effects of increasing the difficulty of too-easy tasks. *Journal of Positive Behavior Interventions* 2004; 6: 13–20.

15. Hackman JR, Oldham GR. Motivation through the design of work: test of a theory. *Organizational Behavior and Human*

Performance 1976; 16: 250–79.

16. Daugherty JR, Brase GL. Taking time to be healthy: predicting health behaviors with delay discounting and time perspective. *Personality and Individual Differences* 2010; 48: 202–7.

17. Goodin RE, Rice JM, Parpo A, Eriksson L. Discretionary time: a new measure of freedom. Cambridge University Press, 2008.

18. Wang M, Sunny Wong MC. Leisure and happiness in the United States: evidence from survey data. *Applied Economics Letters* 2011; 18: 1813–16.

19. Geiselman RE. Enhancement of eyewitness memory: an empirical evaluation of the cognitive interview. *Journal of Police Science & Administration* 1984.

20. Gilbert D. Stumbling on happiness. HarperCollins, 2009.

21. Gilbert D, Killingsworth MA, Eyre RN, Wilson TD. The surprising power of neighborly advice. *Science* 2009; 323: 1617–19.

22. Dobewall H, Realo A, Allik J, Esko T, Metspalu A. Self-other agreement in happiness and life-satisfaction: the role of personality traits. *Social Indicators Research* 2013; 114: 479–92.

23. Lyubomirsky S, Lepper H. A measure

of subjective happiness: preliminary reliability and construct validation. *Social Indicators Research* 1999; 46: 137–55.

24. Roberts J, Hodgson R, Dolan P. "It's driving her mad": gender differences in the effects of commuting on psychological health. *Journal of Health Economics* 2011; 30: 1064–76.

25. Seidlitz L, Diener E. Sex differences in the recall of affective experiences. *Journal of Personality and Social Psychology* 1998; 74: 262–71.

26. Schwartz B. The paradox of choice: why more is less. Harper Perennial, 2005.

27. Bisson JI, Jenkins PL, Alexander J, Bannister C. Randomised controlled trial of psychological debriefing for victims of acute burn trauma. *British Journal of Psychiatry* 1997; 171: 78–81.

28. Bonanno GA. Loss, trauma, and human resilience: have we underestimated the human capacity to thrive after extremely aversive events? *American Psychologist* 2004; 59: 20.

29. Rule NO, Ambady N. Brief exposures: male sexual orientation is accurately perceived at 50ms. *Journal of Experimental Social Psychology* 2008; 44: 1100–1105.

30. Dijksterhuis A, van Olden Z. On the

benefits of thinking unconsciously: unconscious thought can increase post-choice satisfaction. *Journal of Experimental Social Psychology* 2006; 42: 627–31.

31. Creswell JD, Bursley JK, Satpute AB. Neural reactivation links unconscious thought to decision-making performance. *Social Cognitive and Affective Neuroscience* 2013.

32. Payne JW, Samper A, Bettman JR, Luce MF. Boundary conditions on unconscious thought in complex decision making. *Psychological Science* 2008; 19: 1118–23.

33. Newell BR, Wong KY, Cheung JC, Rakow T. Think, blink or sleep on it? The impact of modes of thought on complex decision making. *Quarterly Journal of Experimental Psychology* 2009; 62: 707–32; Dijksterhuis A, Van Baaren RB, Bongers KC, Bos MW, Van Leeuwen ML, Van der Leij A. The rational unconscious: conscious versus unconscious thought in complex consumer choice. *Social Psychology of Consumer Behavior* 2009: 89–108.

34. Hsee CK, Zhang J, Yu F, Xi Y. Lay rationalism and inconsistency between predicted experience and decision. *Journal of Behavioral Decision Making* 2003; 16: 257–72.

6. Designing Happiness

1. Thaler RH, Sunstein CR. Nudge: improving decisions about health, wealth, and happiness. Yale University Press, 2008.
2. Leventhal H, Singer R, Jones S. Effects of fear and specificity of recommendation upon attitudes and behavior. *Journal of Personality and Social Psychology* 1965; 2: 20; Zhao M, Lee L, Soman D. Crossing the virtual boundary: the effect of task-irrelevant environmental cues on task implementation. *Psychological Science* 2012; 23: 1200–1207.
3. Dolan P, Hallsworth M, Halpern D, King D, Metcalfe R, Vlaev I. Influencing behaviour: the MINDSPACE way. *Journal of Economic Psychology* 2012; 33: 264–77. Dolan P, Hallsworth M, Halpern D, King D, Vlaev I. MINDSPACE: influencing behaviour through public policy. Report for the Cabinet Office, 2010.
4. Beshears J, Choi JJ, Laibson D, Madrian BC. Social security policy in a changing environment. In: The importance of default options for retirement saving outcomes: evidence from the United States. University of Chicago Press, 2009: 167–69; Rithalia A, McDaid C, Suekarran S, Myers L, Sowden A. Impact of presumed

consent for organ donation on donation rates: a systematic review. *British Medical Journal* 2009; 338.

5. Team BI. Applying behavioural insights to reduce fraud, error and debt. UK London Cabinet Office, 2012.

6. Dolan P, Metcalfe R. Better neighbors and basic knowledge: a field experiment on the role of non-pecuniary incentives on energy consumption. Unpublished working paper, 2013.

7. Holland RW, Hendriks M, Aarts H. Smells like clean spirit: nonconscious effects of scent on cognition and behavior. *Psychological Science* 2005; 16: 689–93.

8. Birnbach D, King D, Vlaev I, Rosen L, Harvey P. Impact of environmental olfactory cues on hand hygiene behaviour in a simulated hospital environment: a randomized study. *Journal of Hospital Infection* 2013.

9. Shirtcliff EA, Allison AL, Armstrong JM, Slattery MJ, Kalin NH, Essex MJ. Longitudinal stability and developmental properties of salivary cortisol levels and circadian rhythms from childhood to adolescence. *Developmental Psychobiology* 2012; 54: 493–502.

10. Holzman DC. What's in a color? The unique human health effects of blue light.

Environmental Health Perspectives 2010; 118: A22–A27.

11. Moore E. A prison environment's effect on health care service demands. *Journal of Environmental Systems* 1981; 11: 17–34; Ulrich R. View through a window may influence recovery from surgery. *Science* 1984; 224: 420–21.

12. Park SH, Mattson RH, Kim E. Pain tolerance effects of ornamental plants in a simulated hospital patient room. In: Relf D, ed. *XXVI International Horticultural Congress: Expanding Roles for Horticulture in Improving Human Well-Being and Life Quality* 639, 2002: 241–47; Katcher A, Segal H, Beck A. Comparison of contemplation and hypnosis for the reduction of anxiety and discomfort during dental surgery. *American Journal of Clinical Hypnosis* 1984; 27: 14–21.

13. Wansink B. Mindless eating: why we eat more than we think. Random House, 2010.

14. Wansink B, Sobal J. Mindless eating: the 200 daily food decisions we overlook. *Environment and Behavior* 2007; 39: 106–23.

15. Wansink B. Super bowls: serving bowl size and food consumption. *Journal of the American Medical Association* 2005; 293:

1723–28.

16. Chiou W, Yang C, Wan C. Ironic effects of dietary supplementation illusory invulnerability created by taking dietary supplements licenses health-risk behaviors. *Psychological Science* 2011; 22: 1081–86.

17. Kaptchuk TJ, Friedlander E, Kelley JM, et al. Placebos without deception: a randomized controlled trial in irritable bowel syndrome. *PLoS ONE* 2010; 5: e15591.

18. Plassmann H, Mazar N, Robitaille N, Linder A. The origin of the pain of paying. *Advances in Consumer Research* 2011; 39: 146.

19. Werner CM, Turner J, Shipman K, et al. Commitment, behavior, and attitude change: an analysis of voluntary recycling. *Journal of Environmental Psychology* 1995; 15: 197–208.

20. Turner-McGrievy G, Tate D. Weight loss social support in 140 characters or less: use of an online social network in a remotely delivered weight loss intervention. *Translational Behavioral Medicine: Practice, Policy, Research* 2013: 1–8.

21. Ryan RM. Further examining the American dream: differential correlates of intrinsic and extrinsic goals. *Personality and Social Psychology Bulletin* 1996; 22: 280–87.

22. Koo M, Fishbach A. The small-area hypothesis: effects of progress monitoring on goal adherence. *Journal of Consumer Research* 2012; 39: 493–509.

23. Giné X, Karlan D, Zinman J. Put your money where your butt is: a commitment contract for smoking cessation. *American Economic Journal: Applied Economics* 2010; 2: 213–35.

24. Dunn E, Norton M. Happy money: the science of smarter spending. Simon & Schuster, 2013.

25. Thaler R. Toward a positive theory of consumer choice. *Journal of Economic Behavior & Organization* 1980; 1: 39–60.

26. De La Ronde C, Swann WB. Partner verification: restoring shattered images of our intimates. *Journal of Personality and Social Psychology* 1998; 75: 374.

27. Surowiecki J. The wisdom of crowds. Knopf Doubleday, 2005.

28. Bargh JA, Williams EL. The automaticity of social life. *Current Directions in Psychological Science* 2006; 15: 1–4.

29. Dimberg U, Thunberg M. Unconscious facial reactions to emotional facial expressions. *Psychological Science* 2000; 11: 86.

30. Parkinson B, Simons G. Affecting others: social appraisal and emotion conta-

gion in everyday decision making. *Personality and Social Psychology Bulletin* 2009; 35: 1071–84.

31. Fowler JH, Christakis NA. The dynamic spread of happiness in a large social network. *British Medical Journal* 2008; 337: a2338.

32. Totterdell P. Catching moods and hitting runs: mood linkage and subjective performance in professional sport teams. *Journal of Applied Psychology* 2000; 85: 848.

33. McIntosh DN. Spontaneous facial mimicry, liking and emotional contagion. *Polish Psychological Bulletin* 2006; 37: 31.

34. Larson RW, Richards MH. Family emotions: do young adolescents and their parents experience the same states? *Journal of Research on Adolescence* 1994; 4: 567–83.

35. Putnam RD. Bowling alone: the collapse and revival of American community. Simon & Schuster, 2001.

36. Luttmer E. Neighbors as negatives: relative earnings and well-being. *Quarterly Journal of Economics* 2005; 120: 963–1002.

37. Card D, Mas A, Moretti E, Saez E. Inequality at work: the effect of peer salaries on job satisfaction. *American*

Economic Review 2012; 102: 2981–3003.

38. Senik C. When information dominates comparison: learning from Russian subjective panel data. *Journal of Public Economics* 2004; 88: 2099–2123; Akay A, Bargain O, Zimmermann KF. Relative concerns of rural-to-urban migrants in China. *Journal of Economic Behavior & Organization* 2012; 81: 421–41.

39. Blanton H, Crocker J, Miller DT. The effects of in-group versus out-group social comparison on self-esteem in the context of a negative stereotype. *Journal of Experimental Social Psychology* 2000; 36: 519–30.

40. Wadsworth T. Sex and the pursuit of happiness: how other people's sex lives are related to our sense of well-being. *Social Indicators Research* 2013; 1–21.

41. Duhigg C. The power of habit: why we do what we do, and how to change. Random House, 2012.

42. Hofmann W, Friese M, Wiers RW. Impulsive versus reflective influences on health behavior: a theoretical framework and empirical review. *Health Psychology Review* 2008; 2: 111–37.

43. Henningfield JE, Cohen C, Slade JD. Is nicotine more addictive than cocaine? *Brit-*

ish *Journal of Addiction* 1991; 86: 565–69.

44. Christakis NA, Fowler JH. The collective dynamics of smoking in a large social network. *New England Journal of Medicine* 2008; 358: 2249–58.

45. Lally P, van Jaarsveld C, Potts H, Wardle J. How are habits formed: modelling habit formation in the real world. *European Journal of Social Psychology* 2010; 40: 998–1009.

46. Verplanken B, Wood W. Interventions to break and create consumer habits. *Journal of Public Policy & Marketing* 2006; 25: 90–103.

47. Bernheim BD, Rangel A. Addiction and cue-triggered decision processes. *American Economic Review* 2004; 94: 1558–90.

48. Wood W, Tam L, Witt MG. Changing circumstances, disrupting habits. *Journal of Personality and Social Psychology* 2005; 88: 918.

7. Doing Happiness

1. Csikszentmihalyi M. Flow: The psychology of optimal experience. HarperCollins, 2008.

2. Van Boven L, Gilovich T. To do or to have? That is the question. *Journal of*

Personality and Social Psychology 2003; 85: 1193–1202.

3. Frank RH. How not to buy happiness. *Daedalus* 2004; 133: 69–79.

4. Carter TJ, Gilovich T. The relative relativity of material and experiential purchases. *Journal of Personality and Social Psychology* 2010; 98: 146–59.

5. Van Boven L, Campbell MC, Gilovich T. Stigmatizing materialism: on stereotypes and impressions of materialistic and experiential pursuits. *Personality and Social Psychology Bulletin* 2010; 36: 551–63.

6. Nicolao L, Irwin JR, Goodman JK. Happiness for sale: do experiential purchases make consumers happier than material purchases? *Journal of Consumer Research* 2009; 36: 188–98.

7. Olsson LE, Gärling T, Ettema D, Friman M, Fujii S. Happiness and satisfaction with work commute. *Social Indicators Research* 2013; 111: 255–63.

8. Nelson LD, Meyvis T, Galak J. Enhancing the television-viewing experience through commercial interruptions. *Journal of Consumer Research* 2009; 36: 160–72.

9. Baird B, Smallwood J, Mrazek MD, Kam JW, Franklin MS, Schooler JW. Inspired by distraction: mind wandering facilitates

creative incubation. *Psychological Science* 2012; 23: 1117–22.

10. Dolan P, Metcalfe R. The relationship between innovation and subjective wellbeing. *Research Policy* 2012; 41: 1489–98.

11. Ruef M. Strong ties, weak ties and islands: structural and cultural predictors of organizational innovation. *Industrial and Corporate Change* 2002; 11: 427–49.

12. Taylor S. Making time: why time seems to pass at different speeds and how to control it. Totem Books, 2009.

13. Block RA, Zakay D, Hancock PA. Developmental changes in human duration judgments: a meta-analytic review. *Developmental Review* 1999; 19: 183–211.

14. Ahn H-K, Liu MW, Soman D. Memory markers: how consumers recall the duration of experiences. *Journal of Consumer Psychology* 2009; 19: 508–16.

15. DeNeve K, Cooper H. The happy personality: a meta-analysis of 137 personality traits and subjective well-being. *Psychological Bulletin* 1998; 124: 197–229.

16. Koelsch S. Towards a neural basis of music-evoked emotions. *Trends in Cognitive Sciences* 2010; 14: 131–37.

17. Guzzetta CE. Effects of relaxation and music therapy on patients in a coronary

care unit with presumptive acute myocardial infarction. *Heart & Lung: The Journal of Critical Care* 1989; 18: 609; Nayak S, Wheeler BL, Shiflett SC, Agostinelli S. Effect of music therapy on mood and social interaction among individuals with acute traumatic brain injury and stroke. *Rehabilitation Psychology* 2000; 45: 274; Bensimon M, Amir D, Wolf Y. Drumming through trauma: music therapy with post-traumatic soldiers. *The Arts in Psychotherapy* 2008; 35: 34–48; Gold C, Voracek M, Wigram T. Effects of music therapy for children and adolescents with psychopathology: a meta-analysis. *Journal of Child Psychology and Psychiatry* 2004; 45: 1054–63.

18. Sacks O. The power of music. *Brain* 2006; 129: 2528–32.

19. Szabo A. The acute effects of humor and exercise on mood and anxiety. *Journal of Leisure Research* 2003; 35: 152–62.

20. Berk LS, Felten DL, Tan SA, Bittman BB, Westengard J. Modulation of neuroimmune parameters during the eustress of humor-associated mirthful laughter. *Alternative Therapies in Health and Medicine* 2001; 7: 62–76.

21. Yovetich NA, Dale TA, Hudak MA.

411

Benefits of humor in reduction of threat-induced anxiety. *Psychological Reports* 1990; 66: 51–58.

22. Tse M, Lo A, Cheng T, Chan E, Chan A, Chung H. Humor therapy: relieving chronic pain and enhancing happiness in older adults. *Journal of Aging Research* 2010.

23. Van Wormer K, Boes M. Humor in the emergency room: a social work perspective. *Health Social Work* 1997; 22: 87–92.

24. Potter C, Carpenter J. Fathers' involvement in Sure Start: what do fathers and mothers perceive as benefits? *Practice: Social Work in Action* 2010; 22: 3–15.

25. Ruch W. The sense of humor: explorations of a personality characteristic. Vol. 3. Walter de Gruyter, 1998.

26. Carpenter KM, Stoner SA, Mundt JM, Stoelb B. An online self-help CBT intervention for chronic lower back pain. *Clinical Journal of Pain* 2012; 28: 14–22.

27. Brown LA, Gaudiano BA, Miller IW. Investigating the similarities and differences between practitioners of second- and third-wave cognitive-behavioral therapies. *Behavior Modification* 2011; 35: 187–200.

28. Davidson RJ, Kabat-Zinn J, Schumacher J, et al. Alterations in brain and im-

mune function produced by mindfulness meditation. *Psychosomatic Medicine* 2003; 65: 564–70; Teasdale JD, Segal ZV, Mark J, et al. Prevention of relapse/recurrence in major depression by mindfulness-based cognitive therapy. *Journal of Consulting and Clinical Psychology* 2000; 68: 615–23.

29. Lim C, Putnam RD. Religion, social networks, and life satisfaction. *American Sociological Review* 2010; 75: 914–33.

30. Stevens N. Gender and adaptation to widowhood in later life. *Ageing & Society* 1995; 15: 37–58.

31. Demir M, Özen A, Dougan A, Bilyk NA, Tyrell FA. I matter to my friend, therefore I am happy: friendship, mattering, and happiness. *Journal of Happiness Studies* 2011; 12: 983–1005.

32. Lehrer J. Imagine: how creativity works. Canongate Books, 2012.

33. Cain S. Quiet: the power of introverts in a world that can't stop talking. Penguin, 2012; Lucas RE, Diener E. Understanding extraverts' enjoyment of social situations: the importance of pleasantness. *Journal of Personality and Social Psychology* 2001; 81: 343–56.

34. Meiran N, Chorev Z, Sapir A. Component processes in task switching. *Cognitive*

Psychology 2000; 41: 211–53.

35. Buser T, Peter N. Multitasking. *Experimental Economics* 2012: 1–15.

36. Wang Z, Tchernev JM. The "myth" of media multitasking: reciprocal dynamics of media multitasking, personal needs, and gratifications. *Journal of Communication* 2012; 62; 493–513.

37. Kavetsos G, Koutroumpis P. Technological affluence and subjective well-being. *Journal of Economic Psychology* 2011; 32: 742–53; Brown JR, Goolsbee A. Does the Internet make markets more competitive? Evidence from the life insurance industry. *Journal of Political Economy* 2002; 110: 481–507; Czernich N, Falck O, Kretschmer T, Woessmann L. Broadband infrastructure and economic growth. *Economic Journal* 2011; 121: 505–32.

38. Spira J, Feintuch J. The cost of not paying attention: how interruptions impact knowledge worker productivity. Basex, 2005.

39. Jackson TW, Culjak G. Can seminar and computer-based training improve the effectiveness of electronic mail communication within the workplace? *Proceedings of the 17th Australasian Conference on Information Systems* 2006. Centre for Informa-

tion Studies, Charles Sturt University.

40. Zhu E. Hypermedia interface design: the effects of number of links and granularity of nodes. *Journal of Educational Multimedia and Hypermedia* 1999; 8: 331–58.

41. Worthen B. The perils of texting while parenting. *Wall Street Journal,* Sept. 29, 2012.

42. Schwebel DC, Stavrinos D, Byington KW, Davis T, O'Neal EE, de Jong D. Distraction and pedestrian safety: how talking on the phone, texting, and listening to music impact crossing the street. *Accident Analysis & Prevention* 2012; 45: 266–71.

43. Levy J, Pashler H, Boer E. Central interference in driving: is there any stopping the psychological refractory period? *Psychological Science* 2006; 17: 228–35.

44. DeVoe SE, Pfeffer J. Time is tight: how higher economic value of time increases feelings of time pressure. *Journal of Applied Psychology* 2011; 96: 665.

45. DeVoe SE, House J. Time, money, and happiness: how does putting a price on time affect our ability to smell the roses? *Journal of Experimental Social Psychology* 2012; 48: 466.

46. Aguiar M, Hurst E. Measuring trends

in leisure: the allocation of time over five decades. *Quarterly Journal of Economics* 2007; 122: 969–1006.

47. Shah AK, Mullainathan S, Shafir E. Some consequences of having too little. *Science* 2012; 338: 682–85.

48. Dolan P, Metcalfe R. With my money on my mind: income, happiness and intrusive financial thoughts. Unpublished working paper, 2011.

49. Smallwood J, Schooler JW. The restless mind. *Psychological Bulletin* 2006; 132: 946.

50. Mason MF, Norton MI, Horn JDV, Wegner DM, Grafton ST, Macrae CN. Wandering minds: the default network and stimulus-independent thought. *Science* 2007; 315: 393–95.

51. Ziauddeen H, Farooqi IS, Fletcher PC. Obesity and the brain: how convincing is the addiction model? *Nature Reviews Neuroscience* 2012; 13: 279–86.

52. Killingsworth MA, Gilbert DT. A wandering mind is an unhappy mind. *Science* 2010; 330: 932.

53. Nolen-Hoeksema S, McBride A, Larson J. Rumination and psychological distress among bereaved partners. *Journal of Personality and Social Psychology* 1997; 72: 855–62.

54. Dolan P. Thinking about it: thoughts about health and valuing QALYs. *Health Economics* 2011; 20: 1407–16.

55. Gilkey JG. You can master life. Macmillan, 1938.

56. Bennett P, Phelps C, Brain K, Hood K, Gray J. A randomized controlled trial of a brief self-help coping intervention designed to reduce distress when awaiting genetic risk information. *Journal of Psychosomatic Research* 2007; 63: 59–64.

57. Wood W, Quinn JM, Kashy DA. Habits in everyday life: thought, emotion, and action. *Journal of Personality and Social Psychology* 2002; 83: 1281–97.

58. Powers W. Hamlet's BlackBerry. HarperCollins, 2011.

59. Spitzer M. Demencia digital (Digital dementia). Ediciones B, 2013.

60. Yuan K, Qin W, Wang G, et al. Microstructure abnormalities in adolescents with Internet addiction disorder. *PloS ONE* 2011; 6: e20708.

61. Hofmann W, Vohs KD, Baumeister RF. What people desire, feel conflicted about, and try to resist in everyday life. *Psychological Science* 2012; 23: 582–88.

62. Turkle S. Alone together: why we expect more from technology and less from each

other. Basic Books, 2011.

63. Rothberg MB, Arora A, Hermann J, Kleppel R, Marie PS, Visintainer P. Phantom vibration syndrome among medical staff: a cross sectional survey. *British Medical Journal* 2010; 341.

64. The phone stacking game changes everything. *Huffington Post,* Oct. 1, 2012.

65. The communications market report. United Kingdom: a nation addicted to smartphones. OfCom, 2011.

66. The communications market report. United Kingdom: UK is now texting more than talking. OfCom, 2012.

8. Decide, Design, and Do

1. Ferrari JR, Harriott JS, Zimmerman M. The social support networks of procrastinators: friends or family in times of trouble? *Personality and Individual Differences* 1998; 26: 321–31.

2. Borkovec TD, Ray WJ, Stober J. Worry: a cognitive phenomenon intimately linked to affective, physiological, and interpersonal behavioral processes. *Cognitive Therapy and Research* 1998; 22: 561–76.

3. O'Donoghue T, Rabin M. Choice and procrastination. *Quarterly Journal of Eco-*

nomics 2001; 116: 121–60.

4. Bui NH. Effect of evaluation threat on procrastination behavior. *Journal of Social Psychology* 2007; 147: 197–209.

5. Jeanmonod R, Jeanmonod D, Ngiam R. Resident productivity: does shift length matter? *American Journal of Emergency Medicine* 2008; 26: 789–91.

6. Kahneman D, Tversky A. Intuitive prediction: biases and corrective procedures. DTIC Document, 1977.

7. Roy M, Christenfeld N. Effect of task length on remembered and predicted duration. *Psychonomic Bulletin & Review* 2008; 15: 202–7.

8. Van Eerde W. A meta-analytically derived nomological network of procrastination. *Personality and Individual Differences* 2003; 35: 1401–18.

9. Buehler R, Griffin D, Ross M. Exploring the "planning fallacy": why people underestimate their task completion times. *Journal of Personality and Social Psychology* 1994; 67: 366–81.

10. Amabile TM, Hadley CN, Kramer SJ. Creativity under the gun. *Harvard Business Review* 2002; 80: 52–61.

11. Frost RO, Marten P, Lahart C, Rosenblate R. The dimensions of perfectionism.

Cognitive Therapy and Research 1990; 14: 449–68.

12. Dolan P, Rudisill C. Babies in waiting: why increasing the IVF age cut-off is likely to lead to fewer wanted pregnancies. Under review, 2013.

13. Cadena X, Schoar A, Cristea A, Delgado-Medrano HM. Fighting procrastination in the workplace: an experiment. National Bureau of Economic Research, 2011.

14. Roy M, Christenfeld N, McKenzie C. Underestimating the duration of future events: memory incorrectly used or memory bias? *Psychological Bulletin* 2005; 131: 738–56.

15. Wohl MJ, Pychyl TA, Bennett SH. I forgive myself, now I can study: how self-forgiveness for procrastinating can reduce future procrastination. *Personality and Individual Differences* 2010; 48: 803–8.

16. Steel P. The nature of procrastination: a meta-analytic and theoretical review of quintessential self-regulatory failure. *Psychological Bulletin* 2007; 133: 65.

17. Shu SB, Gneezy A. Procrastination of enjoyable experiences. *Journal of Marketing Research* 2010; 47: 933–44.

18. Ariely D, Wertenbroch K. Procrastination, deadlines, and performance: self-

control by precommitment. *Psychological Science* 2002; 13: 219–24.

19. Kruger J, Evans M. If you don't want to be late, enumerate: unpacking reduces the planning fallacy. *Journal of Experimental Social Psychology* 2004; 40: 586–98.

20. Duflo E, Saez E. The role of information and social interactions in retirement plan decisions: evidence from a randomized experiment. National Bureau of Economic Research, 2002.

21. Lee E. The relationship of motivation and flow experience to academic procrastination in university students. *Journal of Genetic Psychology* 2005; 166: 5–14; Read D, Loewenstein G, Kalyanaraman S. Mixing virtue and vice: combining the immediacy effect and the diversification heuristic. *Journal of Behavioral Decision Making* 1999; 12: 257–73.

22. Johns G, Jia Lin Xie, Yongqing Fang. Mediating and moderating effects in job design. *Journal of Management* 1992; 18: 657.

23. Lavoie JAA, Pychyl TA. Cyberslacking and the procrastination superhighway: a web-based survey of online procrastination, attitudes, and emotion. *Social Science Computer Review* 2001; 19: 431–44.

24. Dolan P, Olsen JA. Equity in health: the importance of different health streams. *Journal of Health Economics* 2001; 20: 823–34; Dolan P, Tsuchiya A. The social welfare function and individual responsibility: some theoretical issues and empirical evidence. *Journal of Health Economics* 2009; 28: 210–20.

25. Dolan P, Shaw R, Tsuchiya A, Williams A. QALY maximisation and people's preferences: a methodological review of the literature. *Health Economics* 2005; 14: 197–208; Edlin R, Tsuchiya A, Dolan P. Public preferences for responsibility versus public preferences for reducing inequalities. *Health Economics* 2012; 21: 1416–26.

26. Amiel Y, Cowell F, Gaertner W. Distributional orderings: an approach with seven flavors. *Theory and Decision* 2012; 73: 381–99.

27. Dolan P, Edlin R, Tshuchiya, A. The relative societal value of health gains to different beneficiaries — final report. National Co-ordinating Centre for Research Methodology, 2008.

28. Dolan P, Robinson A. The measurement of preferences over the distribution of benefits: the importance of the reference point. *European Economic Review* 2001; 45: 1697–1709.

29. Clark A, Flèche S, Senik C. The great happiness moderation. IZA Discussion Paper No. 6761, 2012.

30. Alesina A, Di Tella R, MacCulloch R. Inequality and happiness: are Europeans and Americans different? *Journal of Public Economics* 2004; 88: 2009–42.

31. Oshio T, Kobayashi M. Income inequality, perceived happiness, and self-rated health: evidence from nationwide surveys in Japan. *Social Science & Medicine* 2010; 70: 1358–66; Jiang S, Lu M, Sato H. Identity, inequality, and happiness: evidence from urban China. *World Development* 2012; 40: 1190–1200; Graham C, Felton A. Inequality and happiness: insights from Latin America. *Journal of Economic Inequality* 2006; 4: 107–22.

32. Knight J, Song L. Subjective well-being and its determinants in rural China. *China Economic Review* 2009; 20; 635–49.

33. Meier S, Stutzer A. Is volunteering rewarding in itself? *Economica* 2008; 75: 39–59.

34. Dunn EW, Aknin LB, Norton MI. Spending money on others promotes happiness. *Science* 2008; 319: 1687–88.

35. Mogilner C, Chance Z, Norton MI. Giving time gives you time. *Psychological*

Science 2012; 23: 1233–38.

36. Cacioppo JT, Fowler JH, Christakis NA. Alone in the crowd: the structure and spread of loneliness in a large social network. *Journal of Personality and Social Psychology* 2009; 97: 977–91.

37. Luo Y, Hawkley LC, Waite LJ, Cacioppo JT. Loneliness, health, and mortality in old age: a national longitudinal study. *Social Science & Medicine* 2012; 74: 907–14.

38. Andreoni J. Impure altruism and donations to public goods: a theory of warm-glow giving. *Economic Journal* 1990; 100: 464.

39. Dawkins R. The selfish gene. Oxford University Press, 2006.

40. Wilkinson GS. Reciprocal food sharing in the vampire bat. *Nature* 1984; 308: 181–84.

41. Lloyd K. Happiness and the wellbeing of young carers: extent, nature, and correlates of caring among 10 and 11 year old schoolchildren. *Journal of Happiness Studies* 2013; 14: 67–80.

42. Bourassa D. Examining self-protection measures guarding adult protective services social workers against compassion fatigue. *Journal of Interpersonal Violence* 2012; 27: 1699–1715.

43. Fellner CH, Schwartz SH. Altruism in

disrepute: medical versus public attitudes toward the living organ donor. *New England Journal of Medicine* 1971; 284: 582–85.

44. Sandstrom GM, Dunn EW. The virtue blind spot: do affective forecasting errors undermine virtuous behavior? *Social and Personality Psychology Compass* 2011; 5: 720–33.

45. Otake K, Shimai S, Tanaka-Matsumi J, Otsui K, Fredrickson BL. Happy people become happier through kindness: a counting kindness intervention. *Journal of Happiness Studies* 2006; 7: 361–75.

46. Aknin LB, Dunn EW, Whillans AV, Grant AM, Norton MI. Making a difference matters: impact unlocks the emotional benefits of prosocial spending. *Journal of Economic Behavior & Organization* 2013; 88: 90–95.

47. Rand DG, Nowak MA. Human co-operation. *Trends in Cognitive Sciences* 2013.

48. Nelson LD, Norton MI. From student to superhero: situational primes shape future helping. *Journal of Experimental Social Psychology* 2005; 41: 423–30.

49. Jonas E, Schimel J, Greenberg J, Pyszczynski T. The Scrooge effect: evidence that

mortality salience increases prosocial attitudes and behavior. *Personality and Social Psychology Bulletin* 2002; 28: 1342–53.

50. Dolan P, Metcalfe R, Navarro-Martinez D. The determinants of default acceptance in charity donations. Working paper, 2013.

51. Apicella CL, Marlowe FW, Fowler JH, Christakis NA. Social networks and cooperation in hunter-gatherers. *Nature* 2012; 481: 497–501.

52. Cotterill S, Moseley A, Richardson L. Can nudging create the Big Society? Experiments in civic behaviour and implications for the voluntary and public sectors. *Voluntary Sector Review* 2012; 3: 265–74.

53. Dolan P, Olsen JA. Distributing health care: economic and ethical issues. Oxford University Press, 2002.

54. Veblen T. The theory of the leisure class. MacMillan, 1899.

55. Glazer A, Konrad KA. A signaling explanation for charity. *American Economic Review* 1996; 86: 1019–28.

56. Griskevicius V, Tybur JM, Van den Bergh B. Going green to be seen: status, reputation, and conspicuous conservation. *Journal of Personality and Social Psychol-*

ogy 2010; 98: 392–404; Iredale W, van Vugt M, Dunbar R. Showing off in humans: male generosity as a mating signal. *Evolutionary Psychology* 2008; 6: 386–92.

57. Ariely D, Bracha A, Meier S. Doing good or doing well? Image motivation and monetary incentives in behaving prosocially. *American Economic Review* 2009; 99: 544–55.

58. Duffy J, Kornienko T. Does competition affect giving? *Journal of Economic Behavior & Organization* 2010; 74: 82–103.

59. Goldinger SD, Kleider HM, Azuma T, Beike DR. "Blaming the victim" under memory load. *Psychological Science* 2003; 14: 81–85.

Conclusion

1. Potter M, Vu J, Croughan-Minihane M. Weight management: what patients want from their primary care physicians. *Journal of Family Practice* 2001; 50: 513–19.

ABOUT THE AUTHOR

Paul Dolan, PhD, is an internationally renowned expert on happiness, behavior, and public policy. He is currently Professor of Behavioral Science at the London School of Economics and Political Science and has been a visiting research scholar at Princeton University with Professor Daniel Kahneman. Among various other roles, he advises the National Academy of Sciences on measurement issues in happiness research. He lives in Brighton, UK with his wife and two children.